INTRODUCTION TO

HTML

5

Advanced APIs

Introduction to HTML5 Advanced APIs

© 2016 Kevin Ruse + Associates Inc.

Part Number: 2016HTML5API

Edition Number: 1.1

ISBN-13: 978-0-9969797-2-6

Author: Kevin Ruse

Disclaimer

Third-Party Information

Copyright

HELP US IMPROVE OUR COURSEWARE

Please send your comments and suggestions via email to kevin@kevinruse.com.

About the Author

Kevin Ruse

Kevin Ruse is the President and lead trainer at Kevin Ruse + Associates, Inc. Kevin conducts on-site, instructor-led training throughout the world. He is also the project manager for various web applications and Internet of Things projects. The firm has been in business since 1990 and specializes in delivering custom training rooted in a thoughtful needs-analysis approach.

Kevin is a dedicated and enthusiastic instructor currently teaching HTML5, JavaScript, jQuery, CSS and Responsive Web Design. Kevin has also taught XML, XSLT, e4x, XHTML, ActionScript, Cascading Style Sheets, Flash, Flex, LiveCycle Data Services, BlazeDS, ColdFusion, Dreamweaver, Acrobat, Photoshop, Fireworks, and InDesign.

Kevin specializes in corporate on-site training at government agencies and small to large companies throughout the world. He has served on the faculty of DeAnza Community College, San Francisco State University and the University of California Santa Cruz Extension Program. He has taught the faculty and staff at Stanford University. Kevin has had the pleasure of teaching at Google, Facebook, Cisco Systems, You Tube, Applied Materials, KLA Tencor and Adobe as well as the United States Air Force and the Canadian Forces.

When not teaching, Kevin serves as a technical reviewer for computer industry book publishers including Peach-Pit, Sams Publishing and Friends of Ed. Kevin also records video training for Video2Brain and has appeared on Adobe TV.

About the Tech Editor

August 'Augie' Schau

Augie has been providing web, desktop and data developer training services to organizations in Europe, Asia and North America for over twenty years. Originally a Mechanical Engineer, he discovered the joy of computers with the Apple II, and has never looked back.

Copy Editor

Elisabeth Beller

Table of Contents

Forms/ConstraintValidation API

XMLHttpRequest Level 2 API

Web Sockets API

Server-Sent Events API

Canvas APIs

Geolocation APIs

Web Workers API

Course setup instructions

1) Download and install the Visual C++ Packages below. These packages are used in compiling various software installations, so some computers would have this already.

   a. Visual C++ 2010 SP1 Redistributable Package from either:

      i. http://www.microsoft.com/download/en/details.aspx?id=8328 (32-bit version) or http://www.microsoft.com/download/en/details.aspx?id=13523 (64-bit version).

   b. Download and install the Visual C++ 2012 Redistributable Package from:

      i. http://www.microsoft.com/en-us/download/details.aspx?id=30679.

2) Please install the WAMP web server stack (Apache + MySQL + PHP) as follows.

   a. Turn off any existing web servers that you are running on your computer (such as IIS, Apache, or Tomcat), especially if they use port 80 or 8080.

   b. Perform a default installation of WAMP for your architecture (32-bit or 64-bit) using the following download link:

      i. http://www.wampserver.com/en/

   c. Use the "download directly" link shown below.

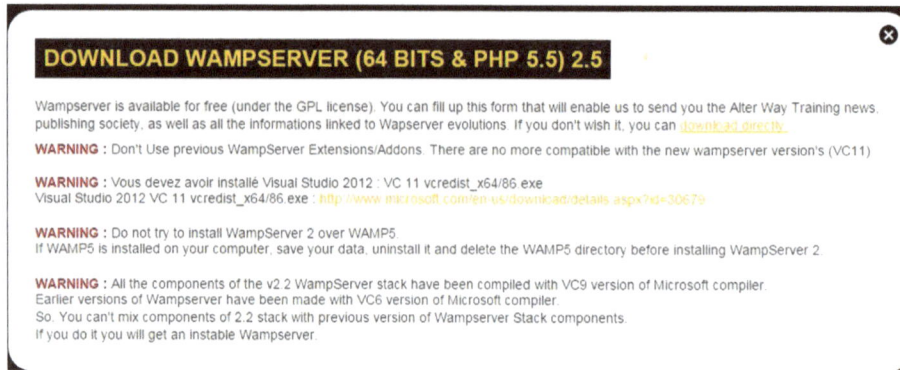

DOWNLOAD WAMPSERVER (64 BITS & PHP 5.5) 2.5

Wampserver is available for free (under the GPL license). You can fill up this form that will enable us to send you the Alter Way Training news, publishing society, as well as all the informations linked to Wapserver evolutions. If you don't wish it, you can download directly.

WARNING : Don't Use previous WampServer Extensions/Addons. There are no more compatible with the new wampserver version's (VC11)

WARNING : Vous devez avoir installé Visual Studio 2012 : VC 11 vcredist_x64/86.exe
Visual Studio 2012 VC 11 vcredist_x64/86.exe : http://www.microsoft.com/en-us/download/details.aspx?id=30679

WARNING : Do not try to install WampServer 2 over WAMP5.
If WAMP5 is installed on your computer, save your data, uninstall it and delete the WAMP5 directory before installing WampServer 2.

WARNING : All the components of the v2.2 WampServer stack have been compiled with VC9 version of Microsoft compiler.
Earlier versions of Wampserver have been made with VC6 version of Microsoft compiler.
So, You can't mix components of 2.2 stack with previous version of Wampserver Stack components.
If you do it you will get an instable Wampserver.

d. Note the download location and locate the executable file "wampserver2.5-Apache-2.4.9-Mysql-5.6.17-php5.5.12-64b" or "wampserver2.5-Apache-2.4.9-Mysql-5.6.17-php5.5.12-32b" (depending on the download you chose earlier: 32-bit or 64-bit) and double-click to run the installer.

e. When prompted, accept the License Agreement.

f. Accept the default settings, including the default directory location (c:\wamp). This is required for several of our scripts and configuration files.

g. If possible, choose the Chrome Web Browser for the default browser (Chrome is typically installed in C:\Program Files (x86)\Google\Chrome\Applications. If you do not have Chrome, choose a different browser (e.g. Firefox).

h. If prompted: "Would you like to install the new WampServer 2 homepage?" click "OK."

i. Accept the default "php Mail parameters."

j. Click "finish."

k. After installing, please go to http://localhost in a browser and verify that you get the WAMP splash screen.

3) Lab file bundle – please download and unzip as follows.

   a. Please download from

      i. www.kevinruse.com/html5apis

   b. Please extract this zip file to the root of your C:\ drive, which should create a folder at "C:\foodPlate". This folder contains the course data files with subdirectories that correspond to the chapters in your courseware.

   c. Navigate to c:\ and right-click the foodPlate folder, and choose Send to > Desktop (create shortcut).

4) Now, we need to add PHP to the path on your machine:

   a. Right click My Computer and choose Properties

   b. Click the Advanced System Settings label

   c. Click the Advanced tab

   d. Click the Environment Variables button

   e. In the bottom half of the dialog, scroll to find the Path environment variable. Select it and choose Edit.

f. Move your cursor to the start of the variable value field and prepend the following:

C :\wamp\bin\php\php5.5.12;

(This is the version of PHP included with your WAMP installation)

g. Click OK repeatedly until all open dialogs disappear.

h. Open a command prompt (To launch a command prompt, type "cmd" in the Windows start menu followed by the enter/return key). In the command prompt, type the following:

php --version

i. Press Enter. Some text confirming the PHP version should appear. Your version of PHP will be 5.5.12.

5) Now, you need to replace the configuration files that have been provided for you. Locate the course data files' config_files directory that correspond to the bit-version of WAMP that you installed (either 32-bit or 64-bit), and make the following replacements:

a. C:\wamp\bin\apache\Apache2.4.9\conf\extra\httpd-vhosts.conf – please overwrite this file with the one from the config files directory.

b. C:\wamp\bin\apache\Apache2.4.9\conf\httpd.conf – please overwrite this file with the one from the config_files directory.

6) Open c:\windows\system32\drivers\etc\hosts for editing.

a. If you are on Vista or Windows 7, you will need to run Notepad as Administrator in order to make these edits (Start menu > All Programs > Accessories > Notepad, right click on it, and choose Run as Administrator).

b. Into this file, please add the following lines. The first line is likely already present in the file – please do not duplicate this line if it is already there:

127.0.0.1 localhost

127.0.0.1 www.foodPlate.local

c. Save and close the file.

7) Confirm that the modified configuration files are working:

a. Restart Apache by left clicking the WAMP tray icon and choosing Apache > Service > Restart Service

b. Start a web browser and go to http://localhost. Confirm the following page is shown:

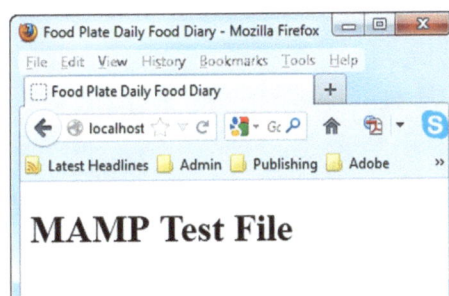

MAMP Test File: www.FoodPlate.local

c. Go to http://www.foodPlate.local in your browser. Confirm the following page is shown:

d. Open the foodPlate directory on your root drive and change the names of the following files:

    i. foodPlate/index.html change to indexX.html

    ii. foodPlate/Sites/LocalSite/index.html to indexX.html

e. Go to your web browser and revisit both http://localhost and http://www.foodPlate.local and you should now see the directories as shown below.

    i. http://localhost:

    ii. http://www.foodPlate.local:

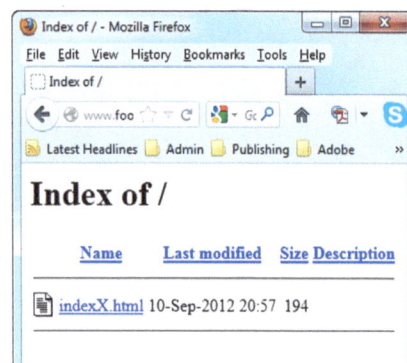

Additional notes

The WAMP setup is used in the following chapters

Chapter 6: WebMessaging API uses the foodplate.local domain for cross-domain messaging.

Chapter 15: XHR Level 2 API uses foodplate.local domain for cross-domain AJAX requests.

Chapter 17: Server-Sent Events API uses php and Apache (for localhost)

Most other chapters simply require a local server to test files.

Troubleshooting tips

Some systems will not work with Skype running. It may be necessary to change the default Skype port or uninstall Skype for the duration of the class. If WAMP will not start consult http://smallcitydesign. com/wamp-wont-start/ for some possible solutions.

About the supplied config files

The supplied config files folder contains httpd.conf and httpd-vhosts.conf. Below is a summary of the changes made to these files. These changes have already been made to the files you moved in step 5 and are noted here for reference only.

C:\wamp\bin\apache\Apache2.4.9\conf\httpd.conf

Removed the # sign from the front of the line, the changed line now looks as follows:

```
#Virtual hosts

Include conf/extra/httpd-vhosts.conf
```

C:\wamp\bin\apache\Apache2.4.9\conf\extra\httpd-vhosts.conf Add the virtual host

Added the following content:

```
<VirtualHost *:80>
    DocumentRoot "C:/foodPlate"
    ServerName localhost
    <Directory "C:/foodPlate">
        Options Indexes FollowSymLinks MultiViews
        AllowOverride None
        Order allow,deny
        Allow from all
    </Directory>
</VirtualHost>
<VirtualHost *:80>
    DocumentRoot "C:/foodPlate/Sites/LocalSite"
    ServerName www.FoodPlate.local
    <Directory "C:/foodPlate/Sites/LocalSite">
        Options Indexes FollowSymLinks MultiViews
        AllowOverride None
        Order allow,deny
        Allow from all
    </Directory>
</VirtualHost>
```

About the icons

Represents a hypertext link. This link can also be found in the bookmarks provided with the course.

Represents a URL that contains the exercise code. You can use this URL to see how the exercise code responds in a mobile device.

Where are the course data files?

You can download the data files that accompany this course at http://www.kevinruse.com/html5apis

About the API specifications

The APIs introduced in this course are derived from two standards bodies: the World Wide Web Consortium (W3C) and the Web Hypertext Application Technology Working Group (WHATWG).

W3C

The W3C (led by Tim Berners-Lee) is responsible for shaping the languages of the web including HTML and CSS and, to some degree, JavaScript. The W3C accomplishes its goal by publishing documents that define various Web technologies. The publication system follows a process that slowly promotes a working draft document to a stable release format that is ready for browser manufacturers to implement.

All W3C standards and drafts can be found at http://www.w3.org/TR/. The process of publishing these documents involves following steps and requirements designed for concenus, fairness, collaboration, public accountability, responsiveness, progress and quality. The standards go through several iterations before becoming mature or final. These iterations are described below.

Working Draft (WD)

A W3C Recommendation (REC) document begins its journey as a "Working Draft (WD)." To become a Working Draft, the web topic will first have been discussed and drafted (aka "Editor Drafts"). The Working Draft is then published for public review. (See the resources below for links to join the W3C mailing lists and participate in the discussions). The Working Drafts are indeed "works in progress" and should not be implemented in production environments, even though some browsers may support the documents features.

Candicate Recommendation (CR)

The CR iteration is more stable that the WD, but still not complete or final. The document is considered final by its editors only in the sense that the draft describes what it set out to. The actual implementation of the spec remains unfinished. So, once again, the document is open to the public for review by developers and browser manufacturers.

Proposed Recommendation (PR)

The document has now passed the two prior levels (WD and CR) and is submitted to the W3C Advisory Council for its final approval. At this point, the document rarely sees additional changes and is well on its way to reaching its final state. To expedite the process, the W3C website will send out a "Last Call" signal for feedback from implementors.

W3C Recommendation (REC)

At this point, the document will have gone through extensive discussion, feedback, review and testing in both an "academic" setting as well as "real-world" settings by browser-developers and web developers. The document is now officially endorsed by the W3C as a standard. It is now the responsibility of browser-developers and web developers to begin implementation.

Historically, some documents in the REC stage have been ambigious leading to incorrect or partial implementation by web browsers. However, there is a notion of "W3C compliance" and it involves complying with two or more levels of compliance as defined by the W3C.

WD Notes

W3C Recommendations are sometimes updated or extended. This is typically done by the publication of separate documents known as Editor Draft Notes. If substantial in size and content, these notes prompt the release of a new Edition or Level of the Recommendation.

W3C community groups

https://www.w3.org/community

Value of Creating Standards at W3C*

W3C continues to evolve to provide the community a productive environment for creating Web standards. W3C standards:

- are created following a consensus-based decision process;
- consider aspects of accessibility, privacy, security, and internationalization;
- reflect the views of diverse industries and global stakeholders;
- balance speed, fairness, public accountability, and quality;
- benefit from Royalty-Free patent licensing commitments from participants;
- are stable (and W3C seeks to ensure their persistence at the published URI);
- benefit from wide review from groups inside and outside W3C;
- are downloadable at no cost;
- are maintained in a predictable fashion;
- are strengthened through interoperability testing;

From: http://www.w3.org/standards/about.html

Resources

W3C vs. WHATWG specifications: http://www.w3.org/wiki/HTML/W3C-WHATWG-Differences

Opinions: http://community.sitepoint.com/t/should-the-w3c-and-whatwg-die/110806

Join the W3C Mailing List: http://www.w3.org/Mail/Request#addr

Join the WHATWG Mailing List: https://whatwg.org/mailing-list

How to contribute to the HTML5 specification: http://html5hub.com/how-developers-can-contribute-to-the-html5-specification/#i.1os11i4f40cpwt

How to "Move the Web Forward:" http://movethewebforward.org/

Chapter 1

Battery Status API

In this chapter, you learn how to obtain the charge status of a device's battery. You determine if the battery is charging and, if so, how much time is required for the device to reach full charge. If the device is not charging, you determine how much time remains before the battery is completely discharged.

The Battery Status API became a W3C Candidate Recommendation on December 9, 2014.

Objectives

- ❑ Describe the Battery Status API.

- ❑ List some use cases for the Battery Status API.

- ❑ Use the Battery Status API to report if a device is charging.

- ❑ Use the Battery Status API to report how much time it will take to fully charge a device.

- ❑ Use the Battery Status API to report how much life is left on a battery that is not charging.

- ❑ List the browsers that support the Battery Status API.

Introduction

Today's mobile apps combined with modern devices and new features present developers with numerous programming decisions. Uploading high-resolution images, sending push notifications, and running camera-accessing code can quickly drain the end user's battery. The Battery Status API allows the developer to gain information about the device's battery status before committing to power-intensive tasks. The developer can write code to both warn the user before commitment to such tasks and automatically defer power-intensive tasks during times of low battery power. By providing programmatic access to the status of the battery in the host device, the application can behave differently depending on the battery strength at any given time.

Why use the Battery Status API?

Today's dynamic web applications perform many client-side tasks, including rendering complex CSS, auto-saving files, making numerous network calls, and storing data offline. Tracking low battery status can trigger the deferral of some of these tasks or mitigation of their use accordingly.

How does the Battery Status API work?

When a document is presented to the user (e.g., a page is viewed in a browser, also known as a *browsing context*), a battery object is created and initially set to null. This battery is a Promise object (see "What is a promise?" below) that holds a `BatteryManager` object. When the `getBattery()` method is invoked, the battery is returned. If the battery is null, the user agent or browser creates a new promise and returns it. The `battery` becomes this object. The battery promise is resolved with the battery Promise object. The user agent should not reject the battery promise.

When the device is unable to report any of the values in the battery status, default values are used. There are a number of scenarios where this may be the case:

- System preference settings
- User preference settings
- Device limitations
- Environment limitations
- No battery attached to the device

The default values emulate a fully charged and plugged in battery.

When the battery is charging, the device should queue a task that sets the `chargingtime` property and fires the `BatteryManager` object's `chargingtimechange` event.

If the device is charging, the `dischargetime` property is not available.

What is a promise?

A JavaScript promise is an object that is a property of the Window object. Its purpose is to execute functions based on the success or failure of another function. Essentially, it is a promise to perform an action based on a value that is not known when the promise is made. The promise, then, is a placeholder that will eventually hold either the successful result value or the reason for the failure to obtain that value. Promises represent a different (and some believe, better) way to handle asynchronous operations (including handling errors that are similar to try/catch blocks) than standard callback functions.

A Promise object can be in one of three states:

Pending: The asynchronous operation is not yet completed; therefore, the promises outcome (or value) has not yet been produced.

Fulfilled: The asynchronous operation has completed, and the promise now holds a value.

Rejected: The asynchronous operation has failed, and the promise will not be fulfilled. The promise value now holds the reason for the failure.

While the promise state is pending, the promise will ultimately be fulfilled or rejected upon completion of the asynchronous operation. The promise will never change state once it is fulfilled or rejected.

First, check for promise support with

```
if(window.Promise)
```

The Promise object is created with the new constructor function:

```
var promise = new Promise(function(resolve, reject) {
    //asynchronous code goes here
  });
```

Notice that the Promise object is a Function object and it takes a function as its one argument. That function argument is a callback function. It takes two arguments that are also functions. Asynchronous or deferred code goes inside the callback function argument of the Promise object. If everything in the callback function argument is successful, the promise is fulfilled and the resolve function is called. If anything in the callback function fails, the promise is rejected and the reject function is called.

For more information about promises, visit https://promisesaplus.com/.

The Battery Status API

Battery Status API met

Name	Description
`getBattery`	Creates a new BatteryManager object
The BatteryManager represents the current battery status of the hosting device. The battery status information is held in properties of the BatteryManager object	

BatteryManager properties

Name	Type	Description	Default Value
`charging`	boolean	The charging state of the systems battery	true
`chargingTime`	unrestricted double	The time remaining (in seconds) until the systems battery is fully charged	positive infinity
`dischargingTime`	unrestricted double	The time remaining in seconds until the system's battery is completely discharged and the system is about to be suspended	0
`level`	double	The level of the systems battery	1.0

BatteryManager events

Name	Description
`dischargingtimechange`	Sets the discharging time and fires when the battery discharging time is updated
`chargingchange`	Sets the charging attributes value and fires when the battery charging state is updated
`chargingtimechange`	Sets the charging attributes value and fires when the battery charging time is updated
`levelchange`	Sets the battery level attribute and fires when the battery level is updated

Note   The definition of how often the `chargingtimechange`, `dischargingtimechange`, and `levelchange` events are fired is left to the implementation.
Browser support

At publication time, the Battery Status API was supported by Chrome version 39 and above, Opera version 25 and above, Firefox 10 through 15 with the moz prefix, Firefox 16 through Firefox 38.5 (and Firefox Nightly 41.0a1 (2015-6-8) with the older specification navigator.battery, Android with Chromium 40, and Firefox for Android. It was not supported in any version of Internet Explorer or Safari.

For the latest information regarding browser support of the Battery Status API, see http://caniuse.com/#-search=battery.

Resources

The W3C specification: http://www.w3.org/TR/battery-status/

Exercise 1.1: Testing for Battery Status API support

In this exercise, you write JavaScript code to determine if the web browser supports the Battery Status API.

Objectives

After completing this exercise, you will be able to do the following:

- Use a conditional statement to determine if the browser supports the Battery Status API.
- Use the original and the more current Battery Status API to check for browser support.
- List the browsers that support the Battery Status API.

Step 1   Using your code editor or IDE, open the file "battery-API/battery-support-starter.html."

Step 2   Enter the code shown below in bold:

```
<!DOCTYPE html>
<html>
<head lang="en">
    <meta charset="UTF-8">
    <title>Battery Status API</title>
</head>
<body>
<h1>Checking for Battery Status API support</h1>
<p>For an article (by David Walsh) with information regarding the older
specification, see <a href="http://davidwalsh.name/battery-api">Older Battery
Status API Specification</a></p>
<p>For an article about the most recent specification, see <a href="http://
davidwalsh.name/javascript-battery-api">Recent Battery Status API Specifica-
tion</a></p>
<p>To check for support, try the following code:</p>
<pre>
    <code>
    &lt;script&gt;
        if (navigator.getBattery || navigator.battery) {
            console.log("Battery Status API is supported.")
        }
        else {
            console.log("Battery Status API is NOT supported.")
        }
    &lt;/script&gt;
    </code>
</pre>
<script>
    if (navigator.getBattery || navigator.battery) {
        console.log("Battery Status API is supported.");
    }
    else {
```

```
        console.log("Battery Status API is NOT supported.");
    }
</script>
</body>
</html>
```

Step 3   Save the file and run it in several web browsers to determine browser support. Be sure to have the browsers Developer Tools open and the console active.

At publication time, the following browsers supported the Battery Status API:

- Chrome Version 42
- Firefox 38.0.5 32-bit
- Opera 30
- Android browser Chromium 40
- Chrome for Android 42

There was no support for Battery Status API in the following browsers:

- Safari
- Internet Explorer/Edge
- Opera Mini

Code explanation

This script block will execute the "if" condition when the page runs, resulting in a log statement output to the console indicating whether or not the Battery Status API is supported. The original Battery Status API proposal used a `battery()` method, whereas, the finished spec uses the `getBattery()` method. Therefore, for the benefit of older browsers that use the `battery()` method, check for the existence of both `battery()` and `getBattery()`.

Exercise 1.2: Obtaining battery status

In this exercise, you write JavaScript to obtain the status of the device battery.

Objectives

After completing this exercise, you will be able to do the following:

- Understand how simple graphics can be created with SVG or CSS.
- Describe the purpose of the ECMAScript 5 "use strict" directive.
- Use the `getBattery()` method of the Battery Status API.
- Understand how the `BatteryManager` object creates a promise.
- List and use the properties of the `BatteryManager` object.

Step 1   Using your code editor or IDE, open the file "battery-API/battery-api-starter.html," and examine the battery graphic code.

The web page contains two images of batteries, neither of which is created with an HTML <img> element that points to a graphic file. Instead, the "images" are code generated. The first battery graphic is created using the Scalable Vector Graphic (SVG) markup language. The second battery image is created with HTML elements that have been styled with the Cascading Style Sheet language (CSS) and appear below on lines 45–48.

Step 2   Review both the SVG and the CSS code that is responsible for creating the battery graphic.

battery-API/battery-api-starter.html

```
1.  <!DOCTYPE html>
2.  <html>
3.  <head>
4.  <meta charset="UTF-8">
5.  <title>Battery Status API-starter</title>
6.  <meta name="viewport" content="width=device-width,initial-scale=1">
7.  <link type="text/css" rel="stylesheet" href="battery.css">
8.  </head>
9.  <body>
10. <h1>Battery Status API</h1>
11. <section id="batteryInfo">
12. <table class="batteryTable">
13. <tr>
14. <td>Attribute</td>
15. <td>Value</td>
16. </tr>
17. <tr>
18. <td>Battery Level: </td>
19. <td id="batLevelElem"></td>
20. </tr>
21. <tr>
22. <td>Battery Charging: </td>
23. <td id="batChargingElem"></td>
24. </tr>
25. <tr>
26. <td>Battery Discharging Time: </td>
27. <td id="dischargeTimeElem"></td>
28. </tr>
29. <tr>
30. <td>Battery Charging Time: </td>
31. <td id="batChargingTimeElem"></td>
32. </tr>
33. </table>
34. </section>
35. <section id="message"></section>
36. <svg width="260" height="140"
                xmlns="http://www.w3.org/2000/svg">
37. <g>
38. <rect id="charge" fill="#ffffff" stroke="#000000"
```

```
                        stroke-width="4" x="33" y="34"
                        width="205" height="86" />
39. <rect id="posTerminal" fill="#000000" stroke="#000000"
                        stroke-width="4" x="241" y="58" z="1"
                        width="10" height="38" />
40. </g>
41. <g display="inline">
42. <rect id="batteryCharge" fill="#ff0000" stroke="#000000"
                        stroke-width="0" stroke-linejoin="null"
                        stroke-linecap="null" x="35" y="36.5" z="5"
                        width="0" height="81" />
43. </g>
44. </svg>
45. <div class="battery">
46. <span id="chargeStripes"></span>
47. <div class="batteryEnd"></div>
48. </div>
49. </body>
50. </html>
```

Step 3   Open the page in a web browser to see the graphics.

Scalable Vector Graphics markup language

SVG is a markup language for describing vector shapes. It is an XML application and can be embedded inside HTML. SVG is widely supported in both desktop and mobile environments. To experiment with SVG, visit Google's online SVG editor here: http://svg-edit.googlecode.com/svn-history/r1771/trunk/editor/svg-editor.html.

More information on SVG is available here:

- http://www.w3.org/TR/SVG/
- http://www.w3schools.com/svg/

Cascading Style Sheet language and CSS shapes

CSS adds presentation information to web pages. It is responsible for the rendering of structured documents including HTML and SVG. It uses a pattern-matching system that locates elements (or tags) on the page (in the CSS Object Model) and then applies style information to those tags.

More information on CSS specifications can be found here:

- http://www.w3.org/Style/CSS/specs.en.html

More information about drawing shapes with CSS can be found here:

- https://css-tricks.com/examples/ShapesOfCSS/

Step 4   Create a script block before the closing body element.

Step 5   Before writing any JavaScript, invoke "strict mode" as shown below.

```
<script>
```

```
        'use strict';
</script>
```

The "use strict" directive

The following explanation is from W3Schools at http://www.w3schools.com/js/js_strict.asp: "use strict"; defines that JavaScript code should be executed in "strict mode."

The "use strict" directive is new in JavaScript 1.8.5 (ECMAScript version 5). It is not a statement, but a literal expression, ignored by earlier versions of JavaScript. The purpose of "use strict" is to indicate that the code should be executed in "strict mode." With strict mode, you cannot, for example, use undeclared variables. Strict mode is supported in these browsers:

- Internet Explorer from version 10
- Firefox from version 4
- Chrome from version 13
- Safari from version 5.1
- Opera from version 12

Step 6   Below the "use strict" directive, declare the following variables:

```
var batLevel, batCharging, batChargingTime, batDischargingTime;
var battery = navigator.battery || navigator.webkitBattery ||
        navigator.mozBattery;
```

The battery variable is set to `navigator.battery` or `navigator.webkitBattery` or `navigator.mozBattery`. By declaring and setting the variable's value in this way, the value will be equal to the battery (object) property of the Browser (Navigator) object in modern standards-compliant browsers as well as in older versions of Chrome and Firefox.

Step 7   Note the `<section>` element with the id equal to "message." Write a function called `showMessage` that will display the battery status inside this section element.

```
        function showMessage(data) {
        document.querySelector('#message').innerHTML = data + '<br />';
}
```

The statement in the `showMessage()` function will locate the DOM element with the `id` of "message" and then set the HTML inside that element to the data argument passed in when the function is called. The data is followed by an HTML line-break element.

Step 8   Add the following "`if`" condition below the `showMessage()` function:

```
if (navigator.getBattery) {
    navigator.getBattery().then(setBatteryPower, function() {
        showMessage('There was an error while getting the battery state or
there is no battery attached to this system');
    });
} else if (battery) {
    setBatteryPower(battery);
} else {
    showMessage('Battery Status API is not supported.');
}
```

This code introduces the JavaScript promise. The `navigator.getBattery()` method returns a promise. Simply put, a *promise* is a block of code assurance. After making a function or method call, the promise assures something will happen if that call is successful and something else will happen if that call fails. Below is the `Promise` constructor function.

```
new Promise(function(resolve, reject) { ... });
```

Here you see the creation of the `Promise` function object. The resolve argument fulfills the promise, and the reject argument rejects it. Now, look at the code you wrote in step 8. The `setBatteryPower()` function will be called upon the success of the `navigator.getBattery()` method. Should the `getBattery()` method fail, the second anonymous function (that calls `showMessage()`) will be called.

Step 9   Add the following function, which is called by the `getBattery()` call from step 8.

```
function setBatteryPower(battery) {
    batLevel = battery.level;
    console.log('batLevel: ' + batLevel);
    batCharging = battery.charging;
    console.log('batCharging: ' + batCharging);
    if(battery.charging === true) {
       batDischargingTime = 'Battery discharging time is not available while
       battery is charging.';
         console.log('batChargingTime: ' + battery.chargingTime);
         batChargingTime = battery.chargingTime;
         var minutesToCharge = (battery.chargingTime * 0.0166667).toFixed(2);
         showMessage('Battery will charge in '+minutesToCharge+' minutes.');
         if (battery.chargingTime === 'Infinity') {
             batChargingTime = 'Battery chargingTime is at default value of
             Infinity.';
         }
    }
    else {
         showMessage('The system is unable to report the remaining charging
time.');
         console.log('The system is unable to report the remaining charging
time.');
    }
}
```

Step 10   Run the page in your mobile, laptop, or desktop web browser. Try plugging and unplugging your device. Refresh the page after you swap the plug in and out. Notice the status change.

Next, modify the `setBatteryPower()` function so that it includes an event watcher to watch for changes in the battery status. Also add code to update the battery graphics.

Step 11   Modify the `setBatteryPower()` function so that it matches the code below (the code added in this step is shown in bold):

```
function setBatteryPower(battery) {
    batLevel = battery.level;
    console.log('batLevel: ' + batLevel);
    batCharging = battery.charging;
```

```
        console.log('batCharging: ' + batCharging);
        if(battery.charging === true) {
            document.querySelector('#chargeStripes').setAttribute('class',
'charging');
            batDischargingTime = 'Battery discharging time is not available
while battery is charging.';
            console.log('batChargingTime: ' + battery.chargingTime);
            batChargingTime = battery.chargingTime;
            var minutesToCharge = (battery.chargingTime * 0.0166667).toFixed(2);
            showMessage('Battery will charge in '+minutesToCharge+' minutes.');
            if (battery.chargingTime === 'Infinity') {
                batChargingTime = 'Battery chargingTime is at default value of
                Infinity.';
            }
        }
        else {
            showMessage('The system is unable to report the remaining charging
time.');
            console.log('The system is unable to report the remaining charging
time.');
        }
        if (battery.charging===false) {
          document.querySelector('#chargeStripes').setAttribute('class', '');
          batDischargingTime = battery.dischargingTime;
          var minutesToDischarge = (batDischargingTime * 0.0166667).toFixed(2);
          batDischargingTime = minutesToDischarge;
          batChargingTime = 'Battery charging time is not available when not
charging.';
          if (battery.dischargingTime == 'Infinity') {
            console.log(battery.dischargingTime);
            batDischargingTime = 'Battery dischargingTime is at default value of
' + 'Infinity.';
          }
        }
        battery.addEventListener('chargingchange', function() {
            showMessage('Battery chargingchange event: ' + battery.charging);
            console.log('battery level: ' + battery.level);
            setBatteryPower(battery);
        }, false);
        battery.onlevelchange = function() {
            showMessage('Battery levelchange event: ' + battery.level);
            console.log(battery.level);
            setBatteryPower(battery);
        }
        showBatteryPower(battery, batCharging);
    }
```

Step 12   Run the file in a web browser and be sure the Developer Tools console is active. The file shown below represents Chrome Version 43.0.2357.81 m (64-bit). Note the log statements in the console.

You will get an error message in the console regarding the `showBatteryPower` function:

`Uncaught ReferenceError: showBatteryPower is not defined`

Fix this error by writing the `showBatteryPower` function next.

Step 13   Add the following function below the `setBatteryPower()` function:

```
function showBatteryPower(battery, chargeStatus) {
    document.querySelector('#batLevelElem').innerHTML = batLevel;
    document.querySelector('#batChargingElem').innerHTML = batCharging;
    document.querySelector('#dischargeTimeElem').innerHTML = batDischarging-
Time;
    document.querySelector('#batChargingTimeElem').innerHTML = batCharging-
Time;
    var batteryWidth = (battery.level * 100) - 22;
    batteryWidth = batteryWidth + "%";
    console.log('batteryWidth: ' + batteryWidth);
    document.querySelector('#batteryCharge').setAttribute('width', battery-
Width);
    if(battery.level <= .35) {
        document.querySelector('#batteryCharge').setAttribute('fill',
'#F00');
    }
    //if level is equal to or below .5
    else if(battery.level < .5) {
        document.querySelector('#batteryCharge').setAttribute('fill',
'#ffff00');
    }
    //if level is above.5
    else if(battery.level >= .5) {
        document.querySelector('#batteryCharge').setAttribute('fill',
'#00ff00   ');
    }
}
```

Step 14   Run the page in your mobile, laptop, or desktop web browser.

The battery-api file showing the value of the variables batLevel, batCharging and batChargingTime.

Step 15   Try plugging and unplugging your device. With the event listeners you added in step 11, you should no longer need to refresh the page after you swap the plug in and out. Notice the status change.

Battery Status API

Attribute	Value
Battery Level:	0.47
Battery Charging:	false
Battery Discharging Time:	Battery dischargingTime is at default value of Infinity.
Battery Charging Time:	Battery charging time is not available when not charging.

The system is unable to report the remaining charging time.

The finished Battery Status API file as seen in the Chrome Version 43.0.2357.81 m (64-bit) web browser while charging.

Battery Status API

Attribute	Value
Battery Level:	0.35
Battery Charging:	false
Battery Discharging Time:	Battery dischargingTime is at default value of Infinity.
Battery Charging Time:	Battery charging time is not available when not charging.

The system is unable to report the remaining charging time.

The finished Battery Status API file as seen in the Chrome Version 43.0.2357.81 m (64-bit) web browser not charging.

Exercise 1.2: Finished file

```
<!DOCTYPE html>
<html>
<head>
    <meta charset="UTF-8">
    <title>Battery Status API</title>
    <meta name="viewport" content="width=device-width,initial-scale=1">
    <link type="text/css" rel="stylesheet" href="battery.css">
</head>
<body>
<h1>Battery Status API</h1>
<section id="batteryInfo">
    <table class="batteryTable">
        <tr>
            <td>Attribute</td>
            <td>Value</td>
        </tr>
        <tr>
            <td>Battery Level: </td>
            <td id="batLevelElem"></td>
        </tr>
        <tr>
            <td>Battery Charging: </td>
            <td id="batChargingElem"></td>
        </tr>
        <tr>
            <td>Battery Discharging Time: </td>
            <td id="dischargeTimeElem"></td>
        </tr>
        <tr>
            <td>Battery Charging Time: </td>
            <td id="batChargingTimeElem"></td>
        </tr>
    </table>
</section>
<section id="message">Battery Power Message</section>
<svg width="260" height="140" xmlns="http://www.w3.org/2000/svg">
    <g>
        <rect id="charge" fill="#ffffff" stroke="#000000" stroke-width="4"
x="33" y="34" width="205" height="86" />
        <rect id="posTerminal" fill="#000000" stroke="#000000" stroke-
width="4" x="241" y="58" z="1" width="10" height="38" />
    </g>
    <g display="inline">
        <rect id="batteryCharge" fill="#ff0000" stroke="#000000" stroke-
width="0" stroke-linejoin="null" stroke-linecap="null" x="35" y="36.5" z="5"
```

```
width="0" height="81" />
    </g>

</svg>
<div class="battery">
    <span id="chargeStripes"></span>
    <div class="batteryEnd"></div>
</div>
<!-- add script block here -->
<script>
    'use strict';

    var batLevel, batCharging, batChargingTime, batDischargingTime;
    var battery = navigator.battery || navigator.webkitBattery || navigator.
mozBattery;
    function showMessage(data) {
        document.querySelector('#message').innerHTML = data + '<br>';
    }
    if(navigator.getBattery) {
        navigator.getBattery().then(setBatteryPower, function() {
            showMessage("There was an error while getting the battery state
or there is no battery attached to this system.");
        });
    }
    else {
        showMessage("Battery Status API is not supported.");
    }

    function setBatteryPower(battery) {
        batLevel = battery.level;
        console.log('batLevel: ' + batLevel);
        batCharging = battery.charging;
        console.log('batCharging: ' + batCharging);
        if(battery.charging === true) {
            document.querySelector('#chargeStripes').setAttribute('class',
'charging');
            batDischargingTime = 'Battery discharging time is not available
while battery is charging.';
            console.log('batChargingTime: ' + battery.chargingTime);
            batChargingTime = battery.chargingTime;
            var minutesToCharge = (battery.chargingTime * 0.0166667).to-
Fixed(2);
            showMessage('Battery will charge in ' + minutesToCharge + ' min-
utes.');
            if (battery.chargingTime === 'Infinity') {
                batChargingTime = 'Battery chargingTime is at default value
```

```
of Infinity.';
            }
        }
        else {
            showMessage('The system is unable to report the remaining
charging time.');
            console.log('The system is unable to report the remaining
charging time.');
        }
        if (battery.charging===false) {
            document.querySelector('#chargeStripes').setAttribute('class',
'');
            batDischargingTime = battery.dischargingTime;
            var minutesToDischarge = (batDischargingTime * 0.0166667).to-
Fixed(2);
            batDischargingTime = minutesToDischarge;
            batChargingTime = 'Battery charging time is not available when
not charging.';
            if (battery.dischargingTime == 'Infinity') {
                console.log(battery.dischargingTime);
                batDischargingTime = 'Battery dischargingTime is at default
value of ' + 'Infinity.';
            }
        }
        battery.addEventListener('chargingchange', function() {
            showMessage('Battery chargingchange event: ' + battery.
charging);
            console.log('battery level: ' + battery.level);
            setBatteryPower(battery);
        }, false);
        battery.onlevelchange = function() {
            showMessage('Battery levelchange event: ' + battery.level);
            console.log(battery.level);
            setBatteryPower(battery);
        }
        showBatteryPower(battery, batCharging);
    }

    function showBatteryPower(battery, chargeStatus) {
        document.querySelector('#batLevelElem').innerHTML = batLevel;
        document.querySelector('#batChargingElem').innerHTML = batCharging;
        document.querySelector('#dischargeTimeElem').innerHTML = batDis-
chargingTime;
        document.querySelector('#batChargingTimeElem').innerHTML = batCharg-
ingTime;
        var batteryWidth = (battery.level * 100) - 22;
```

```
        batteryWidth = batteryWidth + "%";
        console.log('batteryWidth: ' + batteryWidth);
        document.querySelector('#batteryCharge').setAttribute('width', bat-
teryWidth);
        if(battery.level <= .35) {
            document.querySelector('#batteryCharge').setAttribute('fill',
'#F00');
        }
        //if level is equal to or below .5
        else if(battery.level < .5) {
            document.querySelector('#batteryCharge').setAttribute('fill',
'#ffff00');
        }
        //if level is above .5
        else if(battery.level >= .5) {
            document.querySelector('#batteryCharge').setAttribute('fill',
'#00ff00  ');
        }
    }
</script>
</body>
</html>
```

To test this file on your mobile device, go to www.kevinruse.com/battery

Exercise summary

In this exercise, you learned how to use the Battery Status API to retrieve information about a device's charging state and battery life. You were briefly introduced to the new JavaScript Promise object as well.

Challenge exercise

1. Using your IDE, open the file "battery-api-challenge-starter.html" from the challenge subdirectory.

2. Run the file in a web browser.

3. The map represents a Google map and the button represents a potential geolocation call. Your job is to respond to the click and check the battery power before allowing the geolocation call. If the battery level is below .2, pop-up an alert box that reads: "Your battery power is at or below 20%". This operation may deplete your battery." If the battery level is above .2, log to the console: "make geolocation call."

4. If you get stuck, "battery-api-challenge-finished.html" is a possible solution.

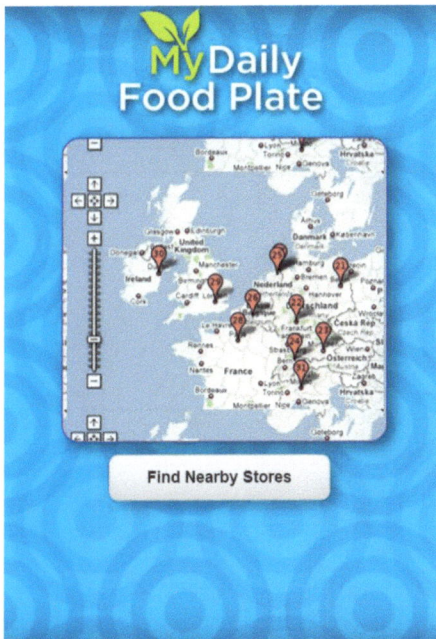

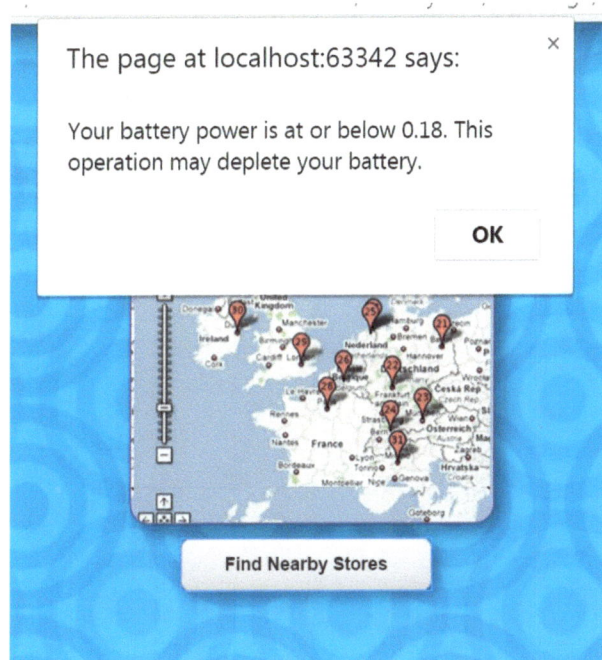

Chapter summary

In this chapter, you learned the API responsible for providing Battery Status updates. You learned the Battery Status API's `getBattery()` method and the properties and methods of the `BatteryManager` object.

Chapter 2

Vibration API

In this chapter, you learn how to gain end users' attention via their sense of touch by providing a form of haptic feedback using an API that allows developers to vibrate a device in a steady or alternating pattern.

The Vibration API became a W3C Candidate Recommendation on February 10, 2015.

Objectives

❑   Describe the Vibration API.

❑   List some use cases for the Vibration API.

❑   Use the Vibration API to make a device vibrate for a given number of seconds.

❑   Use the Vibration API to make a device vibration pattern.

❑   List the browsers that support the Vibration API.

Introduction

While the notification API may be sufficient for alerting users to emails and other messages, sometimes applications require tactile feedback from a device. The Vibration API is designed to fill this need. Therefore, this API is not intended for use cases that require some form of generic notification.

Why use the Vibration API?

The Vibration API has a very simple use case: simple tactile feedback *only*. When a complex notification involving text, icons, and other message formats is required, developers should look to the notification API. When simulating a collision or shaking effect, vibration can enhance a gaming experience. Vibrating the device can be used to mimic other devices (e.g., pagers). Use cases include enhanced accessibility, simulations, gaming effects, and any time that you want to get the user's attention without resorting to visual or audio effects.

How does the Vibration API work?

The Vibration interface is both small and simple, consisting of a single method of the Browser (Navigator) object called vibrate that accepts a vibration pattern as an argument.

Vibration API methods

Name	Type	Parameters
vibrate()	boolean	pattern (type=VibratePattern)

Implementers of the Vibration API must invoke a set of rules for processing vibration patterns. These rules are out of the scope of this chapter; however, details can be found in the W3C specification document at http://www.w3.org/TR/vibration/.

Code example

```
// vibrate for one second (1000 ms):
navigator.vibrate(1000);

// can also be written as:
navigator.vibrate([1000]);

// to cancel any existing vibrations:
navigator.vibrate(0);

// can also be written as:
navigator.vibrate([]);
```

Resources

Specification: http://www.w3.org/TR/vibration/

Exercise 2.1: Test for Vibration API support and vibrate the device

In this exercise, you write JavaScript to determine if the browser supports the Vibration API and then vibrate the device.

Objectives

After completing this exercise, you will be able to do the following:

- Understand the Vibration API and its `vibrate()` method.
- Recognize the required vendor prefixes currently used with the Vibration API.
- Use the `vibrate()` method of the Vibration API.

Step 1 Using your code editor or IDE, open the file "vibration-API/vibration-1-starter.html."

Step 2 Add the code shown in bold below.

```
<!DOCTYPE html>
<html>
<head lang="en">
    <meta charset="UTF-8">
    <title>Vibration 1</title>
    <meta name="viewport" content="width=device-width,initial-scale=1">
</head>
<body>
<button id="vibrateDeviceBtn">Vibrate</button>
<script>
    if(navigator.vibrate || navigator.webkitVibrate || navigator.mozVibrate
|| navigator.msVibrate) {
        console.log("Vibration API is supported.");
        }
    else {
            console.log("Vibration API is NOT supported.");
    }
</script>
</body>
</html>
```

This code checks for support by confirming the existence of the global property/method called `vibrate`. The `||` syntax serves as the "or" operator, thus you are checking for Chrome, Opera, Microsoft, and Firefox versions of the `vibrate()` method. Then, you simply log a result to the console.

Step 3 Test the file in various web browsers with the console running and identify the browsers that support the Vibration API.

Step 4 To make the device vibrate, add the following code shown in bold below:

```
<script>
    if(navigator.vibrate || navigator.webkitVibrate || navigator.mozVibrate
|| navigator.msVibrate) {
```

```
            console.log("Vibration API is supported.");
document.querySelector('#vibrateDeviceBtn').addEventListener('click',
 function() {
            navigator.vibrate = navigator.vibrate ||
                    navigator.webkitVibrate ||
                    navigator.mozVibrate ||
                    navigator.msVibrate;
            console.log("vibrate device");
            navigator.vibrate(1000);
        })
    }
    else {
            console.log("Vibration API is NOT supported.");
    }
</script>
```

Step 5   Test the file in various devices.

Exercise 2.1: Finished file

```
<!DOCTYPE html>
<html>
<head lang="en">
    <meta charset="UTF-8">
    <title>Vibration 1</title>
    <meta name="viewport" content="width=device-width,initial-scale=1">
</head>
<body>
<button id="vibrateDeviceBtn">Vibrate</button>
<script>
    if(navigator.vibrate || navigator.webkitVibrate || navigator.mozVibrate
|| navigator.msVibrate) {
        console.log("Vibration API is supported.");
        document.querySelector('#vibrateDeviceBtn').addEventListener('click',
function() {
            navigator.vibrate = navigator.vibrate ||
                    navigator.webkitVibrate ||
                    navigator.mozVibrate ||
                    navigator.msVibrate;
            console.log("vibrate device");
            navigator.vibrate(1000);
        })
    }
    else {
            console.log("Vibration API is NOT supported.");
    }
</script>
</body>
</html>
```

Exercise summary

In this exercise, you learned how to check for support of the Vibration API and made the phone vibrate for a specified amount of time. In the next exercise, the phone will vibrate on and off according to a specified pattern.

Exercise 2.2: Vibrate the device with a pattern

In this exercise, you write JavaScript to vibrate the phone according to a specified pattern.

Objectives

After completing this exercise, you will be able to do the following:

- Use the Vibration API and its `vibrate()` method to stop and start the phone from vibrating.

Step 1   Using your code editor or IDE, open the file "vibration-API/vibration-2-starter.html."

Step 2   Locate the comment and add the following call to the `vibrate()` method:

```
//vibrate for half a second (500 milliseconds), be still for one second and
then vibrate again for 500 ms
    navigator.vibrate([500, 1000, 500]);
```

Notice how an array is passed in to the `vibrate()` method. This syntax can be used when passing in only one number, as you will see later in step 4.

Step 3   Save the file and test it in various device browsers.

Step 4   Change the code so that the phone vibrates continuously when the Constant Vibrate button is clicked. The additional code is shown in bold below:

```
<script>
    if(navigator.vibrate || navigator.webkitVibrate || navigator.mozVibrate
|| navigator.msVibrate) {
        console.log("Vibration API is supported.");
        document.querySelector('#vibrateConstantBtn').addEventListen-
er('click', constantVibrate);
        document.querySelector('#vibrateDeviceBtn').addEventListener('click',
function() {
            navigator.vibrate = navigator.vibrate ||
                navigator.webkitVibrate ||
                navigator.mozVibrate ||
                navigator.msVibrate;
            console.log("vibrate device");
            navigator.vibrate([500, 1000, 500]);
        })
    }
    else {
        console.log("Vibration API is NOT supported.");
    }
```

```
var vibrateConstant;
function  constantVibrate() {
        vibrateConstant = setInterval(function() {
            navigator.vibrate([1500]);
        }, 1000);
    }
</script>
```

In step 4, you add the event listener to the Constant Vibrate button. Then you write the `constantVibrate()` function. In this function, you use the JavaScript `setInterval()` method to call a function (`navigator.vibrate()`) every second. The first argument to the `setInterval()` method is the function you wish to call, and the second argument is how often to call that function (in milliseconds).

Step 5   Save the file and test it in various device browsers.

Next, write a function to stop vibrating the device.

Step 6   Add the `stopVibrate()` function below the last function you wrote in step 4.

```
function stopVibrate() {
    if(vibrateConstant) {
        clearInterval(vibrateConstant);
    }
    navigator.vibrate(0);
}
```

In step 6, stop the device from vibrating by first checking if the constantVibrate function is executing and, if so, call `clearInterval()` to stop the vibrate code from executing every second.

Step 7   Add the event listener to the Stop Vibrate button. Place this code beneath the previous event listener.

```
document.querySelector('#vibrateStopBtn').addEventListener('click', stopVi-
brate);
```

Step 8   Save the file and test it in various device browsers. Be sure to click the Constant Vibrate button before clicking the Stop Vibrate button.

Exercise 2.2: Finished file

```
<!DOCTYPE html>
<html>
<head lang="en">
    <meta charset="UTF-8">
    <title>Vibration with Pattern</title>
    <meta name="viewport" content="width=device-width,initial-scale=1">

</head>
<body>
<button id="vibrateDeviceBtn">Vibrate</button>
<button id="vibrateConstantBtn">Constant Vibrate</button>
<button id="vibrateStopBtn">Stop Vibrate</button>
<script>
```

```
       if(navigator.vibrate || navigator.webkitVibrate || navigator.mozVibrate
|| navigator.msVibrate) {
           console.log("Vibration API is supported.");
       document.querySelector('#vibrateConstantBtn').addEventListener('click',
constantVibrate);
           document.querySelector('#vibrateStopBtn').addEventListener('click',
stopVibrate);
           document.querySelector('#vibrateDeviceBtn').addEventListener('click',
function() {
               navigator.vibrate = navigator.vibrate ||
                   navigator.webkitVibrate ||
                   navigator.mozVibrate ||
                   navigator.msVibrate;
           console.log("vibrate device");
           //vibrate for half a second (500 milliseconds), be still for one
second and then vibrate    again for 500 ms
           navigator.vibrate([500, 1000, 500]);
       })
    }
    else {
       console.log("Vibration API is NOT supported.");
    }
    var vibrateConstant;
    function constantVibrate() {
       vibrateConstant = setInterval(function() {
           navigator.vibrate([1500]);
       }, 1000);
    }
    function stopVibrate() {
    if(vibrateConstant) {
       clearInterval(vibrateConstant);
    }
    navigator.vibrate(0);
}
</script>
</body>
</html>
```

To test this file on your mobile device, go to www.kevinruse.com/vibration

Exercise summary

In this exercise, you learned how to invoke a constant vibration, a vibration pattern, and how to stop the device from vibrating.

Challenge exercise

1. Using your IDE, open the file "vibration-challenge-starter.html" from the challenge subdirectory.

2. Run the file in a web browser.

3. The pager is programmed to display a message five seconds after the page loads. Your job is to vibrate the phone for two seconds at the same time that the message displays.

4. If you get stuck, "vibration-challenge-finished.html" is a possible solution.

Page at startup:

Page five seconds after startup:

Chapter summary

In this chapter, you learned the API responsible for providing a form of haptic feedback consisting of a vibration effect on the device.

Chapter 3

Notifications API

In this chapter, you learn how to send the end user notifications that appear outside the web browser. With the Notifications API, you can send the user alerts for a variety of reasons such as letting the user know he or she has received messages and email or because of a server-side event.

The Notifications API became a W3C Candidate Recommendation on May 19, 2015.

Objectives

☐ Describe the Notifications API.

☐ List some use cases for the Notifications API.

☐ Use the Notifications API to create a visible notification outside the browser.

☐ Use the Notifications API to make multiple notifications that appear together.

☐ Group notification by type so that notifications of the same type override one another.

☐ List the browsers that support the Notifications API.

Introduction

Many applications would benefit from the ability to send alerts to the user outside the context of the web browser. The Notifications API provides a means to send notifications outside the browser, but the specification does not dictate exactly how the web browser (or user agent) should display any given form of notification. While the specification references sending notifications to the "desktop," this is intended to be interpreted as "outside the web page in a static display area such as a small section of the user's display screen, an area within the web browser Chrome, or possibly the home screen of a mobile device."[1] All presentation options regarding the notifications are left to the implementer of the specification, which attempts to be as platform-independent as possible. Because implementers are required to display the notification outside the web browser, the notification remains visible even when the browser window is closed. The user must grant permission to accept and receive notifications.

Why use the Notifications API?

There are many use cases for notifications. For example, you may want to alert the user when a back-end process has completed. In conjunction with other APIs and device features, the Notifications API becomes even more useful. You can alert the user when incoming messages or email appear. You may be thinking that there are already ways to do this in the browser; however, the driving use case for notifications lies in the appearance of these notifications outside the browser—if the user were to close the browser, the notification would remain open and visible. When your message content is such that it should be available outside the browsing experience, then you have a use case for notifications.

How does the Notifications API work?

First, notifications can be displayed only if the end user grants permission. The request for permission from the web browser on behalf of the user comes in the form of the `requestPermission()` method of the Notification object.

The `requestPermission()` method accepts a single callback function as an argument. The Notifications API provides a permission attribute that comes from the `requestPermission()` method and should be set to one of the following three strings:

"`default`"   This is equivalent to "`denied`" but the user has made no explicit choice thus far.

"`denied`"   This means the user does not want notifications.

"`granted`"   This means notifications can be displayed.

Experiences can vary regarding how often the browser shows its permission request. In addition, settings vary from browser to browser as to making the choice between "always ask for notification permission" and "always accept notifications."

The browser must keep a *list of pending notifications* as well as *active ones*. When the user activates a notification, the user agent should queue a task to fire a click event on the Notification object. This click event will be examined in the upcoming exercises.

---

1   http://www.w3.org/TR/notifications/

Notifications API

Notification object attributes

Attribute	Properties	Description	Value
title	readonly	Returns the notification's title	DOMString *
dir	readonly	Returns the notification's direction	"auto", "ltr", "rtl"
lang	readonly	Returns the notification's language	DOMString
body	readonly	Returns the notification's body or an empty string	DOMString
tag	readonly	Returns the notification's tag or an empty string	DOMString
icon	readonly	Returns the notification's icon URL (serialized) or an empty string	DOMString
*A UTF-16 string that maps directly to the JavaScript type: string			

Notification events

Event Handler	Event Handler Event Type
onclick	click
onshow	show
onerror	error
onclose	close

Notifications API methods

Method	Description
close()	Returns the close steps for the notification per the specification steps shown below: 1. If notification is neither in the list of pending notifications nor in the list of active notifications, terminate these steps. 2. Queue a task to remove notification from either the list of pending notifications or the list of active notifications, and fire an event named "close" on notification.

Resources

The W3C specification: http://www.w3.org/TR/2015/CR-notifications-20150519/

W3C Candidate Recommendation 19 May 2015

Demo: Notifications API permissions

Step 1   Using your web browser, open the file "notification-API/notification-permissions.html."

notification-permissions.html

```
1.  <!DOCTYPE html>
2.  <html>
3.  <head lang="en">
4.      <meta charset="UTF-8">
5.      <title>Notifications API-permissions</title>
6.      <meta name="viewport" content="width=device-width,
        initial-scale=1">
7.      <style>
8.          #iconMessage {
9.              font-family: "Arial", sans-serif;
10.             font-size: 10px;
11.         }
12.     </style>
13. </head>
14. <body>
15. <section>
16.     <p id="message">
17.     </p>
18. </section>
19. <div id="iconMessage">
20.     <p>The icon used in this notification is made by
            <a href="http://www.freepik.com"
                title="Freepik">Freepik</a> from
            <a href="http://www.flaticon.com"
                title="Flaticon">www.flaticon.com</a>
            is licensed under
            <a href="http://creativecommons.org/licenses/by/3.0/"
                title="Creative Commons BY 3.0">CC BY 3.0</a></p>
21. </div>
22. <script>
23.     if(window.Notification) {
24.     Notification.requestPermission(function() {
25.             var notification = new Notification("New Message
                            Received", {icon: "images/message.png"});
26.             if (Notification.permission === "denied") {
27.             console.log(Notification.permission);
28.             console.log("no permission granted");
29.             document.querySelector('#message').innerHTML =
                    "You've been notified of a message but have denied
                        the notification.";
30.             }
```

```
31.          else if (Notification.permission === "granted") {
32.              console.log(Notification.permission);
33.              console.log("Permission granted");
34.          document.querySelector('#message').innerHTML =
                  "You've been notified of a message.";
35.          }
36.      })
37.  }
38.  </script>
39.  </body>
40.  </html>
```

Code explanation

Line 23 is the browser support check. This is followed by line 24 containing the call to requestPermission() that returns (and sets) the permission attribute. Recall in the "How does the Notifications API work?" section, the possible values of default, denied, and granted. If the permission attribute is "granted," the notification appears.

Step 2   Close the browser window and observe that the notification remains.

Step 3   In preparation for upcoming demos and exercises, close the notification.

Demo: Notification events

Step 1   Using your web browser, open the file "notification-API/notification-events.html."

notification-API/notification-events.html

```
1.  <!DOCTYPE html>
2.  <html>
3.  <head lang="en">
4.      <meta charset="UTF-8">
5.      <title>Notifications API: Events-Demo
6.  </title>
7.      <style>
8.          #iconMessage {
9.              font-family: "Arial", sans-serif;
10.             font-size: 10px;
11.         }
12.     </style>
13. </head>
14. <body>
15. <section>
16. <p id="message">
17.     </p>
18. </section>
19. <h1>Notifications API: Events</h1>
```

```
20. <section>
21. <p id="message">
22. </p>
23. </section>
24. <div id="iconMessage">
25. <p>The icon used in this notification is made by
        <a href="http://www.freepik.com" title="Freepik">Freepik</a>
        from <a href=http://www.flaticon.com
        title="Flaticon">www.flaticon.com</a> is licensed under
26. <a href="http://creativecommons.org/licenses/by/3.0/"
        title="Creative Commons BY 3.0">CC BY 3.0</a></p>
27. </div>
28. <script>
29.     if(window.Notification) {
30.         var notification;
31.         Notification.requestPermission(function() {
32.             notification = new Notification("New Message
                    Received", {icon: "images/message.png"});
33.             if (Notification.permission === "denied") {
34.                 console.log(Notification.permission);
35.             console.log("no permission granted");
36.             }
37.         else if (Notification.permission === "granted") {
38.             console.log(Notification.permission);
39.             console.log("Permission granted");
40.             document.querySelector('#message').innerHTML =
                    "You've been notified of a message.";
41.             }
42.         notification.onshow = function() {
43.             console.log("you've been notified");
44.             setTimeout(closeNotification, 3000);
45.         };
46.         notification.onclick = function() {
47.             console.log('You clicked the notification');
48.             document.querySelector('#message').innerHTML =
                    "You've clicked the notification.";
49.         };
50.         notification.onclose = function() {
51.             console.log('You closed the notification');
52.             document.querySelector('#message').innerHTML =
                    "You've closed the notification.";
53.         };
54.     })
55. }
56. function closeNotification() {
57.     notification.close();
```

```
58. }
59. </script>
60. </body>
61. </html>
```

Step 2   Examine the event handlers used in this file. The Notifications events being acknowledge here include:

```
onshow
onclick
onclose
```

Code explanation

The beginning of this file is similar to that in the previous demo, but here event handlers have been added on lines 36, 40, and 44; the events (in code order) are `onshow` (the notification has appeared on the device), `onclick` (the user has clicked anywhere on the notification window), and `onclose` (the user has clicked the window's close box). Each event listener locates the html element with the `id` of "message" and inserts content into that element that describes the event. The onshow eventhandlers' line 38 waits three seconds and then calls the `closeNotification` function.

Exercise 3.1: Create a notification and set notification options

In this exercise, you use the Notifications API to create a notification that contains a title, an icon, and a message body. You send multiple notifications. You also group notifications, so that instead of creating additional notification popups, you replace existing notifications with new ones.

Objectives

After completing this exercise, you will be able to do the following:

- Use the Notifications API to send notifications to the end user.
- Set properties of the Notification object to give your notification a title, an icon, and a message.
- Group notifications into categories.

Step 1   Using your code editor or IDE, open the file "notification-API/notification-starter.html."

Notice the script block on line 25. Line 26 is the call to the `requestPermission()` method introduced in an earlier demo file. The function passed into request permission consists of the declaration of a single variable called `notification`. This will hold the notification, which will be created in step 2.

Step 2   Locate the `notification` variable and modify the code as shown in bold below:

```
<script>
    Notification.requestPermission(function() {
     var notification;
     //create Notification here
     notification = new Notification("New Message Received", {icon:
"images/message.png", dir: "rtl", body: "This is the body of the first notifi-
cation."});
        if(Notification.permission === "denied") {
```

```
        console.log(Notification.permission);
        console.log("no permission granted");
    }
    else if (Notification.permission === "granted") {
        console.log(Notification.permission);
        console.log("Permission granted");
    }
});
```

When calling the Notification's constructor function, the first argument, "New Message Received," serves as the title of the notification. The second argument sets the notification options. First, an icon is set to display message.png, followed by the text direction of the notification: "rtl" (right to left). Finally, the body of the message is set: "This is the body of the notification." The notification constructor's parameters are shown below.

Parameter	Description
title	Defines a title for the notification, which is typically displayed at the top of the notification window
options	An object that contains notification settings

Options Argument	Description	Possible Vallues
dir	Defines the text direction of the notification	auto (default value set at the browser's language setting) ltr (left to right) rtl (right to left)
lang	The notifications language	An ISO two-letter language code; see http://www.sitepoint.com/web-foundations/iso-2-letter-language-codes/ for more information
body	The notifications body text typically displayed below the title	DOMString
icon	The URL of an icon to be displayed within the notification window	Valid path to the graphical icon
data	Arbitrary data that should be associated with the notification	Any data type
tag	A string that identifies the notification	DOMString
sound *	The URL of a sound file to be associated with the notification	Not supported by any browser at publication time
Renotify *	Sets a renotify preference	Not supported by any browser at publication time
Silent *	Sets the silent preference	Not supported by any browser at publication time
Noscreen *	Sets the screen-off preference	Not supported by any browser at publication time
Sticky *	Sets the sticky preference	Not supported by any browser at publication time

*For information that is more recent, see the Living Standard at https://notifications.spec.whatwg.org/#dom-notification-notificationtitle-options

Step 3   Save and test the file in a compliant web browser. See the notification pop up with a title, a body, and an icon. The image below shows the notification as it appears in Chrome Version 43.0.2357.124 m (64-bit).

For additional information at runtime, be sure to open the web browser's Developer Tools and activate the Console.

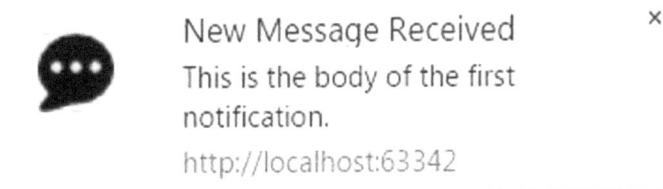

New Message Received   ✕
This is the body of the first
notification.
http://localhost:63342

The notification popup, showing a title, a body and an icon.

Next, write code that will invoke a second notification when the user clicks the "Create Notification" button located below the form. The form allows the user to enter a title and body for the new notification.

Step 4   Locate the comment: `//Second notification goes here.` and add the code shown below in bold:

```
//Second notification goes here
document.querySelector('#createNotification').addEventListener('click',
function(event) {
    event.preventDefault();
    var newNotificationTitle = document.getElementById('notificationTitle').
value;
    console.log(newNotificationTitle);
    var newNotificationBody=document.getElementById('notificationBody').value;
    console.log(newNotificationBody);
    var notification2 = new Notification(newNotificationTitle, {icon: "images/
        message.png", body: newNotificationBody});
});
```

Invoke a notification

Notification Title:

Second Message Title

Notification Body:

This is the second message

Create Notification

The filled-out web page form that will invoke a notification.

Step 5   Save the file, run the page in a web browser, and fill out the form as shown in this screenshot.

Step 6   Click the Create Notification button and you should see a second notification pop up as shown below in the Chrome web browser. For additional information at runtime, be sure to open the web browser's Developer Tools and activate the Console.

Second Message Title
This is the second message
http://localhost:63342

×

New Message Received
This is the body of the first
notification.
http://localhost:63342

×

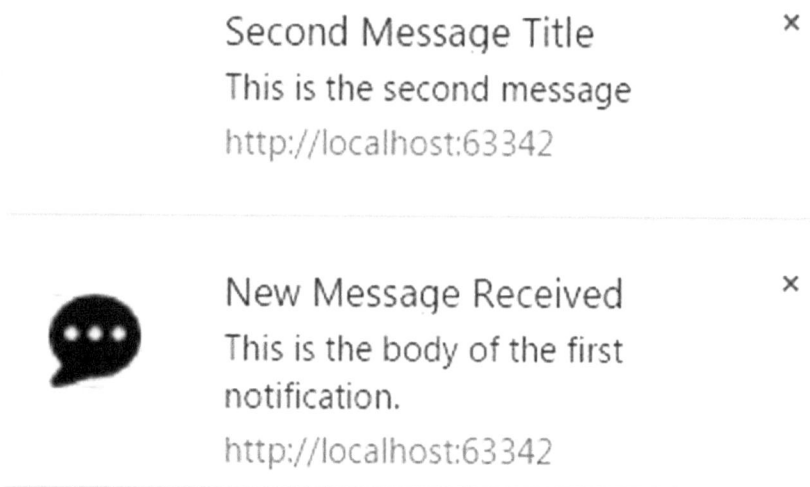

The two notification popups as seen in Chrome.

In the next step, set the tag option that will associate all notifications with equivalent tag values. Therefore, by providing the same tag value to both the initial notification and the second notification, the second notification will replace the first. In step 5, both notifications are shown. After you add the tag option, only one notification will appear.

Step 7   Return to your code editor or IDE and modify the first notification code to add the tag option. The modified code is shown below in bold.

```
//create Notification here
notification = new Notification("New Message Received", {icon: "message.png",
dir: "rtl", body: "This is the body of the first notification.", tag:
  "kevin"});
var notification2 = new Notification(newNotificationTitle, {icon: "images/mes-
sage.png", body: newNotificationBody, tag: "kevin"});
```

Step 8   Save the file, run the page in a web browser, and fill out the form as shown in the screenshot.

Invoke a notification

Notification Title:

Second Message Title

Notification Body:

This is the second message

Create Notification

The filled-out web page form that will invoke a notification.

Step 9   Click the Create Notification button. As in the last test, you should initially see the first notification.

After creating the second notification, the second one replaces the first.

Second Message Title   ✕
This is the second message
http://localhost:63342

The second notification after replacing the first.

The Notifications Living Standard specification (https://notifications.spec.whatwg.org/#dom-notification-tag) describes a use case for tags when there is a single instance of a notification as opposed to this exercise, which uses multiple notifications. Section 3.5.3 of the Notifications API – Living Standard is shown below.

3.5.3. Using the `tag` member for a single instance

The `tag` member can also be used by a single instance of an application to keep its notifications as current as possible as state changes.

For example, if Alice is using a chat application with Bob, and Bob sends multiple messages while Alice is idle, the application may prefer that Alice not see a desktop notification for each message.

```
// Bob says "Hi"
new Notification("Bob: Hi", { tag: 'chat_Bob' });

// Bob says "Are you free this afternoon?"
new Notification("Bob: Hi / Are you free this afternoon?", { tag: 'chat_Bob'
});
```

The result of this situation is a *single* notification; the second one replaces the first having the same tag. In a platform that queues notifications (first-in-first-out), using the tag allows the notification to also maintain its position in the queue. Platforms where the newest notifications are shown first, a similar result could be achieved using the `close()` method.

To test this file on your mobile device, go to www.kevinruse.com/notification

Exercise summary

In this exercise, you learned how to set the notification options, including the addition of an icon, a title, and a body. You also learned how to group notifications by tag value for both multiple and single instance notifications.

Chapter summary

In this chapter, you learned how to alert the user outside the browsing context. The alert or notification is created with standard client-side JavaScript; however, the resulting notification "lives" outside the browser and remains open even after the browser window is closed. The resulting notification look and feel is left entirely up to the browser. Therefore, the developer should test the code in various devices and desktop browsers to learn how each browser and/or device will respond.

Challenge exercise

1. Using your IDE, open the file "notification-challenge-starter.html" from the challenge subdirectory.

2. Run the file in a web browser.

3. The file displays an image of a pager. After five seconds, the pager displays a message.

4. Your job is to fire a notification at the same time that the message appears on the pager.

5. The notification should read: "You have an urgent message" and show the icon of a pager (icon is included in the challenge folder).

5. If you get stuck, "notification-api-challenge-finished.html" is a possible solution.

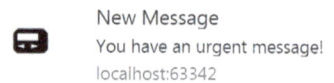

Chapter 4

DeviceOrientation Event API

In this chapter, you learn how to tap into the device's physical orientation. The ability to move a character, vehicle, or component by moving the device in your hand is popular in mobile gaming and device simulation. This API makes these types of features possible by giving the developer access to the devices' motion and orientation along x-, y-, and z-axes, numbers that can, in turn, be used by the application.

The DeviceOrientation Event API became a W3C Working Draft on December 1, 2011.

Objectives

☐   Describe the DeviceOrientation Event API.

☐   List some use cases for the DeviceOrientation Event API.

☐   Understand the difference between device orientation and device motion.

☐   Use the DeviceOrientation Event API to access both the orientation and the motion of a device.

Introduction

This DeviceOrientation Event API allows developers to obtain information about the orientation, motion, and acceleration of a device, that is, the physical orientation of the browsing device. By responding to the API's Document Model Object (DOM) events, the developer can access the device's rotation from a specified local coordinate frame. The DeviceMotion DOM events allow the developer to ascertain the acceleration of the device, expressed as a Cartesian coordinate that is based on a coordinate frame defined in the device. In addition, the developer can also determine the rotation rate of the device around that same coordinate frame. Similar to the Geolocation API, this API cannot distinguish between the means through which this data is obtained. Thus, the information provided to the device is agnostic of the source of information, which can be any mechanism capable of obtaining the information, including accelerometers, gyroscopes, and compasses.

Why use the DeviceOrientation Event API?

Probably the most compelling reason to obtain device orientation information is to provide the best viewing experience for users. For example, the user may want to change the aspect ratio of a movie they are watching based on whether the device is in portrait or landscape view. Another use case for DeviceOrientation is to make the device a natural steering mechanism that can simulate the use of tools or machinery as well as for enhancing game play. The position of characters, the direction they move, how fast they run, and how high they jump can be controlled by gestures that invoke code responses based on the orientation and motion of the device. The DeviceOrientation specification document suggests the following use cases:

5.1.1 Controlling a game: A gaming web application monitors the device's orientation and interprets tilting in a certain direction as a means to control an on-screen sprite.

5.1.2 Gesture recognition: A web application monitors the device's acceleration and applies signal processing in order to recognize certain specific gestures. For example, using a shaking gesture to clear a web form.

5.1.3 Mapping: A mapping web application uses the device's orientation to correctly align the map with reality.[1]

DeviceOrientation Event API

DeviceOrientation events

Event	Description
deviceorientation event	Fires on the Window object whenever a significant change in orientation occurs

DeviceOrientation event properties

DeviceOrientation Event Property
alpha
beta
gamma
absolute

---

1   http://www.w3.org/TR/orientation-event/

How does the DeviceOrientation Event API work?

To understand how acknowledging the orientation and motion of a device works, you must first understand how the API sets initial values regarding the position of the device (in other words, the base coordinate system). The starting or normal position is based on the phone or device lying on a flat level surface with the screen up and the top of the device pointing directly north. From this normal position, you can determine the device's orientation.

DeviceOrientation

Now, imagine a bar running through the top of the device, all the way through it, and coming out the bottom end, as shown in the image below.

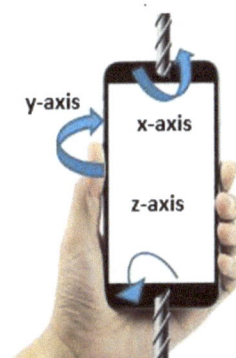

A view of the x, y and z-axes.

In this position, the x-axis value will increase as you rotate the device to the right. The y-axis value will increase as you tilt the bottom of the device forward and the z-axis will increase as you tilt the top of the device forward.

DeviceMotion

Device motion can be understood in a similar fashion. A coordinate frame forms the basis for acceleration data. For motion purposes, the x-axis (gamma) runs side to side across the device's screen and returns an increasing positive number if the device is tilted to the right and an increasing negative number if the device is tilted to the left. The y-axis (beta) runs from the top to the bottom of the devices' screen and returns an increasing negative number if the device bottom is tilted upward (an increasing positive number if the device top is tilted downward). The numbers returned by the API are the number of degrees difference from normal. Therefore, beta represents how much the device is tilted front to back while gamma represents how much the device is tilted side to side and alpha represents how much the device has been rotated around the z-axis.

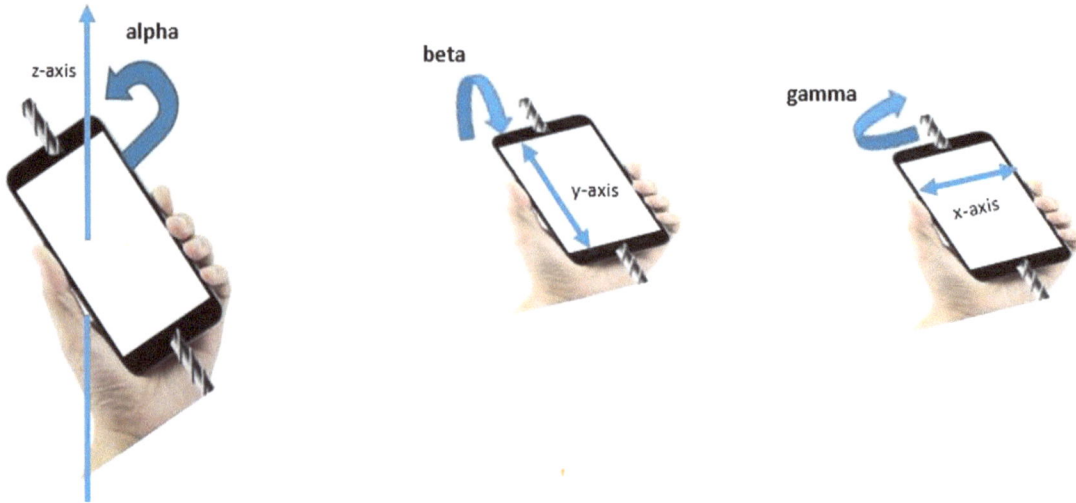

The device motion's x, y and z-axes described via alpha, beta and gamma.

The figure below was created using the Chrome web browser Ripple extension and represents a phone turned 180 degrees so that it is facing south. In other words relative to the normal position, the phone has been turned upside down.

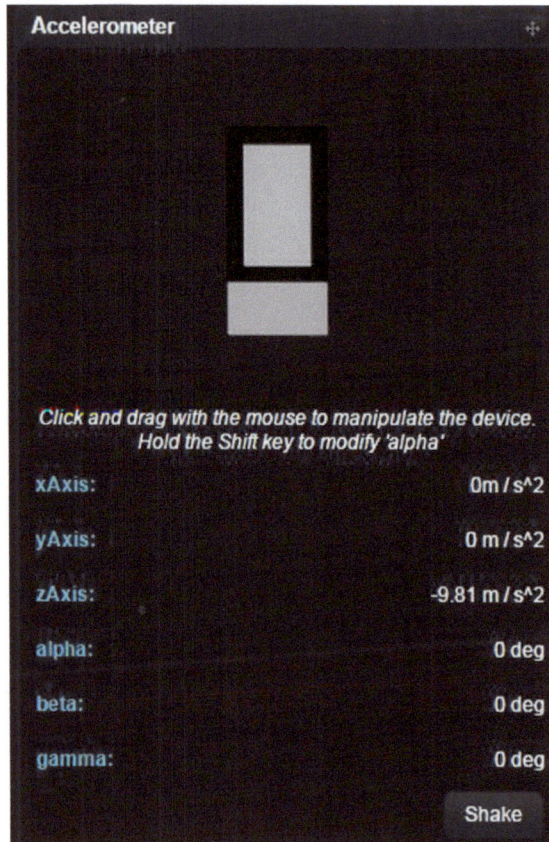

The x, y and z-axes as shown in the Ripple Chrome extension.

DeviceOrientation Event API

The following API description comes from the specification document found at http://www.w3.org/TR/orientation-event/

The DeviceOrientation Event API fires on the Window object whenever a significant change in orientation occurs (as determined by the implementing device).

The `alpha`, `beta`, and `gamma` properties of the event must specify the orientation of the device in terms of the transformation from a coordinate frame fixed on the Earth to a coordinate frame fixed in the device. The coordinate frames must be oriented as described below.

The Earth coordinate frame is an "East, North, Up" frame at the user's location. It has the following three axes, where the ground plane is tangent to the spheriod of the World Geodetic System 1984 [WGS84], at the user's location:

- East (X) is in the ground plane, perpendicular to the North axis and positive to the East.

- North (Y) is in the ground plane and positive toward True North (toward the North Pole).

- Up (Z) is perpendicular to the ground plane and positive upward.

For a mobile device such as a phone or tablet, the device coordinate frame is defined relative to the screen in its standard orientation, typically portrait. This means that slide-out elements such as keyboards are not deployed and swiveling elements such as displays are folded to their default position. If the orientation of the screen changes when the device is rotated (or a slide-out keyboard is deployed), this doesn't affect the orientation of the coordinate frame relative to the device. Users wishing to detect these changes in screen orientation may be able to do so with the existing `orientationchange` event. For a laptop computer, the device coordinate frame is defined relative to the integrated keyboard.[2]

According to the specification document found at http://www.w3.org/TR/orientation-event/:

a device lying flat on a horizontal surface with the top of the screen pointing West has the following orientation:

```
{alpha: 90,
 beta: 0,
 Gamma: 0};
```

To get the compass heading, you would simply subtract `alpha` from 360 degrees. As the device is turned on the horizontal surface, the compass heading is (360 -`alpha`).

A user is holding the device in his or her hand, with the screen in a vertical plane and the top of the screen pointing upward. The value of `beta` is 90, regardless of the value of `alpha` and `gamma`.

A user facing a compass heading of alpha degrees is holding the device in his or her hand, with the screen in a vertical plane and the top of the screen pointing to his or her right. Here is the orientation of the device:

```
{alpha: 270 - alpha,
 beta: 0,
 gamma: 90};
```

---

2 http://www.w3.org/TR/orientation-event/

See the images below (generated via the Ripple Emulator for Google Chrome browser extension; to download go to https://chrome.google.com/webstore/category/apps and search for Ripple Emulator). To understand the DeviceOrientation numbers obtained from the API, use this Chrome extension in the next exercise.

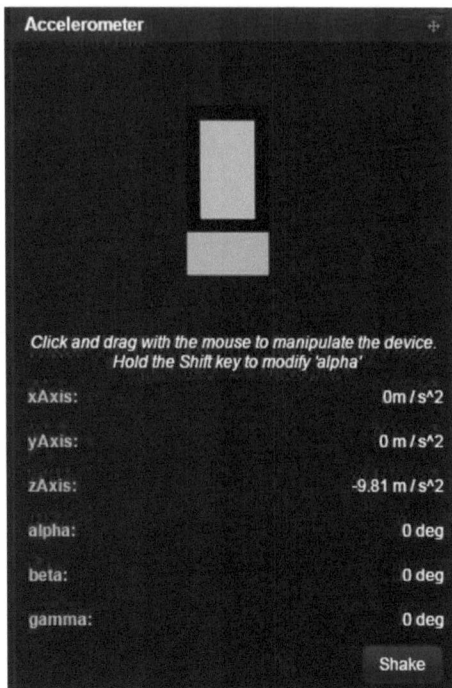

Ripple Chrome extension showing 0 deg for alpha, beta and gamma.

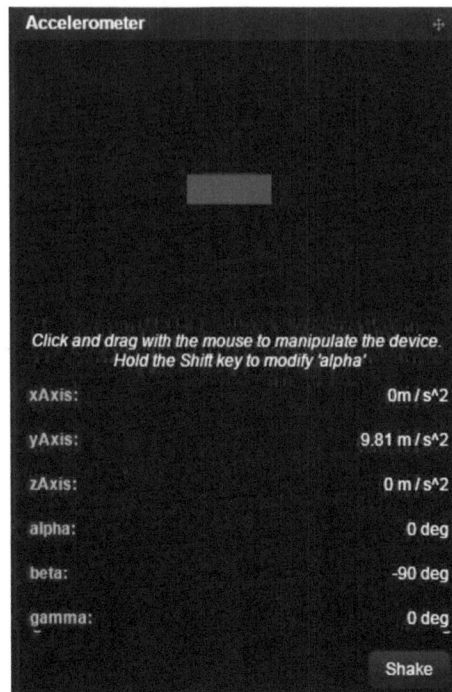

Ripple Chrome extension showing the device at 0 degrees alpha, 90 degrees beta and 0 degrees gamma.

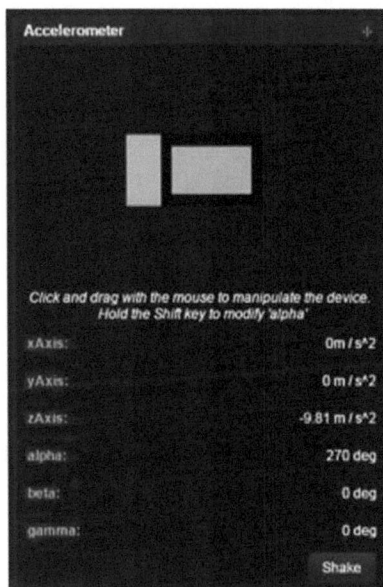

Alpha 270 degrees (z-axis)

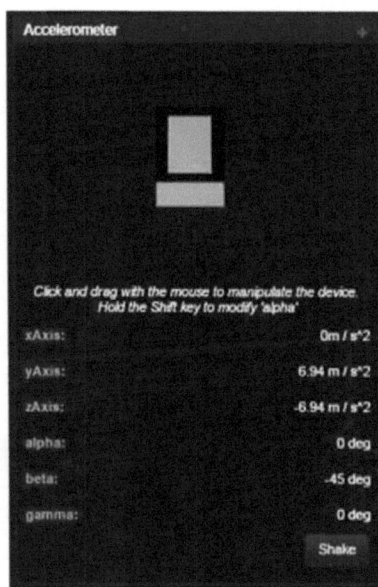

Beta -45 degrees (x-axis)

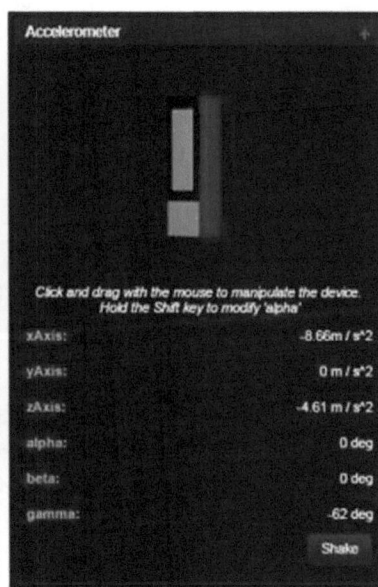

Gamma -62 degrees (y-axis)

Exercise 4.1: Understanding device orientation

In this exercise, you use the Chrome web browser Ripple extension to help you understand the DeviceOrientation Event API properties and values.

Objectives

After completing this exercise, you will be able to do the following:

- Understand and describe the deviceOrientation x-, y-, and z-axes.
- Understand and describe the alpha, beta, and gamma deviceMotion properties.

Step 1   Using the Chrome web browser, launch the Google search engine website and search for "Ripple Emulator."

Step 2   Click on the result with the Chrome Web Store URL (shown below).

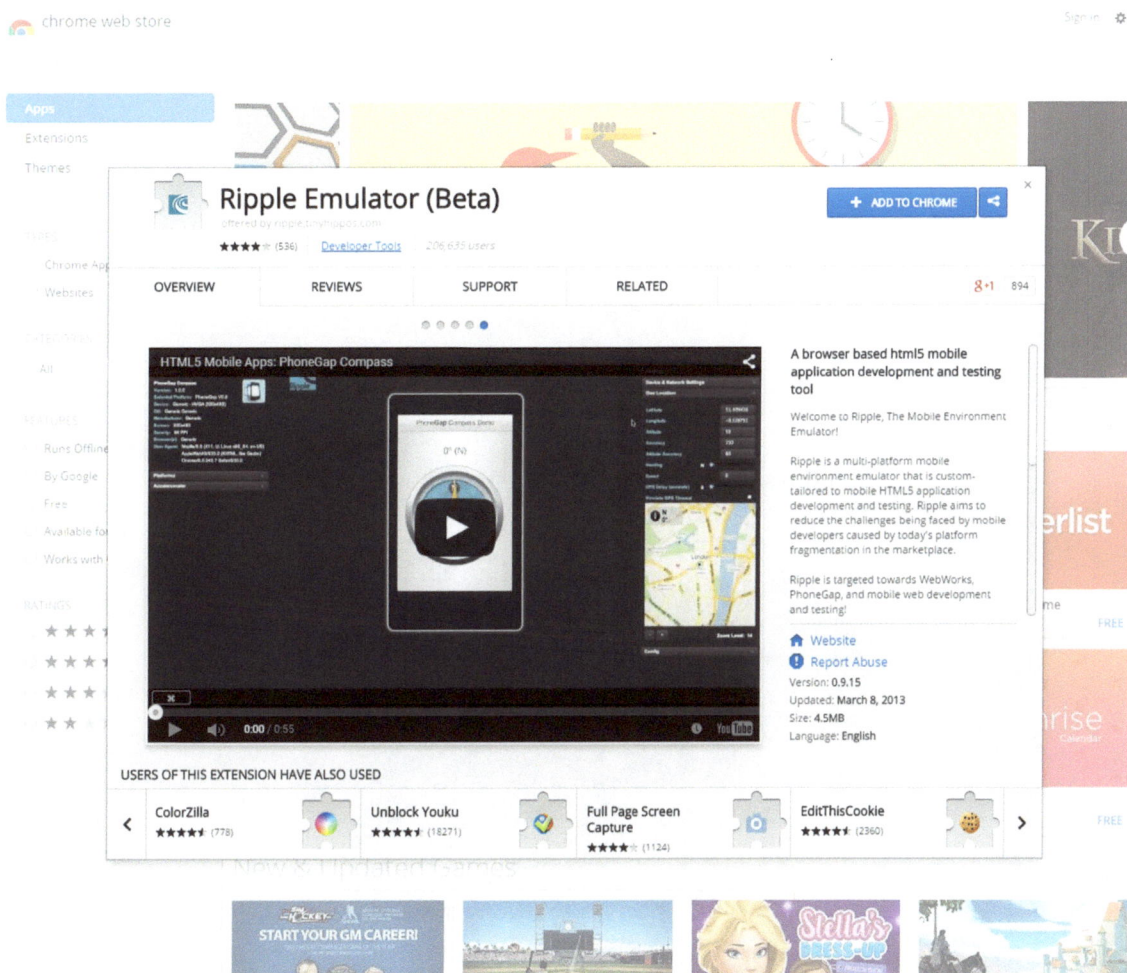

The "ADD TO CHROME" button on the Ripple Emulator (Beta) download screen as shown in Chrome.

Step 3   To install the Chrome extension, click on the + ADD TO CHROME button (circled above in red).

Step 4   After the Confirm New Extension prompt appears; confirm the download by clicking the Add button.

The "ADD TO CHROME" button after installation is complete.

Step 5   Confirm that the upper-right corner of the Ripple Emulator (Beta) window appears as shown below. An additional popup in the browser window should confirm the installation.

Step 6   While still in the Chrome web browser, open deviceOrientationMotion-API/deviceorientation.html.

Step 7   To enable the Ripple extension, use one of the techniques below:

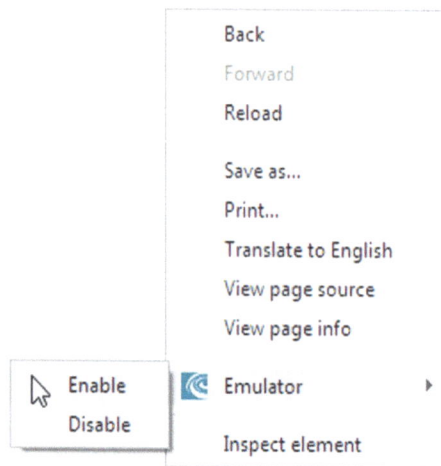

- Right-click the browser window and choose Emulator → Enable.

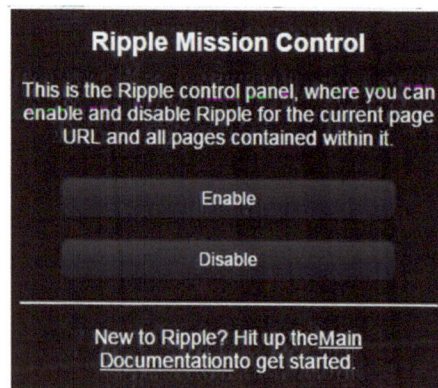

- Locate the Ripple button on the Chrome toolbar at the top of the browser and click it. Then click the Enable button.

Note: If you cannot install the Chrome Ripple extension, you may complete this exercise using the Chrome Developers Tools.

1. Launch Chrome.

2. Press Control + Shift + I to open the Developer Tools .

3. Click the "Dock to right" button on the far right of the Dev Tools.

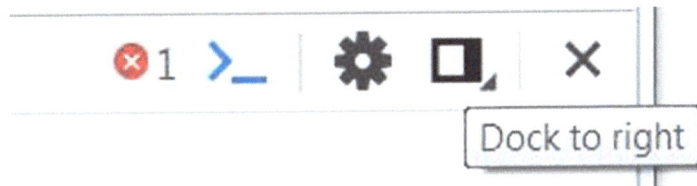

4. Click the "Emulation" tab and then click the "Enable emulation" button.

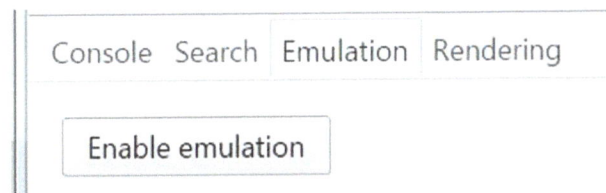

5. Click the "Accelerometer" check box. You should be able to simulate rotating the device.

Step 8   Using the DevTools or Ripple's Accelerometer section in the lower-left corner of the browser window, rotate the device simulator by pressing the mouse down over the simulator and moving to the right in a straight line.

See the screenshot below as an example.

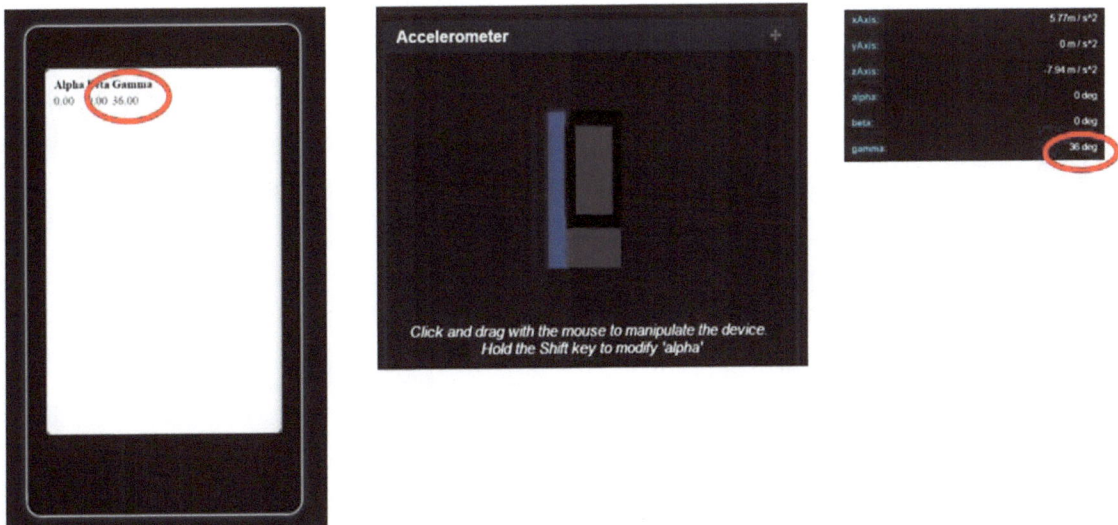

Step 9   Keep moving the phone and watch the `gamma` values increase both on the phone and in the ripple extension.

Step 10   Try altering the `alpha` and `beta` values by moving the phone.

Step 11   Using your code editor or IDE, open the same file and examine the code that handles the DeviceOrientation event:

```
<script>
    if (window.DeviceOrientationEvent) {
        console.log("DeviceOrientation is supported.");
        window.addEventListener("deviceorientation", function (event) {
            document.querySelector('#alpha').innerHTML = event.alpha.to-
Fixed(2);
            document.querySelector('#beta').innerHTML = event.beta.to-
Fixed(2);
            document.querySelector('#gamma').innerHTML = event.gamma.to-
Fixed(2);
            console.log(event.alpha);
            console.log(event.beta);
            console.log(event.gamma);
        }, true);
    }
</script>
```

Step 12   You can view this page on a mobile device at http://www.kevinruse.com/device

Step 13   Check out some of these DeviceOrientation event demos on the Internet:

- http://www.ikdoeict.be/leercentrum/slides/html5/demos/02_js/orientation.html
- http://www.smartjava.org/examples/deviceorientation/
- http://www.html5rocks.com/en/tutorials/device/orientation/deviceorientationsample.html
- http://sandbox.juurlink.org/accelerometer/
- http://wellcaffeinated.net/demos/device-orientation

Exercise summary

In this exercise, you learned how to invoke the DeviceOrientation event and verified the event-handling code by using the Chrome Ripple extension. In doing so, you learned the alpha, beta, and gamma properties of the event.

DeviceMotion

DeviceMotion supplies the acceleration and rotation rates of the device. The DeviceMotion event fires on the Window object.

The DeviceMotion event properties can be somewhat complex. The specification document defines the properties as follows:

> The `acceleration` property must provide the acceleration of the hosting device relative to the Earth frame, expressed in the body frame, as defined in section 4.1. The acceleration must be expressed in m/s^.

> Implementations that are unable to provide acceleration data without the effect of gravity (for example, because they lack a gyroscope) may instead supply the acceleration including the effect of gravity. This is less useful in many applications but is offered here as a means of providing best-effort support. In this case, the `accelerationIncludingGravity` property must provide the acceleration of the hosting device, plus an acceleration equal and opposite to the acceleration

due to gravity. Again, the acceleration must be given in the body frame defined in section 4.1 and must be expressed in m/s^.

The `rotationRate` property must provide the rate of rotation of the hosting device in space. It must be expressed as the rate of change of the angles of the defined in section 4.1 and must be expressed in deg/s.

The `interval` property must provide the interval at which data is obtained from the underlying hardware and must be expressed in milliseconds. It must be a constant, to simplify filtering of the data by the web application.

Implementations that are unable to provide all properties must set the values of the unknown properties to null. If an implementation can never provide motion information, the event should be fired with all properties set to null.[3]

Exercise 4.2: Understanding device motion

In this exercise, you use the Chrome web browser Ripple extension to help you understand the devicemotion properties and values.

Objectives

After completing this exercise, you will be able to do the following:

- Understand and describe the deviceMotion properties: `acceleration.x`, `acceleration.y`, and `acceleration.z`
- Understand the difference between the `acceleration` property and the `accelerationIncludingGravity` property

Note   This file may not work in an emulator. To view the finished file, use a mobile device and go to http://www.kevinruse.com/devicemotion.html.

Step 1   Using your code editor or IDE, open deviceOrientationMotion-API/devicemotion.html.

Step 2   Run the file in the Chrome browser with the Ripple extension enabled.

Step 3   Use the Accelerometer in the Ripple extension to rotate the phone while watching the x-, y-, and z-axes.

Step 4   Review the code in the editor that is responsible for the table data in the web page.

The relevant code is shown here:

```
<script>
    if (window.DeviceMotionEvent) {
        console.log("DeviceMotionEvent supported");
        window.addEventListener("devicemotion", function(event) {
            var acceleration = event.acceleration;
            console.log("Acceleration x: " + acceleration.x);
            console.log("Acceleration y: " + acceleration.y);
            console.log("Acceleration z: " + acceleration.z);
            document.querySelector('#dmx').innerHTML = acceleration.x.to-
```

---

[3] http://www.w3.org/TR/orientation-event/

```
Fixed(2);
            document.querySelector('#dmy').innerHTML = acceleration.y.to-
Fixed(2);
            document.querySelector('#dmz').innerHTML = acceleration.z.to-
Fixed(2);
            accelerationGravity = event.accelerationIncludingGravity;
            console.log("Acceleration Including Gravity x: " +
                    accelerationGravity.x);
            console.log("Acceleration Including Gravity y: " +
            accelerationGravity.y);
            console.log("Acceleration Including Gravity z: " +
            accelerationGravity.z);
            document.querySelector('#ax').innerHTML = accelerationGravity.x.
              toFixed(2);
            document.querySelector('#ay').innerHTML = accelerationGravity.y.
              toFixed(2);
            document.querySelector('#az').innerHTML = accelerationGravity.z.
              toFixed(2);
            var rotation = event.rotationRate;
            console.log("Rotation Alpha: " + rotation.alpha);
            console.log("Rotation Beta: " + rotation.beta);
            console.log("Rotation Gamma: " + rotation.gamma);
            console.log("Device Motion Interval: " + event.interval);
            document.querySelector('#ra').innerHTML = rotation.alpha;
            document.querySelector('#rb').innerHTML = rotation.beta;
            document.querySelector('#rg').innerHTML = rotation.gamma;
            document.querySelector('#int').innerHTML = event.interval;
        }, true);
    }
</script>
```

Acceleration and accelerationIncludingGravity

The acceleration property provides the acceleration of the device relative to the earth frame—in other words, the movement of the device relative to the x-, y-, and z-axes defined earlier.

The earth frame is defined in some detail in the specification and is shown here for reference:

The Earth coordinate frame is an "East, North, Up" frame at the user's location. It has the following three axes, where the ground plane is tangent to the spheriod of the World Geodetic System 1984 [WGS84], at the user's location.

- East (X) is in the ground plane, perpendicular to the North axis and positive toward the East.

- North (Y) is in the ground plane and positive toward True North (toward the North Pole).

- Up (Z) is perpendicular to the ground plane and positive upward.

For a mobile device such as a phone or tablet, the device coordinate frame is defined relative to the screen in its standard orientation (typically portrait). This means that slide-out elements such as keyboards are not deployed, and swiveling elements such as displays are folded to their default position. If the orientation of the screen changes when the device is rotated or a slide-out keyboard is deployed, the orientation of the coordinate frame relative to the device is not affected. Users wishing to detect these changes in screen orientation may be able to do so with the existing `orientationchange` event. For a laptop computer, the device coordinate frame is defined relative to the integrated keyboard.

- x is in the plane of the screen or keyboard and is positive toward the right-hand side of the screen or keyboard.

- y is in the plane of the screen or keyboard and is positive toward the top of the screen or keyboard.

- z is perpendicular to the screen or keyboard and is positive out of the screen or keyboard.[4]

  The `accelerationIncludingGravity` property provides the acceleration of the device, plus an acceleration equal and opposite to the acceleration due to gravity.

rotationRate

The rotationRate property provides the rate of rotation in space and is returned as the change in the angles around the x-, y-, and z-axes. The rotationRate that returns this change in angles is expressed in degrees.

To test this file on your mobile device, go to www.kevinruse.com/device

Exercise summary

In this exercise, you learned the properties of deviceMotion that are used to measure acceleration and rotation.

Chapter summary

In this chapter, you learned how to recongize and respond to a user moving their device. You learned the terminology used to describe the various motions. You followed and debugged the motion through the use of Chromes' Developer Tools.

---

4 http://www.w3.org/TR/orientation-event/

Chapter 5

ContentEditable API

In this chapter, you learn how to make portions of your web page editable by the end-user. You will use the new contentEditable HTML attribute. You also learn how to make an entire web page editable.

The contenteditable attribute became part of the W3C HTML5 specification on October 28, 2014

Objectives

- ❑ Describe the contentEditable HTML attribute.

- ❑ List some use cases for the contentEditable attribute.

- ❑ Create HTML elements that can be edited in a web browser by the end user.

- ❑ Allow the user to edit entire HTML documents.

Introduction

The contentEditable attribute allows regions of the HTML page to be edited in the browser by the end user. The attributes' value could be any one of the following:

true   Content of the element is editable.

false   Content of the element is not editable.

inherit   Content element is editable if its parents' content is editable.

Changes made to the document can be stored permanently with the localStorage API. Alternatively, changes can be stored for the duration of the browsing session with sessionStorage. (See the chapter on Web Storage, for more information.)

Why use contentEditable?

There are numerous use cases for making parts of your page editable. Before the existence of the contentEditable attribute, user-entered text was accomplished mainly through text-input and textarea elements which results in the look and feel of a form. Some user interfaces, such as online text editors, are not and should not look like forms. By making any element including simple headings and paragraphs editable, the contentEditable attribute allows for any look and feel on the front end. Other use cases include applications designed for document collaboration. The user is presented with a normal looking document, but can freely edit it. Although it is beyond the scope of the contentEditable attribute, user-entered changes can be pushed to a back-end database or stored locally on the client. Another use case is an online grammer or spelling game or exercise. The user is presented with paragraphs containing misspelled words or improper use of grammar rules and is challenged to edit them directly in their current context.

contentEditable API

Property	Description
contentEditable	Returns "true," "false," or "inherit," based on the state of the contenteditable attribute.
isContentEditable	Returns true if the element is editable; otherwise, returns false. An empty string is equivalent to true.

Resources

http://www.w3.org/TR/html5/editing.html#contenteditable

https://html.spec.whatwg.org/multipage/interaction.html#contenteditable

Exercise 5.1: Using the contentEditable API

In this exercise, you use the contentEditable attribute to allow the end user to edit parts of the web page.

Objectives

After completing this exercise, you will be able to do the following:

- Use the contentEditable HTML attribute.

Step 1   Using your web browser, open the file "contentEditable/contentEditable-starter.html."

Step 2   Add the code shown below in bold.

```
<!DOCTYPE html>
<html>
<head lang="en">
    <meta charset="UTF-8">
    <title>contentEditable</title>
</head>
<body>
    <h1>This is not editable.</h1>
        <!-- make this h1 editable -->
    <h1 contenteditable="true">This is editable.</h1>
<div id="parentDiv" contenteditable="true">
    <p>Content in the parent div.</p>
        <!-- add a script block here -->
        <div id="childDiv">
            <p>Content in the child div.</p>
        </div>
</div>
  <script>
    console.log(document.querySelector('#childDiv').isContentEditable);
  </script>
</body>
</html>
```

Step 3   Test the file in a web browser. Be sure that the browser's Developer tools are active and that the Console is open. Examine the log statement that shows the effect of the `isContentEditable` property.

Step 4   Recall that in step 2, the div with the `id` of `parentDiv` was made editable. Try editing that div element's descendant elements.

Exercise summary

In this exercise, you learned how to make portions of a web page editable by the end user simply by adding the contentEditable attribute to those elements that you want to make editable.

Making entire documents editable with designMode

Developers can make entire web documents editable using the document `designMode` attribute. When enabled, the end user can edit the entire document. Further JavaScript is required to save the users changes either on the client or back to the server if necessary.

designMode

`designMode` is a web Interface Description Language (IDL) attribute. The web IDL describes interfaces intended to be implemented in web-browsing devices. The IDL attributes typically correspond to properties of ECMAScript DOM objects. The web IDL specification can be found at http://www.w3.org/TR/WebIDL/.

The `designMode` attribute is set to "on" to enable designMode and "off" to disable designMode.

designMode (as getter)

If enabled, must return "on"

If disabled; must return "off"

Resources

http://www.w3.org/TR/html5/editing.html#making-entire-documents-editable:-the-designmode-idl-attribute.

Exercise 5.2: Making an entire document editable

In this exercise, you use the html `designMode` property of the `Document` object to allow the end user to edit the entire web page.

Objectives

After completing this exercise, you will be able to do the following:

- Make an entire web page editable.

Step 1   Using your code editor or IDE, open the file "contentEditable/docEditable-starter.html."

Step 2   Add the code shown below in bold.

```
<!DOCTYPE html>
<html>
<head lang="en">
    <meta charset="UTF-8">
    <title>designMode</title>
</head>
<body>
<h1>Making entire documents editable</h1>
```

```
<h2>Document designMode attribute</h2>
<p>HTML documents have a designMode Web IDL<sup>1</sup> attribute.</p>
<p>The designMode attribute is set to "on" to enable designMode and "off" to
disable designMode.</p>
<h3>designMode (as getter)</h3>
<ul>
    <li>if enabled: must return "on"</li>
    <li>if disabled: must return "off"</li>
</ul>

<sup>1</sup><span style="margin-left: 4px;">IDL stands for Interface
Description Language. Web IDL is used to describe interfaces intended to be
implemented in web-browsing devices. The IDL attributes typically correspond
to properties of ECMAScript DOM objects.</span>
<p style="margin-left: 12px;">The web IDL specification can be found at <a
href="http://www.w3.org/TR/WebIDL/">http://www.w3.org/TR/WebIDL/.</a></p>
<button id="editDoc">Edit Document</button>
<!-- add script block here -->

<script>
    document.querySelector('#editDoc').addEventListener('click', function()
    {
        document.designMode = "on";
    })
</script>
</body>
</html>
```

Step 3   Test the file in a web browser. Try editing any portion of the document.

Exercise summary

In this exercise, you learned how to make an entire web page editable by way of the designMode property of the Document object.

Chapter summary

In this chapter, you learned two ways to make a web page editable by the end user. In the first method,
you used an html attribute (contentEditable) to control which portions of the document could be
changed. In the second method, you used the designMode property of the Document object, which
made the entire document editable by the end user.

Challenge exercise

1. Using your IDE, open the file "contenteditable-challenge-starter.html" from the challenge subdirectory.

2. Run the file in a web browser.

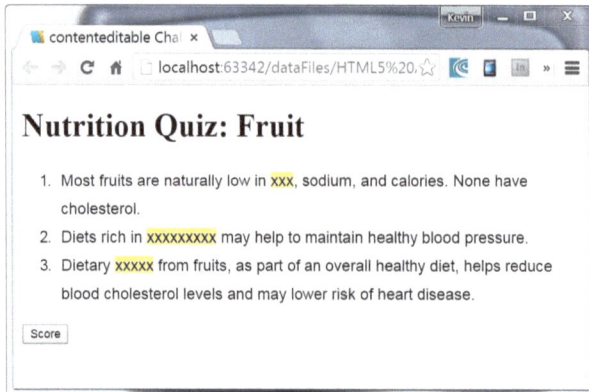

3. Your job is to make the text highlighted in yellow editable by the end user.

4. The "Score" button is already working, however, you need to make the highlighted text uneditable after the user clicks the "Score" button.

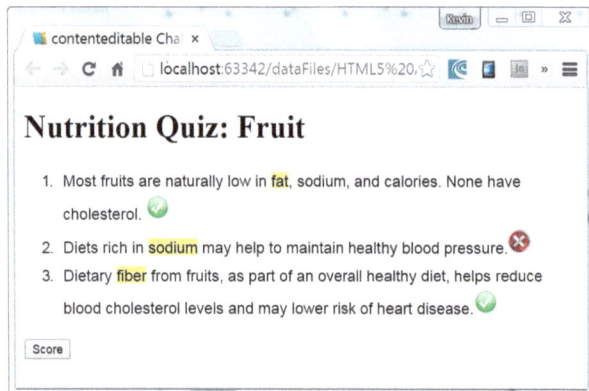

NOTE   The alert box code is supplied in the starter file.

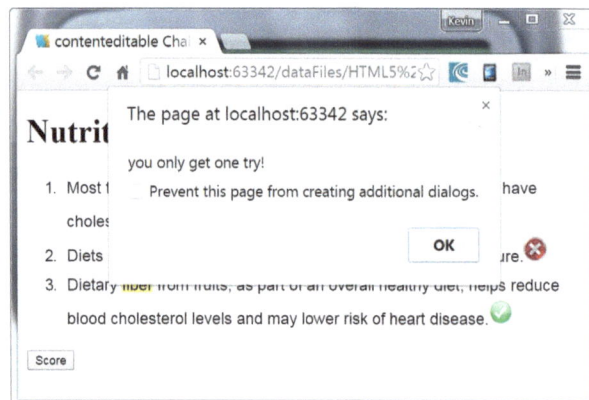

Chapter 6

Fullscreen API

In this chapter, you learn how to display portions of the web page so that they occupy the users' entire screen. You make <div>, <video> and <image> elements display full screen. You learn how to let the user disable the full –screen view and discuss use cases for the full-screen API.

The Fullscreen API was last updated in the WHATWG Living Standard on May 8, 2015.
The Fullscreen API was last edited as a W3C Working Group Note on November 18, 2014.

Objectives

❑   Describe the Fullscreen API.

❑   List some use cases for the Fullscreen API.

❑   Explain how the API pushes a section of a web page or the entire web page into full-screen view.

Introduction

The Fullscreen API allows any element to be viewed full screen. This means that the developer can choose any element, such as an image, a video, a section, and so on, to be displayed full screen. This is different from the browser's Full Screen button or keyboard command, which simply displays the entire web page in full screen. The API also allows the developer to mimic this browser functionality as well. Depending on the browser, a popup message appears that allows the user to accept or deny full-screen mode. A followup message informs the user that they can disable full screen by pressing the ESC key.

Why use the Fullscreen API?

Desktop users typically enjoy the Web via large or sometimes multiple monitors. The typical viewing experience for phone and tablet viewers is, of course, a much smaller screen. The Fullscreen API provides the user with the opportunity to view a web page, or portions of a web page, at a maximum width and height that matches the device screens' width and height. In addition, the full-screen view will remove the browser's chrome. The browser's chrome comprises the window frames, menus, toolbars, and scrollbars that can be distracting when presenting a web page, for example, during a presentation, where the focus should be on the web content and not on the surrounding browser chrome. The Fullscreen API consists of simple methods for enabling and disabling full-screen view and simple properties that return the state of the view and the element that is capable of displaying in full view.

Use cases for full screen include any circumstances in which the user would benefit from seeing the entire page or portions of the page at the maximum resolution of the device screen. This can be invoked to call attention to an area of the page or application, provide a larger viewing experience for small-screen devices, or to invoke a projector-type viewing experience. Remember that the browser's chrome is no longer displayed in full-screen mode, making the experience less like a web browser view and more like a movie screen dedicated entirely to your web page or application.

The Fullscreen API

Fullscreen API methods

Method	Behavior
`requestFullscreen`	Displays an individual element in full-screen view, for example `document.documentElement.requestFullScreen()`
`exitFullscreen`	Stops any element from being displayed in full screen

Note that the WHATWG specification uses a lowercase "s" in all Fullscreen methods; however Firefox, Google Chrome, and Safari use an uppercase one.

Fullscreen API properties

Method	Behavior
`fullscreenEnabled`	Returns true if the document has the ability to display elements in full-screen and full-screen is supported; returns false otherwise
`exitFullScreen`	Stops any element from being displayed in full screen. Older versions of Firefox use cancelFullScreen.
`fullscreenElement`	Returns the element that is displayed full screen, sor null if there is no such element.

Fullscreen API events

Method	Behavior
`onfullscreenchange`	This event is fired whenever the user has moved into or out of full-screen view.
`onfullscreenerror`	Fires whenever a full-screen error is fired.

Notes on the full-screen view

In some browsers (at publication time, these included IE11 and Firefox [including Nightly]), the full-screen element is set to 100 percent width and height. Thus, the element's content may be stretched because the aspect ratio is ignored.

Exercise 6.1: Using the Fullscreen API

In this exercise, you use the Fullscreen API to make an entire web page appear full screen as well as make a `<video>` and/or a `<div>` element on the same page appear full screen. You learn how to programmatically exit Fullscreen and respond to Fullscreen API events. You also learn how to determine whether the user is in fullscreen view.

Objectives

After completing this exercise, you will be able to do the following:

- Make an entire web page appear full screen.
- Make portions (single elements) of a web page appear full screen.
- Disable full-screen view.

Step 1   Using your code editor or IDE, open the file "fullscreen-API/fullscreen-starter.html."

The relevant code in this web page is that for the three children of the body element: the `<video>`, `<div>`, and `<figure>` elements. Below those elements are the buttons that will be used to active full-screen views for the preceding elements.

A quick look at canisuse.com indicates that while supported by several browsers, each requires a vendor prefix. See the screenshot below.

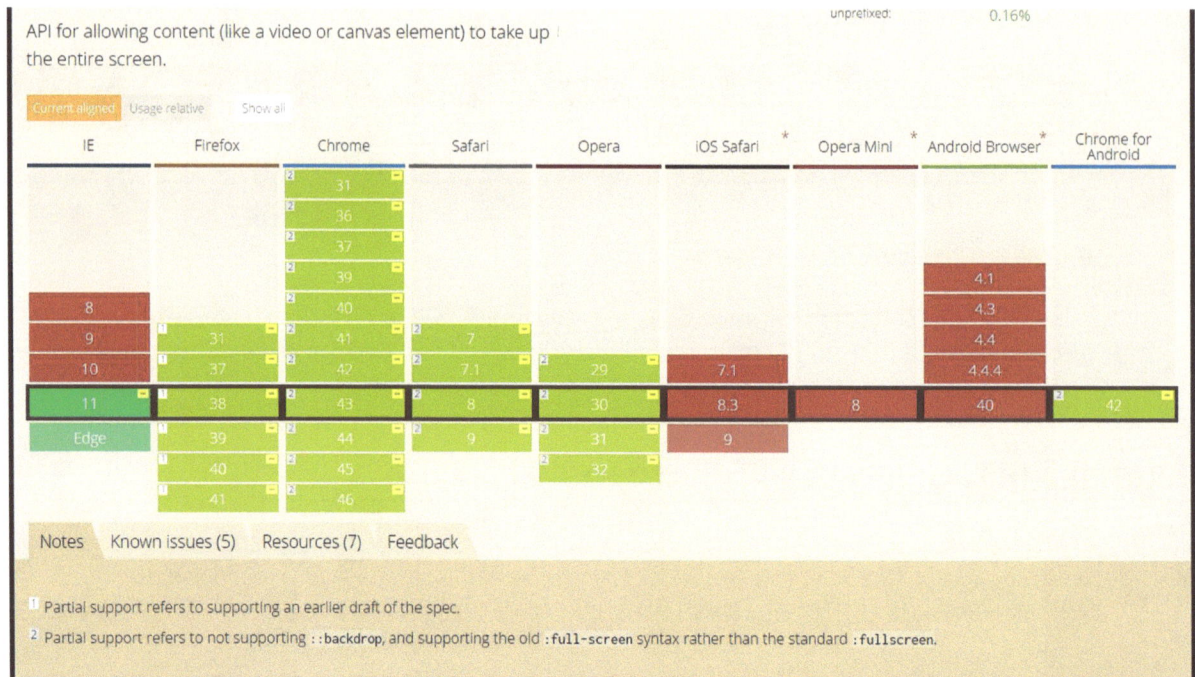

The yellow box in the upper-right corner of each browser version indicating a required vendor prefix.

Step 2   Create a script block below the last button element and before the closing body element. You will find a comment in the file for reference.

Step 3   Create a variable called `canFullScreen` to hold the document's `fullscreenEnabled` property. Assign a value that allows for all vendor-prefixed versions of this property as shown below in bold.

```
<script>
        var canFullScreen = document.fullscreenEnabled || document.web-
kitFullscreenEnabled || document.mozFullScreenEnabled || document.ms-
FullscreenEnabled;
</script>
```

Step 4   Following the variable declaration, check to see if the browser supports fullscreen view by verifying the fullscreenEnabled property and logging the result to the console.

```
if (canFullScreen) {
    console.log(canFullScreen);
}
```

Step 5   Save the file and run it several browsers. Be sure the browser's Developer tools are active and the console is open. Review the log statements.

Step 6   Return to your code editor or IDE and add a variable to store the fullscreenElement property of the Document object. You will log this property to the console; however, at publication time, there were no browsers that returned a value for this property.

```
var fullScreenElem = document.fullscreenElement ||
                     document.webkitFullscreenElement ||
                     document.mozFullScreenElement ||
                     document.msFullscreenElement;
console.log(fullScreenElem);
```

Step 7   Declare variables for all buttons on the page.

```
var viewFullScreenBtn = document.querySelector('#fullScreenBtn');
var exitFullScreenBtn = document.querySelector('#exitFullScreen');
var viewFullScreenVideoBtn = document.querySelector('#fullScreenVideoBtn');
var viewFullScreenDivBtn = document.querySelector('#fullScreenDivBtn');
```

Step 8   Declare variables for the sections of the page that will displayed in full-screen view.

```
var docElem = document.documentElement;
var divElem = document.querySelector('#sampleDiv');
var videoElem = document.querySelector("#dogVideo");
var imgElem = document.querySelector('#logo');
```

Step 9   Add event listeners for all of the buttons and the image element.

```
viewFullScreenBtn.addEventListener("click", function() {
    fullScreenDisplay(docElem);
});

viewFullScreenVideoBtn.addEventListener("click", function() {
    fullScreenDisplay(videoElem);
});

viewFullScreenDivBtn.addEventListener("click", function() {
    fullScreenDisplay(divElem);
});

imgElem.addEventListener("click", function() {
    fullScreenDisplay(imgElem);
});
```

Notice that each event handler function calls the fullScreenDisplay() function and is passed the element that will be displayed in full-screen view. The fullScreenDisplay function will invoke a vendor-prefixed version of the requestFullScreen() method.

Step 10   Write the fullScreenDisplay() method.

```
function fullScreenDisplay(elem) {
    if (elem.requestFullscreen) {
        elem.requestFullscreen();
    } else if (elem.webkitRequestFullScreen) {
        elem.webkitRequestFullScreen();
    } else if (elem.mozRequestFullScreen) {
        elem.mozRequestFullScreen();
    } else if (elem.msRequestFullScreen) {
        elem.msRequestFullScreen();
    }
}
```

Step 11   Save the file and run it several browsers. To see full-screen view, remember to click each button and the HTML5 image. Be sure the browser's Developer tools are active and that the console is open.

Step 12   Now write the function to disable full-screen view.

```
exitFullScreenBtn.addEventListener('click', function() {
    if (document.exitFullscreen) {
        document.exitFullscreen();
    }
    else if (document.msExitFullscreen) {
        document.msExitFullscreen();
    }
    else if (document.mozCancelFullScreen) {
        document.mozCancelFullScreen();
    }
    else if (document.webkitCancelFullScreen) {
        document.webkitCancelFullScreen();
    }
}, false);
```

Step 13   Save the file and run it on several browsers. To test the code that disables full-screen view, first, click the Enable Full Screen Page View button. Allow full-screen view in your browser, then, click the Disable Full Screen View button.

Step 14   Next, add the event listeners that respond to the vendor-prefixed `onfullscreenchange` event.

```
document.addEventListener('fullscreenchange', screenChangeHandler);
document.addEventListener("webkitfullscreenchange", screenChangeHandler);
document.addEventListener("mozfullscreenchange", screenChangeHandler);
document.addEventListener("MSFullscreenChange", screenChangeHandler);
```

Each event handler calls the screenChangeHandler function that you will write in the next step.

Step 15   Write the screenChangeHandler function. The example below uses only the webkit version, so you will have to test the file in the Chrome browser. Alternatively, you can add the additional vendor prefixes.

```
function screenChangeHandler(event) {
    console.log("Full-screen Change Event. Fullscreen is: " +
        document.webkitIsFullScreen);
}
```

Note   This API has undergone many implementation in almost all web browsers, so your results may vary. The main changes have included case-sensitive changes such as FullScreen vs. Fullscreen and CancelFullScreen vs. Exit-FullScreen.

Exercise summary

In this exercise, you learned how to make an entire web page viewable in full-screen view. You also learned that it is possible to make only portions of the web page viewable in full-screen view. You learned how to disable full-screen view and became familiar with the entire fullscreen API.

Resources

Polyfill: https://github.com/sindresorhus/screenfull.js/

Challenge exercise

1. Using your IDE, open the file "fullScreen-challenge-starter.html" from the challenge subdirectory.

2. Run the file in a web browser.

3. The file shows "Tips for increasing your physical activity," followed by three buttons for each category: "At Home," "At Work," and "At Play."

4. Your job is to go to full-screen view when each button is clicked and each full-screen view should display only the text associated with the button.

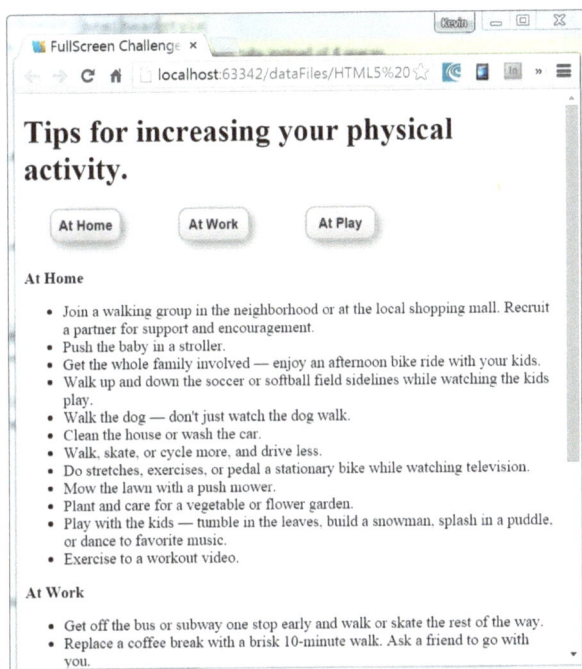

Before clicking the "At Home" button.

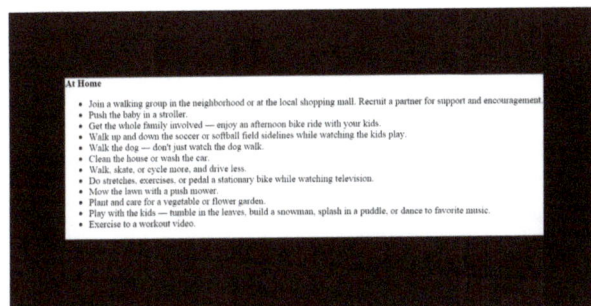

After clicking the "At Home" button.

Chapter summary

In this chapter, you learned the fullscreen API, some possible use cases, and the JavaScript required to invoke full-screen view in a variety of web browsers.

Chapter 7

Speech APIs

In this chapter, you will implement voice recognition and speech synthesis. In the first section, the browser will respond to your voice using the Speech Recognition API. You'll retrieve the weather by stating your city and state. In the second section, the browser will speak based on the text you enter into a text input field.

The WebSpeech specification was published by a W3C Community Group on October 19, 2012

Objectives

❑   Understand and use the SpeechUtterance object.

❑   Understand and use the SpeechRecognition object.

Introduction

The Speech Recognition is not yet a W3C recommendation. This chapter is based partially on the work of the Speech API Community Group's final report. See https://dvcs.w3.org/hg/speech-api/raw-file/tip/speechapi.html#speechreco-section for the complete report. Because the API is not a W3C candidate recommendation, this chapter will not address the specifics of the API. Two exercises will be introduced that use the API. Both exercises will work in Chrome 31 and higher. Since this is a very new technology, it is both buggy and unstable with only partial support from Chrome. Therefore, this chapter will not cover the API in its entirety, but instead, focus on the parts that are currently implemented by the Chrome browser.

Speech Recognition and Speech Synthesis

The primary object in the Speech Synthesis API is the `SpeechSynthesisUtterance` object. The primary object in the SpeechRecognition API is the SpeechRecognition object.

The SpeechSynthesisUtterance Object

This object contains a number of properties that characterize the speech, such as pitch, rate, volume and voice. Another property of the `SpeechSynthesisUtterance` object is the voice property. Each operating system's supporting browsers implement a number of voices. You can get a list of the voices the browser supports by calling the getVoices() method. Some voices include whisper, deranged and more.

The `speechSynthesis` object is a property of the window object. The `SpeechSynthesisUtterance` can be instantiated with a constructor function. The `SpeechSynthesisUtterance` object includes a method called `speak()` that is responsible for actually voicing an utterance.

Partial list of SpeechUtterance Object Properties

text	The text or utterance to be synthesized.
lang	The language to be synthesized (represented as a string; example; en-GB.
voiceUI	A string that identifies the location of a speech synthesis service to be used by the web application. NOTE: Chrome uses a `voice` property instead of the `voiceURI`.
volume	0 to 1 value representing volume.
rate	Speaking rate between 0.1 and 10 with a default value of 1. A rate of 2 indicates twice the default speed.
pitch	Number between 0 and 2 with a default value of 1 representing the speaking pitch.

Partial list of SpeechUtterance Object events

onstart	Dispatched with the speech synthesis begins.
onpause	Dispatched when the speech synthesis is paused.
onresume	Dispatched when the speech synthesis is resumed.
Onend	Dispatched when the speech synthesis in finished.

Exercise 7.1: Using Speech Synthesis

In this exercise, you use the SpeechSynthesis API to give provide a voice to your computer. You use the SpeechUtterance object to say hello.

Objectives

After completing this exercise, you will be able to do the following:

- Check for browser support of the SpeechUtterance object.
- Create a SpeechUtterance object.
- Control the browsers' voice characteristics by using properties of the SpeechUtterance object.
- Activate speech on the Chrome web browser.

Step 1   Using your IDE, open the file speechSynthesis-starter.html from the speech-API folder. To familiarize yourself with the page layout, run the file in a browser.

The speechSynthesis-starter.html as shown in the Chrome web browser.

Step 2   Return to your IDE and add a script block above the closing body element as shown below in bold.

```
</body>
<script>
</script>
```

Step 3   Inside the script block, add two variables; one to store your first name and the other to store the speechUtterance object.

```
var yourName;
var sayHi;
```

Step 4   Below the variable declaration, write an "if" condition to check for browser support of the SpeechSynthesis API.

```
if (window.speechSynthesis) {
        console.log("SpeechSynthesis is supported.");
            }
else {
        console.log("SpeechSynthesis is NOT supported.");
}
```

Step 5   Inside the if block add the following JavaScript as shown below in bold:

```
if (window.speechSynthesis) {
 console.log("SpeechSynthesis is supported.");
 document.getElementById('userName').addEventListener('blur', function()
{
     yourName = document.getElementById('userName').value;
});
 document.getElementById('sayHello').addEventListener('click', function()
{
```

```
            sayHi = new SpeechSynthesisUtterance('Hello ' + yourName);
            window.speechSynthesis.speak(sayHi);
            });
    }
    else {
            console.log("SpeechSynthesis is NOT supported.");
    }
```

Step 6   Run the file in Chrome, type your first name in the text input field and click the "Say Hello" button.

After agreeing to give the browser access to your microphone, you should hear the browser saying hello followed by your name.

Step 7   Add the following code to the sayHello button's click handler as shown below in bold.

```
document.getElementById('sayHello').addEventListener('click', function() {
        sayHi = new SpeechSynthesisUtterance('Hello ' + yourName);
        var voices = window.speechSynthesis.getVoices();
        sayHi.voice = voices[0];
        window.speechSynthesis.speak(sayHi);
})
```

Step 8   Try changing the array index number in voices[0], refresh the page in the browser and you should hear different voices.

Step 9   Add the event handlers for the "Stop Talking," "Pause" and "Resume Talking" buttons as shown below. The finished code is shown below with the additional event handlers shown in bold.

```
<script>
 var yourName;
 var sayHi;
 if (window.speechSynthesis) {
        console.log("SpeechSynthesis is supported.");
        document.getElementById('userName').addEventListener('blur', function() {
            yourName = document.getElementById('userName').value;
        });
        document.getElementById('sayHello').addEventListener('click', function() {
            sayHi = new SpeechSynthesisUtterance('Hello ' + yourName);
            var voices = window.speechSynthesis.getVoices();
            sayHi.voice = voices[2];
            window.speechSynthesis.speak(sayHi);
            });
          document.getElementById('pauseSpeech').addEventListener('click',
          function() {
        speechSynthesis.pause();
            });

          document.getElementById('stopSpeech').addEventListener('click',
          function() {
        speechSynthesis.cancel();
        });
```

```
        document.getElementById('resumeSpeech').addEventListener('click',
        function() {
      speechSynthesis.resume();
    });
  }
 else {
    console.log("SpeechSynthesis is NOT supported.");
    }
</script>
```

Step 10   Save the file and refresh it in the Chrome web browser. Check that all of the buttons work as expected.

Step 11   Try setting some of the other SpeechUtterance properties and see the effect they have in the browser.

Step 12   When you are finished experimenting, close all open files.

To test this file on your mobile device, go to www.kevinruse.com/speech

Exercise summary

In this exercise, you learned how to synthesis speech based on text input by the user. You learned how to create a SpeechUtterance object and use some of its properties. You started, paused, resumed and stop the speech synthesis.

Speech Recognition

The SpeechRecognition object is also a property of the window object. The start() method activates the speech recognizer. The SpeechRecognition object listens for events similar to the SpeechUtterance object events.

Because you will be working in Chrome, you will need to reference the SpeechRecognition object with a vendor prefix: webkitSpeechRecognition. When using this object, the browser will prompt you for permission to use your microphone.

Exercise 7.2: Using Speech Recognition

In this exercise, you use the Recognition API to retrieve the weather by stating your city and state.

Objectives

After completing this exercise, you will be able to do the following:

- Create a SpeechRecognition object.
- React to the user's voice by responding to the onresult event.
- Use the spoken word to activate a link.

Step 1   Using your IDE, open the file speechRecognition-starter.html from the speech-API folder. To familiarize yourself with the page layout, run the file in a browser.

The speechRecognition-starter.html file as seen in the Chrome web browser.

Step 2   Add a click event handler to the "Click to Speak" button as shown below in bold.

```
<input type="button" value="Click to Speak" onclick="recognition.start()">
```

Step 3   Add a script block below the closing `</form>` element.

```
<script>
    var recognition = new webkitSpeechRecognition();
    recognition.onresult = function(event) {
      if (event.results.length > 0) {
        city.value = event.results[0][0].transcript;
        setTimeout(function() {
            var location = event.results[0][0].transcript;
            console.log(location);
            var url = location;
            document.getElementById('weatherForm').action = 'https://www.
google.com/?gws_rd=ssl#q=weather+' + url;
            city.form.submit();
        }, 1250);
      }
    }
</script>
```

Step 4   Save the page and preview the file in a web browser. For this code to execute most browsers will require that the page run through a server and not the file system. You can run the file through the Apache server by directing your browser to http://localhost. Be sure that you have started WAMP. You will see a directory structure. Locate this chapter and file. Clicking the file name will launch the page through the Apache server.

Step 5   In your web browser, click the "Click to Speak" button. You should be prompted by the browser, asking for permission to access your computer's microphone. Provide permission and speak the name of a large city such as New York. The browser should now write the content in the form and your JavaScript will submit the form to the Google weather API, which then provides the weather in the city you spoke.

To test this file on your mobile device, go to www.kevinruse.com/speech

Code explanation

The result event includes a transcript that contains the recorded response. Although, it's not being acknowledge in the code above, the event also include a confidence level between 0 and 1 with a confidence of .5 representing an unreliable transcript.

The `setTimeout()` methods waits 1,250 milliseconds before it retrieves the transcript and passes the information to the Google weather service via a form submission.

Exercise summary

In this exercise, you learned how to implement voice recognition. In doing so, you invoked the Google weather service via the spoken word.

Challenge exercise

1. Using your IDE, open the file "speechRecognition-challenge-starter.html" from the challenge subdirectory.

2. Run the file in a web browser.

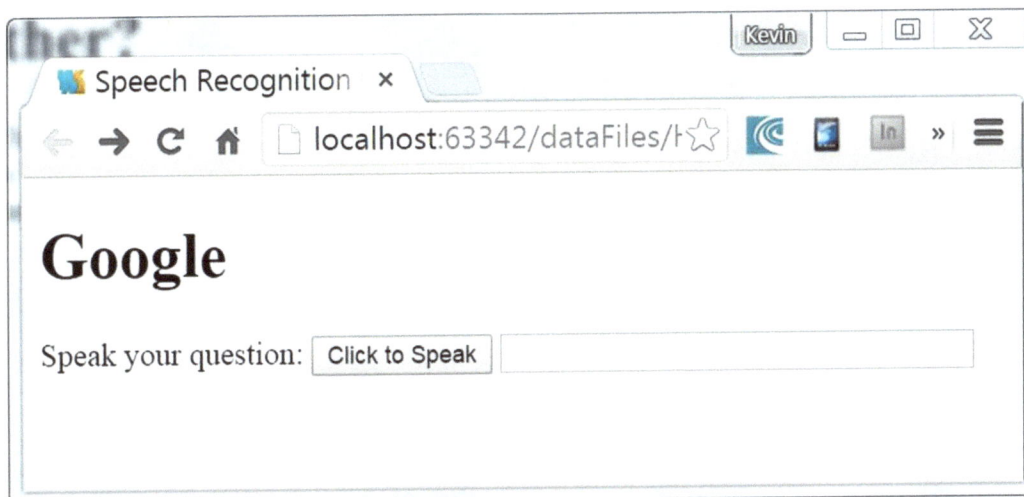

3. Your job is to allow the "Click to Speak" button to recognize speech. After the user asks a question, the question should be directed to Google and the text input element's value is submitted.

4. If you get stuck, "speechRecognition-challenge-finished.html" is a possible solution.

Hints:

The Google URL begins with: https://www.google.com/?gws_rd=ssl#q=

The "q=" at then end of the url represents the beginning of the query string.

The JavaScript method to encode the text input as a url is: encodeURI()

To test this file on your mobile device, go to www.kevinruse.com/speech

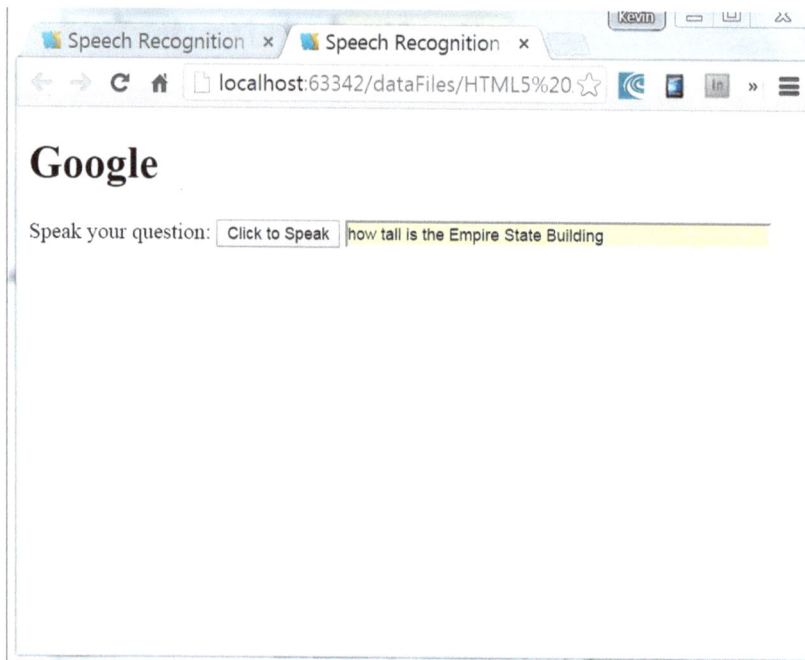

After voice recognition. Question: How tall is the Empire State Building

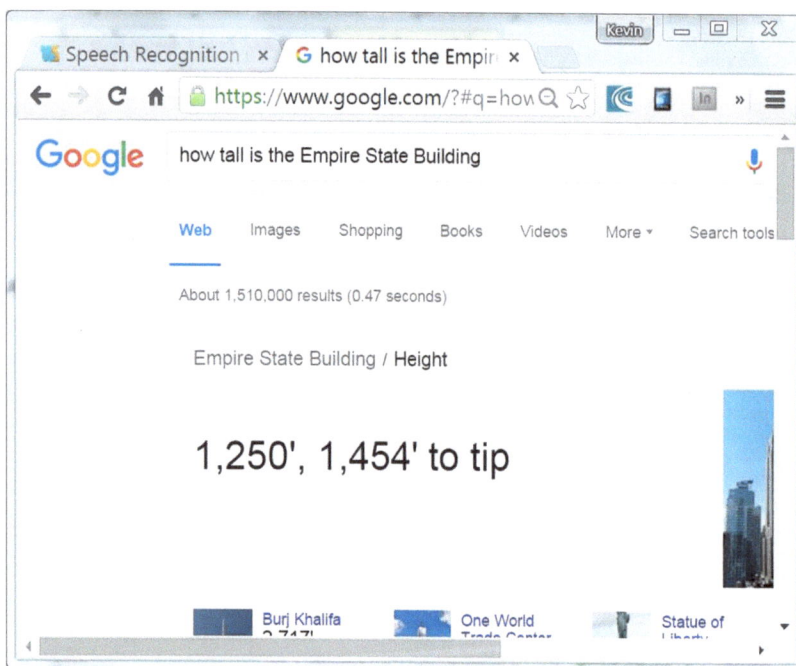

After the programmatic submit.

Chapter summary

Although not complete, the Speech API is on its way toward implementation and currently available in the Chrome web browser. Due to its status, the API was not covered completely. The major objects including SpeechUtterance and SpeechRecognition were used in the exercises along with some of their respective properties and events.

Chapter 8

HTML5 Media Elements and API

In this chapter, you learn the new media elements—audio and video—and the application programming interface (API) behind them. You use these new elements and their attributes and also learn the various codecs used to compress and decompress audio and video for the Web.

The HTML5 media elements were published in the HTML5 W3C Recommendation on October 28, 2014 in the document subtitled: A vocabulary and associated APIs for HTML and XHTML

Objectives

❑   Describe the new media elements.

❑   Understand the role of codecs.

❑   Know when to use the new media elements.

❑   Detect browser support of the new media elements.

❑   Use the new media elements.

❑   Build a simple video player.

❑   Understand the audio and video API.

Introduction

New media elements have been created in an effort to make the Internet more usable for everyone. These elements display multimedia content in the form of audio and video files and can reduce or eliminate the need for browser plug-ins or add-ons that are currently required to view or listen to such files. Flash Player is arguably the most predominant plug-in. The current market penetration of the latest Flash Player makes it the ideal choice as a fallback for browsers that do not fully support these new elements. In addition to supporting these elements, the browser must also support the encoding type of the video or audio itself. This is referred to as the media codec. See the browser charts on page 71 for current browser support.

Audio and video

The media elements

Element	What It's Used For
`<audio>`	To playback audio files
`<video>`	To playback video files

What are the new elements used for?

These elements not only provide a standard for showing video and playing audio, they also provide a common API for the handling of these video and audio files.

Browser support for the new media elements

For the most recent information, please visit these sites:

- http://caniuse.com
- http://html5please.com
- http://mobilehtml5.org
- http://www.findmebyip.com/litmus#html5-web-applications
- http://html5test.com

`<audio>` element attributes

Attribute	Value	What It's Used For
`audio`	muted	Defines the default state of the audio
`autoplay`	autoplay	Plays the video as soon as its ready
`controls`	controls	Displays controls, such as a Play button
`loop`	loop	Plays the audio again after it reaches the end
`preload`	preload	Loads the audio file at page load (ignored if autoplay is present)
`src`	url	Indicates the URL of the audio to play

See http://www.w3.org/wiki/HTML/Elements/audio#HTML_Attributes for more information about the audio element attributes.

`<video>` element attributes

Attribute	Value	What It's Used For
autoplay	autoplay	Plays the video as soon as it's ready
controls	controls	Displays controls, such as a Play button
loop	loop	Plays the audio again after it reaches the end
preload	preload	Loads the audio file at page load (ignored if autoplay is present)
src	url	Indicates the URL of the audio to play

Browser support `<video>`

IE	Firefox	Safari	Chrome	Opera	iOS	Opera Mobile	Android
9.0 +	3.6 +	4.0 +	10.0 +	10.6 +	3.2 +	11.0 +	2.3 +

Browser support Ogg/Theora video format*

IE	Firefox	Safari	Chrome	Opera	iOS	Opera Mobile	Android
No	3.6 +	No	10.0 +	10.6 +	No	11.0 +	No

* Free, lossy video-compression format

Browser support WebM/VP8 video format*

IE	Firefox	Safari	Chrome	Opera	iOS	Opera Mobile	Android
No	3.6 +	No	10.0 +	10.6 +	No	11.0 +	2.3+

* Royalty-free, high-quality open, video-compression format

Browser support MPEG-4/H.264video format*

IE	Firefox	Safari	Chrome	Opera	iOS	Opera Mobile	Android
9.0 +	No	3.2 +	10.0 +	No	3.2 +	No	2.1+

* Common, but not royalty-free, video-compression format

Browser support `<audio>`

IE	Firefox	Safari	Chrome	Opera	iOS	Opera Mobile	Android
9.0 +	3.6 +	4.0 +	10.0 +	10.6 +	4.0 +	11.0 +	2.3 +

Browser support audio codec

Format	IE9	Firefox 3.5	Opera 10.5	Chrome 3.5	Safari 3.0
Ogg Vorbis	No	Yes	Yes	Yes	No
MP3	Yes	No	No	Yes	Yes
Wav	No	Yes	Yes	Yes	Yes

To convert a video from one format/codec to another, try http://video.online-convert.com/convert-to-ogg.

About video codecs

When playing video files, the browser must first determine if it can decode the video codec. Codec is a word like modem (modulate/demodulate) that means compress and decompress. Video codecs, then, are compressed video formats which must be diciphered by the web browser before they can play. The `canplaytype()` method is used when making this determination. The `canplaytype()` method is used in the next exercise to determine browser support.

The codec deciphering is part of the progressive download process of the video by the web browser. The process will be viewed here in two scenarios. In the first scenario, the video element contains an autoplay attribute as shown below.

```
<video autoplay … >
```

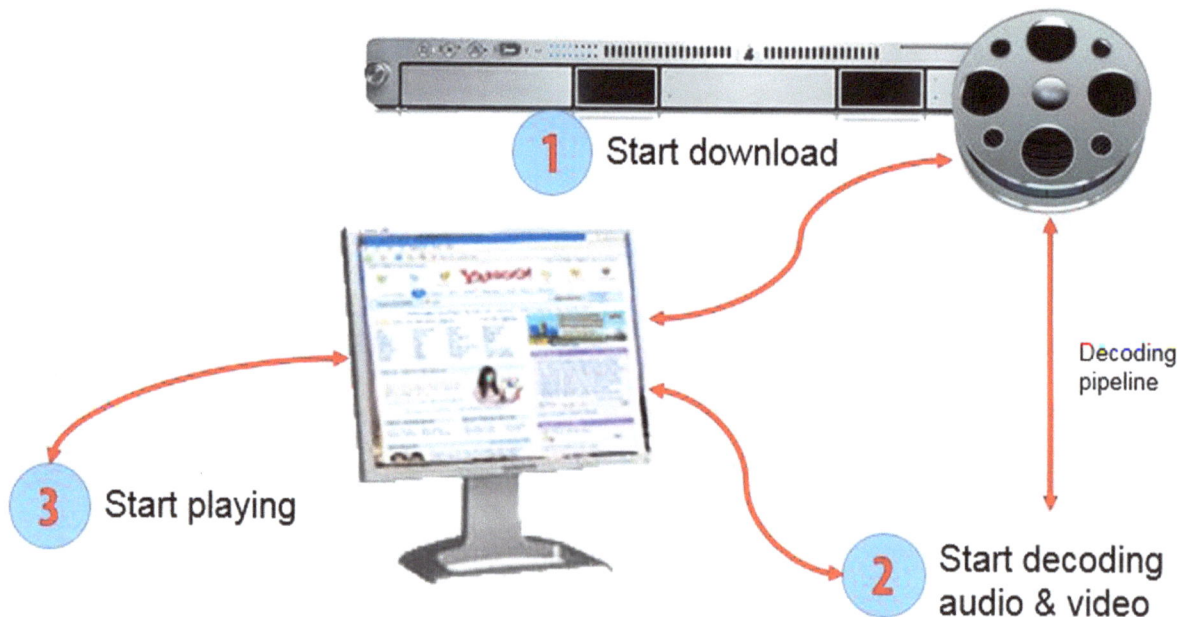

1. The video is set to "autoplay."

2. The video begins to download.

3. The browser starts downloading the video through the decoding pipeline and starts to decode the audio and video.

4. The video begins to play.

`<video autoplay ... >`

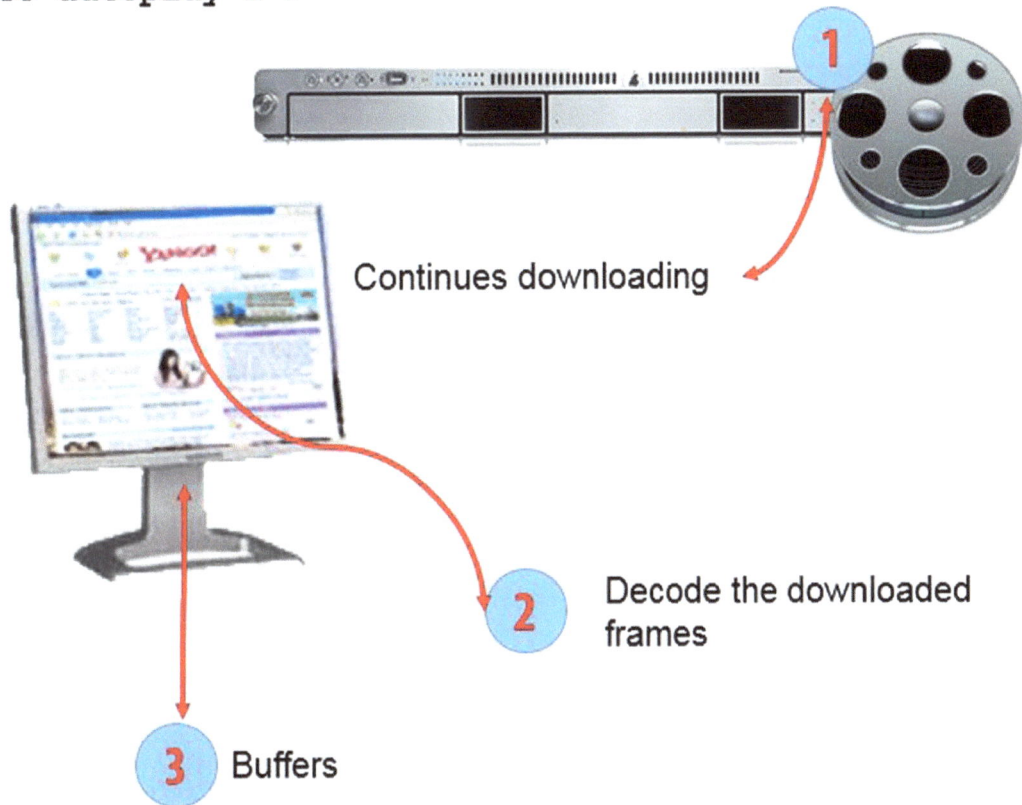

1. The video continues to download to the browser.

2. The browser continues to decode the downloaded frames.

3. The video buffers the frames that have downloaded but not yet played.

In the second scenario, the video tag does not contain the autoplay attribute and there is no poster image associated with the video.

`<video NO AUTOPLAY & NO POSTER IMAGE... >`

1 Download video properties & ONLY the metadata required to set up the decoding pipeline

Decoding pipeline

2 Decode the first image frame

3 Display the first frame

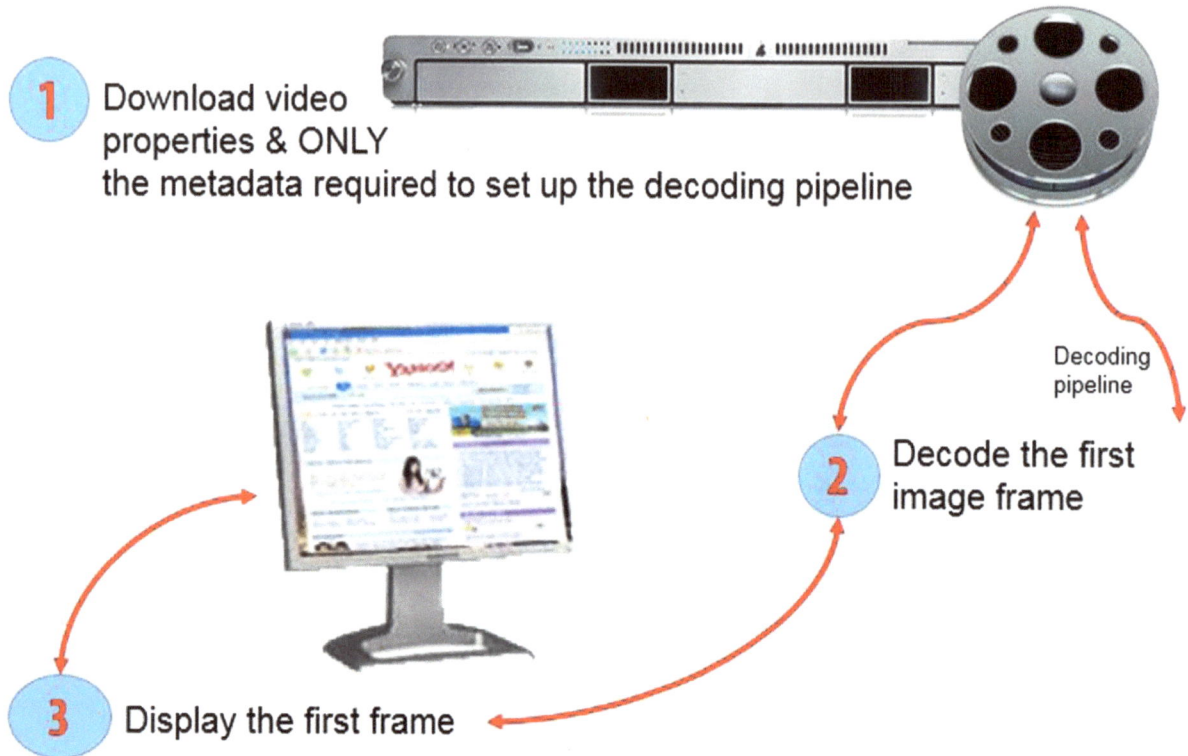

1. Only the video properties and the metadata required to set up the decoding pipeline are downloaded.

2. The browsers decodes frame 1 of the video file to determine if it can play it.

3. The browser displays frame 1 of the video file and can return a value to the `canplaytype()` method.

When do I use these new elements?

You may use the `<video>` element when you want to display video. However, based on the charts above, support is far from universal. Therefore, you need fallback methods such as the Adobe Flash Player.

You may use the `<audio>` element when you want to play audio-only files.

Resources

HTML5 video elements and API: http://www.w3.org/2010/05/video/mediaevents.html

Video converter tool: http://www.mirovideoconverter.com/

Exercise 8.1: Detecting browser support for video

In this exercise, you determine if the user's browser will support the new media elements.

Objectives

After completing this exercise, you will be able to do the following:

- Write JavaScript code that detects if the browser will support the new `<video>` element.
- Use fallback methods for browsers that do not support audio/video or specific codecs.
- Use a JavaScript library to get browser support in all browsers.

Step 1   Open the file "video-support-starter.html" from the media-API folder.

Step 2   In the `<script>` block, locate the `checkVideoSupport()` method.

Step 3   Declare a variable called `hasVideo`, as shown in bold below:

```
function checkVideoSupport(){
            //Step 3: add variable hasVideo here
        var hasVideo

}
```

Step 4   Assign the value of the variable to the document's createElement() method and indicate that the element you wish to create is a `<video>` element, as shown:

```
var hasVideo = document.createElement('video')
```

Now that you have access to the new video DOM object, invoke a method of this DOM object called `canPlayType`. If the browser doesn't support the `<video>` element, the method will not return anything.

Step 5   Reference the `canPlayType()` method of the new video DOM object, as shown in bold below:

```
var hasVideo = document.createElement('video').canPlayType;
```

Step 6   Below the variable declaration (after step 5), invoke the alert() method and display the variable. You may also use the console to display the variable. Both lines of code are shown below.

```
console.log(hasVideo);
alert(hasVideo);
```

Step 7   Save and test the file in the Chrome browser. After the page loads, click the Video Support? button.

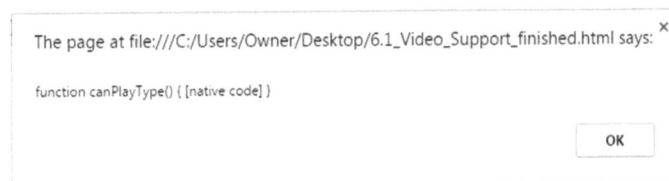

> The page at file:///C:/Users/Owner/Desktop/6.1_Video_Support_finished.html says: ×
>
> function canPlayType() { [native code] }
>
> OK

Alert box after step 6.

Step 8   Convert the method call so that it returns a Boolean value by typing two exclamation points in front of the code, like this. And be sure to add the parenthesis following the "!!" and immediately preceding the final semicolon:

```
!!(document.createElement('video').canPlayType);
```

This page says:

true

OK

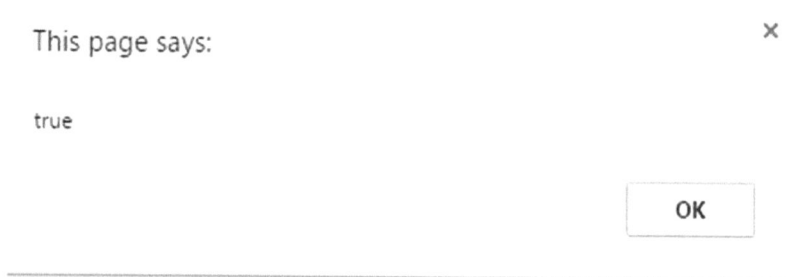

Alert box after step 8.

Step 9   Save and test the file in the Chrome browser by clicking theVideo Support? button,

This indicates that your browser supports the `<video>` element. Remember, however, that the browser may not support the codec used to compress the video for delivery over the Web and will therefore not play the video.

Step 10   Close all open files.

Exercise outcome

The outcome of this exercise is the appearance of the alert box after step 6, indicating a function definition, and again after step 8, indicating a boolean value of "true."

Exercise 8.2: Detecting browser support for `<audio>`

In this exercise, you determine if the user's browser will support the new media elements.

Objectives

After completing this exercise, you will be able to do the following:

- Use JavaScript to check for audio support.

Checking for audio can be accomplished with the same steps as checking for video.

Step 1   Open the file "audio-support-starter.html" from the media-API folder.

Step 2   Modify the code for audio as shown in bold below:

```
function checkAudioSupport() {
        var hasAudio = !!(document.createElement('audio').canPlayType);
        console.log("Audio support = " + hasAudio);
    }
```

Step 3   Run the file in any Web browser. Be sure the console is running and confirm the console log statement is correct.

Step 4   Close all open files.

Exercise outcome

The outcome of this exercise is the appearance of a log statement in the console indicating support or lack of support for the HTML5 <audio> element.

Exercise summary

In this exercise, you learned a JavaScript method that will determine if the end user's web browser will support the use of HTML5 audio.

Exercise 8.3: Using Modernizr to detect video

In this exercise, you determine if the user's browser will support the new media elements by using the Modernizr JavaScript library.

Objectives

After completing this exercise, you will be able to do the following:

- Use Modernizr to detect for video support.

Step 1   Open the file "video-modernizr-starter.html" and reference the Modernizr JavaScript library and include the script that will check for browser support of the <video> element.

```
<script src="scripts/modernizr-2.0.6.js"></script>
<script>
function checkVideoSupport() {
    if (Modernizr.video) {
            console.log("Your browser supports video!");
            }
}
</script>
```

Step 2   Save and test the file in all web browsers.

Step 3   Modify the function to test for a specific codec as shown below:
```
Modernizr.video.webm
```

Step 4   Modify the function to test for a specific codec as shown below:
```
Modernizr.video.ogg
```

Step 5   Modify the function to test for a specific codec as shown below:
```
Modernizr.video.h264
```

Step 6   Save and test the file in all web browsers. You may now close all files.

Exercise outcome

The outcome of this exercise is an alert box indicating support or lack of support for the various codecs accessed via the Modernizr object, such as webm, ogg, and h264.

Exercise summary

In this exercise, you learned a JavaScript method that will determine if the end user's web browser will support the use of HTML5 video.

Exercise 8.4: Playing audio with the `<audio>` element

Now that you have determined whether the browser supports audio, you can use the new HTML5 `<audio>` element. Note that the browser check code has been removed from this exercise for brevity. Also note that the various fallback methods needed should the browser fail to support the `<audio>` element are not discussed. It is best practice to provide a fallback method.

Objectives

After completing this exercise, you will be able to do the following:

- Play audio with the `<audio>` element.
- Use the `<audio>` element and its attributes: type, controls, and codec.

Step 1   Open the file "audio-starter.html" from the media-API folder.

Step 2   Locate the `<h1>Playing Audio</h1>` and below that create an `<audio>` element.

```
<audio src="media/things_to_eat_01_estes_64kb.ogg.ogv" controls>
</audio>
```

Step 3   Add content inside the `<audio>` element that will display if the browser does not support audio as shown below in bold.

```
<audio src="media/things_to_eat_01_estes_64kb.ogg.ogv">
        <p>Your browser does not support HTML5 Audio.</p>
</audio>
```

Step 4   Save and test the file in any browser. You should not hear any audio nor see any indication of an audio file on the page.

The `<audio>` element lacks controls for the user to play the audio. You can add these controls with the single-word attribute `controls`. For those developers who write well-formed HTML, you may be tempted to write the attribute with the following form:

```
controls = "true"
```

This may lead you to believe that controls will be displayed using this format and that controls will not be displayed with controls="false." This is not the case. The existence of the single-word attribute is sufficient to show controls, and nothing following the word "controls" has any effect. Therefore, if you would like to use the attribute="value" form, you might use controls="controls," otherwise the single-word attribute format will suffice.

Step 5   Add the controls attribute as shown below in bold and test the file in the browser.

```
<audio src="media/things_to_eat_01_estes_64kb.ogg.ogv" controls>
```

Note   If you know with certainty the codec used to compress your audio, you can provide this information to the browser to determine if it supports that codec. You can use the `type` attribute only within a `<source>` element, as shown below. This file uses a `src` attribute. In a later exercise you will use the `<source>` element.

```
<source type="audio/ogg; codecs=vorbis"...
```

Step 6   Save the file and open it in the Chrome browser. You should see a screen similar to the figure below.

Step 7   Click the Play button to play the audio in the browser.

Playing Audio

The Audio file as seen in the web browser

Step 8   Close all open files.

Audio/Video Support quick summary*

Ogg Container	supports Theora Video and Vorbis Audio
webM Container	supports VP8 Video and Vorbis Audio
MP4 Container	supports H.264 Video and AAC-low complexity Audio

*As of the publication date of this courseware

Exercise outcome

The outcome of this exercise is the appearance of an audio element along with the ability to play the audio file in browsers that support both the <audio> element and its associated codec.

Exercise summary

In this exercise, you learned how to play audio files with the new HTML5 audio element.

Exercise 8.5: Playing video with the <video> element

Now that you have determined if the browser supports video, you use the <video> element to play a short demo video.

Objectives

After completing this exercise, you will be able to do the following:

- Play video with the <video> element.
- Use the <video> element and its attributes: type and controls.

In this exercise, you use the new HTML5 <video> element. The browser check code has been removed from this exercise for brevity. Note: The various fallback methods needed should the browser fail to support the <video> element are not discussed, but it is best practice to provide a fallback method.

Step 1   Open the file "video-starter.html" from the media-API folder.

Step 2   Locate the `<h1>Playing Video</h1>` element and add a `<video>` element below it.

```
<video src="media/foodPlate_demo.ogg" controls>
          <p>Your browser does NOT support HTML5 Video.</p>
</video>
```

Note   If you know with certainty the codec used to compress your video you can provide this information to the browser to determine if it supports that codec. You can use the `type` attribute only within a `<source>` element, as shown below. This file uses a `src` attribute. In a later exercise you will use the `<source>` element.

```
<source type="video/ogg; codecs=vorbis"...
```

Step 4   Save the file and open it in the Chrome browser. You should see a screen similar to the figure below.

Playing Video

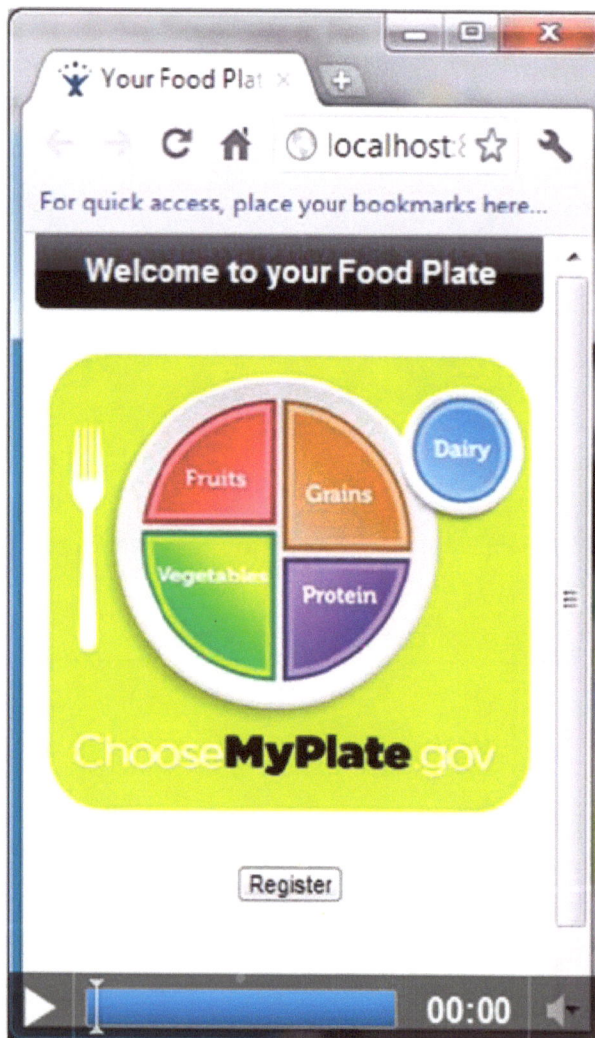

The video as seen in the web application at runtime.

Step 5   Click the Play button to play the video in the browser. To test IE versions lower than 10, use Compatibility View in IE's developer tools.

Step 6   Close all open files.

Demo 8.1: Using the `<video>` element with a fallback

The code shown below is an example of a video element with various fallbacks. The following is taken from:
http://dev.opera.com/articles/view/simple-html5-video-flash-fallback-custom-controls/

Note   A bug in the iPad makes it necessary for a developer to place the MP4 option first.

```
<!DOCTYPE HTML>
<html lang="EN">
<head>
        <title>video</title>
        <meta charset="UTF-8">
        <style type="text/css">
                body {
                        margin:0;
                        padding:50px;
                        background:#444;
                        }
        </style>
</head>
<body>
        <video controls poster="video.jpg" width="854" height="480">
                <source src="video.mp4" type="video/mp4">
                <source src="video.webm" type="video/webm">
                 <object type="application/x-shockwave-flash" data="player.
    swf"width="854" height="504">
                        <param name="allowfullscreen" value="true">
                        <param name="allowscriptaccess" value="always">
                        <param name="flashvars" value="file=video.mp4">
    <!--[if IE]><!--><param name="movie" value="player.swf">
    <!--<![endif]-->
    <img src="video.jpg" width="854" height="480" alt="Video">
    <p>Your browser can't play HTML5 video. <a href="video.webm">
Download it</a> instead.</p>
  </object>
</video>
</body>
</html>
```

Discuss the fallback section of this code with your instructor.

Demo outcome

The result of this demo is that various fallbacks allow you to view and play the video contained on the web page in any web browser you choose. At the very least, an old browser should display a jpeg file of the video's first frame.

Demo summary

In this demo, you learned how to play video files with the new HTML5 `<video>` element. You also saw a demo that plays in all browsers and uses a Flash-based fallback method for browsers that do not understand either the video element or the codec used to compress the video.

Video and audio APIs

The HTML5 `<video>` and `<audio>` elements include a rich API for programmatic access to a Video/Audio object. The tables below describe the properties, methods, and events of the Video/Audio object.

Video/Audio API methods

Property	Description
play()	Plays the video/audio
pause()	Pauses the video/audio
load()	Required if you dynamically create the video/audio
canPlayType()	Tests to see if the browser can play a particular MIME type
addTextTrack	Adds a TextTrack to a media element (e.g., subtitles)
fastSeek	Directly seeks to a given time
setMediaKeys	Sets the MediaKeys keys to use when decrypting media during playback
setSinkID	Sets the id of the audio device through which audio ouput should be rendered

Video/Audio object properties

Property	Description
muted	Gets the video/audio muted property, whatever the volume
paused	Gets the video/audio paused property
played	The ranges of the media source that the browser has played
playbackRate	The current rate at which the media is being played back
currentTime	Gets or sets the current playback position of the video/audio using a float value that represents seconds
currentSrc	Gets the URL of the media resource
duration	Returns the duration of the video/audio (if known) in a float value that represents seconds (if the duration is unknown then duration returns NaN)
volume	Gets or sets the video/audio playback volume measured with a float between 0.0 and1.0
audioTracks	The list of AudioTrack objects contained in the element

autoplay	Represents the autoplay HTML attribute
buffered	The ranges of the media source that a browser has buffered. Represents the buffered amount at the moment the buffered property is accessed
controller	Represents the media controller that has been assigned to the element
controls	Represents the controls HTML attribute
cross-origin	The CORS setting for the media element
defaultMuted	Represents the muted HTML attribute
defaultPlaybackRate	The default playback rate of the media
ended	Indicates whether the media element has ended playback
error	The MediaError object for the most recent error
loop	Represents the loop HTML attribute
mediaGroup	Represents the mediagroup HTML attribute
preload	Represents the preload HTML attribute
readystate	Indicates the readiness of the media to play
seekable	Indicates the time ranges that the user is able to seek to
seeking	Indicates whether the media is in the process of seeking
textTracks	The list of TextTrack objects contained in the element
videoTracks	The list of VideoTrack objects contained in the element
sinkId	The unique id of the device delivering the output
initialTime	The initial playback position in seconds
mediaKeys	Returns a reference to the MediaKeys interface (a set of keys that the associated media element can use for decryption of data during playback)

Video/Audio object events

Property	Description
loadeddata	Dispatched when the browser has loaded enough data to begin playing the video/audio
play	Dispatched when the video/audio begins playing
pause	Dispatched when the video/audio has been paused
timeupdate	Dispatched when the current playback position of the video/audio has changed
ended	Dispatched when the video/audio has reached the end of the clip
abort	Dispatched when playback is aborted, for example, when playing media is restarted from the beginning
canplay	Dispatched when enough data is available that the media can be played (even for just a couple of frames)
canplaythrough	Dispatched when the readystate changes to CAN_PLAY_THROUGH (when the entire media can be played without interruption)
emptied	Dispatched when the media has become empty, for example, when the media is or has been loading and the load() method is called to reload it
encrypted	Dispatched when the browser has encountered initialization data in the media data
error	Dispatched when an error occurs
seeking	Dispatched when a seek operation begins

stalled	Dispatched when the browser is trying to fetch media data, but data is not forthcoming
volumeChange	Dispatched when the audio volume is changed
waiting	Dispatched when a requested operation is delayed, pending the completion of another operation
suspend	Dispatched when loading of the media is suspended
rateChange	Dispatched with the playback speed changes
playing	Dispatched when the media begins or resumes play
progress	Dispatched periodically to indicate downloading progress of the media
loadedata	Dispatched after the first frame of the media has finished loading
loadstart	Dispatched when the loading of the media begins

See http://www.w3.org/wiki/HTML/Elements/video#HTML_Attributes.

Exercise 8.6: Using the `<video>` element's attributes

In this exercise, you use some of the attributes of the `<video>` tag to control various aspects of video display, control, and playback.

Objectives

After completing this exercise, you will be able to do the following:

- Describe attributes of the `<video>` element: `height, width, poster, autoplay,preload`.
- Understand properties of the Video object: `volume, duration, currentSrc,currentTime`.

As with images, video should not be resized via height and width. Downsizing a large video with height and width does not prevent the download of the larger video size. Always provide height and width to allow space for the video in your layout.

Video files may take some time to display, so it is advisable to use a placeholder graphic that will display in place of the video until the user plays the video, at which time the placeholder image will go away and the video will play. This placeholder image is known as a "poster" and is an attribute of the `<video>` element. The value supplied to the poster attribute is an image file in the format .png, .gif, or .jpg.

Step 1   Open the file "video-attributes-starter.html" from the media-API folder, and add a height and a width property to the `<video>` element, for example, height = 300 and width = 150.

Step 2   Save and test the file in any browser. Note the resizing of the video itself (which remains proportional) and then remove the `height` and `width` attributes and values.

Step 3   Add the poster image "videoPoster.png" to the `<video>` element as shown in bold below:

```
<video id="myVid" src="media/FoodPlate.ogg" controls poster="../images/vid-
eoPoster.png">
```

Note the use of the graphic in place of the video at startup. The static .png image is replaced by the video when the user clicks the Play button.

Many HTML5 attributes are Booleans. In other words, single-word attributes such as `autoplay` are sufficient for setting the attribute to "true." For example, the following code snippets are functionally equivalent:

```
<video src="myVid" autoplay>
<video src="myVid" autoplay="true">
<video src="myVid" autoplay="false">
```

Note Use of spacebars around the equals (=) sign is optional and typically added for readability. While this bit of syntax remains the developer's choice, consistency should be the rule. Ideally, a style guide exists that indicates your company's preference regarding this and other issues of syntax and code styling.

Step 4 Create and set the autoplay attribute of the `<video>` element to "`true`."

Step 5 Save and test the file in all browsers. Note that the video begins playing automatically.

Step 6 Set the autoplay attribute to "`false`" and save and test the file. The video still plays automatically.

Step 7 Change the autoplay attribute to a single word.

Step 8 Save and test the file in all browsers.

Step 9 Create and set the preload attribute to "`none`."

If the preload attribute is not set, the default value is "auto," which loads the video at page load. The default value is ignored if autoplay is set to "`true`."

Step 10 Remove the `autoplay` and confirm the preload attribute is set to "`none`."

Step 11 Test the page in the browser and click the "Get Property" button.

The Get Duration button is designed to display the total duration of the video; however, because the video is not yet loaded, the `getDuration` function returns "NaN" or "Not a Number." Next you will set the preload attribute to metadata, which will cause the videos' metadata to load at startup. This metadata contains the duration of the video, so the button will now return a value.

Step 12 Set the preload property to "`metadata`."

Step 13 Test in the browser and click the Get Duration button. You should now receive a value for the video's duration.

Step 14 Set the loop attribute and test the file in all browsers. Wait for the video to complete and see if it plays again.

Step 15 Reset the preload attribute to "auto."

Step 16 Change the `getProperty()` function to check for volume, as shown in bold below:

```
function getProperty(){
        var vid = document.getElementById("myVid");
        console.log("video property is " + vid.volume);
}
```

Step 17 Save and test the file in all browsers. You should see the video's volume after clicking the Get Property button.

Step 18 Change the `getProperty()` function to check for currentSrc as shown in bold below:

```
function getProperty(){
        var vid = document.getElementById("myVid");
        console.log("video property is " + vid.currentSrc);
}
```

Step 19 Save and test the file in all browsers. You should now see the current source location of the video after clicking the Get Property button.

Step 20   Change the `getProperty()` function to check for the muted property as shown in bold below:

```
function getProperty(){
        var vid = document.getElementById("myVid");
        console.log("video property is " + vid.muted);
}
```

Step 21   Save and test the file in all browsers. Mute the video and click the button to see the muted property.

Step 22   Change the `getProperty()` function to check for currentTime as shown in bold below:

```
function getProperty() {
        var vid = document.getElementById("myVid");
        console.log("video property is " + vid.currentTime);
}
```

Step 23   Save and test the file in all browsers. Click the Play button before clicking the Get Property button to see the videos current playing time. You may now close all files.

Exercise summary

In this exercise, you learned some of the properties of the video element and how to use them.

Exercise 8.7: Controlling video

Along with the new `<video>` element, HTML5 provides a common API for controlling the `<video>`. In this exercise, you use the new HTML5 `<video>` element with a small amount of jQuery.

Objectives

After completing this exercise, you will be able to do the following:

- Use jQuery to determine if the Document Object Model (DOM) has been loaded.
- Create a Play button that will play the video.

We will use jQuery for the following tasks:

- Wait for the DOM to completely load.
- Locate the Play button placed at the bottom of the page (`id` attribute is "play_btn").
- Invoke the `play()` method.

You will encounter some errors along the way, but don't worry: it's all in an effort to explain JavaScript and will ultimately prove helpful in your understanding of jQuery.

Step 1   Open the file "control-video-starter.html" from the media-API folder.

Step 2   Locate the `<h1>Controlling Video</h1>` element and note the `<video>` element beneath it.

Step 3   Locate the `<script>` block at the top of the page. Create a second `<script>` block that will reference the JavaScript file you will write to control the video.

```
<script src="scripts/videoPlayer.js"></script>
```

Step 4   Create a new JavaScript file named "videoPlayer.js" and save it in the scripts folder.

Step 5   Write the code below, which uses the jQuery `$()` syntax that calls the jQuery method (which in turn creates the jQuery object), which will then invoke the `ready()` method. The `document.ready()` function causes the functions inside to be evaluated only after the page's DOM is completely loaded.

```
$(document).ready(function() {
})
```

Step 6   Now write the additional functionality that will be executed after the DOM is completely loaded. This code uses the jQuery function $(), which locates elements on the page. In this case, it is locating the <input> element with the `id` of "play_btn". Now that the Play button on the page is accessed, you invoke the jQuery `click()` method, which assigns a click handler function to the "play_btn" button. This function uses further jQuery by locating the element with the id of "myVid," which is the <video> element and uses the `play()` method of the video API. This is important: the `play()` method is a method of the Video object and not a jQuery method (like `click()` and `ready()`).

```
$(document).ready(function() {
        $('#play_btn').click(function(){
         $('#demo').play();
        })
})
```

Step 7   Save the .js file and run the .html file in the Chrome browser. If you click the Play button, the video will not play. This is because you have located the HTML5 element with the id property of "demo," which is the <video> element. After locating the element with the jQuery method (and syntax) $('element name')—known as a jQuery selector—jQuery expects a jQuery function to follow. However, `play()` is not a function or method of jQuery; it is a method of the HTML5 DOM object <video>.

The solution is to get out of jQuery and into the DOM. This is accomplished with a jQuery method called `get()`, which returns a DOM object by its index number in relationship to the jQuery selector (in this case, the <#myVid video> element).

Step 8   Delete the `$('#myVid').play();` and replace it with the following:

```
$('#play_btn').click(function(){
        $('#demo').get(0).play();
})
```

Note   In this case, the use of jQuery is ultimately inefficient and should be replaced with the "`document.getElementById()`" DOM method. (See the commented section of code in step 10.)

Step 9   Save the file and run it in the Chrome browser. You should be able to play the video by clicking the Play button.

Step 10   Next you add the jQuery to control the Pause button. Locate the existing jQuery `document.ready()` function and add the following code shown below in bold:

```
$(document).ready(function() {
        $('#play_btn').click(function(){
        $('#demo').get(0).play();
        //document.getElementById('demo').play();
   })
$('#pause_btn').click(function(){
        $('#demo').get(0).pause();
   })
})
```

Step 11   Save and test the Pause button in the browser.

Step 12 Next declare some global variables to reference the seekbar and the video. Write the two variables below inside the `document.ready()` function, as shown below in bold:

```
$(document).ready(function() {
    var seekbar = document.getElementById('seekbar');
    var video = document.getElementById('demo');
```

Step 13 Next add the function that controls the volume slider; add it below the previous code.

```
$('#volumeControl').change(function() {
    video.volume = this.value;
})
```

Step 14 Save and test the volume control in the browser.

Step 15 Return to the JS file.

Step 16 Next call the `init()` function, which will initialize the seekbar and add the event listeners. Call the `init()` function directly below the code in step 12 as shown below in bold:

```
$(document).ready(function() {
    var seekbar = document.getElementById('seekbar');
    var video = document.getElementById('demo');
    init();
```

Step 17 Write the `init()` function below the code that controls the volume as shown below in bold:

```
$('#volumeControl').change(function(event, value) {
    video.volume = this.value;
        })
function init() {
        video.addEventListener('timeupdate', updateSeekbar, false)   ;
        video.addEventListener('durationchange', initSeekbar, false);
        seekbar.addEventListener('change', changeVidTime, false);
        initSeekbar();
}
```

Line 1 references the seekbar range control. The next two lines listen for the timeupdate and durationchange events of the Video object. The seekbar range control also listens for its change event, which is dispatched whenever the user moves the slider. These events will control both the seekbar and the video through their event handlers. Finally, the `initSeekbar()` function that will set the initial properties of the seekbar range control is called.

Step 18 Write the initSeekbar() function as shown below. Place this code below the init() function you just wrote.

```
function initSeekbar() {
        seekbar.min = 0;
        seekbar.max = video.duration;
}
```

The file is still missing the callback functions from our event listeners. You will write them next.

Step 19 Write the event handlers for the listeners you added in step 17.

```
function updateSeekbar() {
        seekbar.value = video.currentTime;
}
```

```
function changeVidTime() {
        video.currentTime = seekbar.value;
}
```

Step 20   Save and test the file.

Optional Task

Step 21   Change the play button to a play-pause button.

Hint   Use the following pseudo-code as a guide:

1.   Create a reference to the Play-Pause button.

   a.   Change the name and id of the play button to something more appropriate.

   b.   Declare a variable and set the variable's value to the getElementById method (getting the new play-pause button).

   c.   When the button is clicked:

      i.   If the video is paused, invoke the play() method and change the button label from "Play" to "Pause."

      ii.   If the video is playing, invoke the pause() method and change the button lable from "Pause" to "Play."

      iii.   If the video has ended, change the currentTime property to 0, play the video and change the button label from "Pause" to "Play."

Step 22   Open the videoPlay-pause-finished.js file, which also uses unobtrusive JavaScript, and review its contents. You may now close all files.

Exercise summary

In this exercise, you learned how to control video using the HTML5 video API. This exercise used the jQuery JavaScript library so that less code writing was required compared to standard JavaScript. You learned how to play and pause the video, control the volume, and add a functional seekbar. In addition, you respected the separation of concerns principle and wrote unobtrusive JavaScript.

The `<source>` element

Both the audio and video element may have a child element called source to identify a video or audio file. The code looks like this:

```
<video controls>
    <source src="sample-video.ogv" type='video/ogg;
                              codecs="theora, vorbis"'>
    <source src="sample-video.mp3" type="video/webm">
</video>
```

In the next exercise, you will use multiple source element in an effort to be cross-browser compatible. Remember that no single browser currently supports all video and audio formats or codecs. If the developer supplies multiple source element children as shown in the sample code above, the browser will grab the first file it can play and look no further. Adding the type attribute is a way to help the browser and save on network traffic.

The browser will use the type attribute to determine if it can play the video and therefore avoid any unnecessary downloads. Sometimes the type attribute can be ambiguous. For example:

`type = "audio/ogg"`

Is it Ogg Vorbis? Ogg Flac? Ogg Speex?

... what about:

`type = "audio/mpeg"`

Is it MPEG-1 or MPEG-2?

In such cases, the browser simply guesses. The canPlayType() method returns the following possible responses:

- `YES`   it does support the resource type.
- `MAYBE`   there is a chance the resource type is supported.
- `PROBABLY`   the browser is confident of support.

You can also add the media attribute to the source element to query the browser to determine its screen size. This will determine which video to send.

```
<video controls>
    <source src="hi-res_video.ogv" type='video/ogg;
        codecs="theora, vorbis"'
            media="(min-device-width:768px)">
    <source src="low-res_video.ogv">
</video>
```

If the browser has a minimum device width of 768 pixels, the high resolution version of the file is served. If the minimum width is less, the file named in the first source element is ignored and the browser moves on and downloads the low resolution version.

Exercise 8.8: Using multiple audio/video formats

In this exercise, you use multiple audio files for maximum browser support. The browser will select the audio file that it is capable of playing.

Objectives

After completing this exercise, you will be able to do the following:

- Add multiple file formats for audio playback.

As you've seen from the support charts at the beginning of this chapter, not all browsers support all audio or video formats. You can, however, place multiple file formats of the same video to gain maximum support. For example, the MP3 audio format (at the time of publication) is understood by Internet Explorer 9.0 but not by Firefox; the Ogg Vorbis audio format is understood by Firefox but not by Internet Explorer. In this exercise, you add both file formats to the `<audio>` tag, and the browser will play the one that it supports.

Step 1   Open the file "multiple-audio-starter.html" from the media-API folder.

Step 2   In the `<body>` section, create an `<audio>` tag that shows controls. Place fallback text between the opening and closing `<audio>` tags.

```
<audio controls>
    <p>An introduction to the Food Plate.</p>
</audio>
```

Step 3   Now you place the two source elements (which use different format types) inside the audio element, as shown in bold below.

```
<audio controls>
    <p>An introduction to the Food Plate.</p>
    <source src="media/KidsHealth_Food_Guide_Pyramid_Becomes_a_Plate.ogg">
    <source src="media/KidsHealth_Food_Guide_Pyramid_Becomes_a_Plate.mp3">
</audio>
```

Step 4   Save the file and test it in Internet Explorer 9.0 and Firefox. Then test it in all browsers. The audio should play in all modern web browsers.

Step 5   Try commenting the first source element and then test again in Internet Explorer 9.0 and Firefox. The audio codec is not supported in one of these browsers.

Step 6   Remove the comment from the first source element, comment the second source element, and retest the file in Internet Explorer 9.0 and Firefox. Again, the codec is not supported in one of these two web browsers. You may now close all files and browsers.

Exercise summary

In this exercise, you learned how to designate multiple audio files for playback by providing a different audio format to the source element for the same audio. The browser plays the file format that it supports.

Demo 8.2: Video Tracks

In this demo, you examine the use of video tracks.

Objectives

After completing this demo, you will be able to do the following:

- Recognize the use of video tracks.
- Understand the additional markup required to use video tracks.

Video tracks add additional information to multimedia content. You can use text tracks to assist users with visual impairments as well as those who temporarily have the volume turned down. You can also use it simply to add descriptions or metadata to your multimedia file.

First create a text file with a .vtt extension, which serves as the text track that accompanies your video. The file has a strict format, particularly when it comes to setting up the timing cues. Timing cues are the indications to the video player that the text track should be displayed. Timing cues take this format:

```
hh:mm:ss.mls or 01:30:30:200
```

This represents double-digit hours, double-digit minutes, double-digit seconds, and triple-digit milliseconds. You can find a WEBVTT file syntax checker at https://quuz.org/webvtt/.

Step 1   In your IDE, open the files "video-tracks.html" and "video-tracks.vtt" from the media-API folder and the media subdirectory.

Step 2   Run the file in the Chrome web browser and examine the "subtitles."

Step 3   Return to your IDE and examine the additional code inside the video element.

Step 4   Examine the WEBVTT file and note the timing cues.

Step 5   For an excellent demonstration of implementing a text track to sync DOM elements, see http://simpl.info/track/map/index.html.

Chapter summary

In this chapter, you learned the new `<video>` and `<audio>` elements of HTML5 as well as some of the new media elements attributes. You also explored the associated API.

Chapter 9

Forms/ConstraintValidation API

In this chapter, you learn the new `<form>` elements and attributes that are designed to make your form more effective for the end user and easier to build for the developer. You will also be introduced to the ConstraintValidation API, which provides built-in form validation (for compliant browsers).

The HTML5 form elements and API were published in the HTML5 W3C Recommendation on October 28, 2014 in the document subtitled: A vocabulary and associated APIs for HTML and XHTML

Objectives

- ☐ Recite the new form elements and attributes.

- ☐ Know when to use the new `<form>` elements and attributes.

- ☐ Determine browser support for the new `<form>` elements.

- ☐ Validate your forms using the ConstraintValidation API.

Introduction

HTML5 introduces new form features including new input types, new elements and attributes, better accessibility and a form validation API. In this chapter you'll begin by learning the new HTML features. The chapter concludes with the ConstraintValidation API used for form validation that is now built-in to most modern web browsers.

New form `<input>` types

HTML5 introduces several new features for form development. These new features include new attributes for existing elements, new `type` attributes for `<input>` elements, new `<form>` elements, and a new Form API, which includes functions and objects to aid in client-side form validation.

What are the new `<input>` type attributes?

New `<input>` types

- `color`
- `date`
- `email`
- `number`
- `range`
- `search`
- `url`

New attributes for `<input>` elements

- `autocomplete`
- `autofocus`
- `form`
- `form overrides`
- `height`
- `list`
- `max`
- `min`
- `multiple`
- `novalidate`
- `pattern`
- `placeholder`
- `required`
- `step`
- `width`

New <form> elements

- datalist
- keygen
- output

In addition to the new elements and attributes, HTML5 introduces a new Form API with useful objects and functions that can aid in client-side form validation. The new functions include the following:

- checkValidity (a function)
- customError
- patternMismatch
- rangeOverflow
- rangeUnderflow
- stepMismatch
- tooLong
- typeMismatch
- validityState (an object)
- valueAsNumber (a function that converts the value of a control from text to number)
- validationMessage (an attribute)
- valueMissing

When do I use these new elements?

These new <form> elements provide more information to the browser or device rendering the web page or application. For example, using the new input type attribute "number" provides numerous benefits. If the application is being viewed on a mobile device, then the device will pop up the numeric keyboard because it now knows that the expected input will be a number. In conjunction with the new ValidityState object, the developer can use the typeMismatch property, which returns "true" if the field for which the type value was a number returns a string. The same is true for the remaining type attributes, such as URL, email, and so on.

The best part about using the new <form> elements and attributes is that they will simply be ignored by browsers that do not support them. Instead, the type attribute will be rendered with a standard text-input field. Therefore, you won't have to worry about markup breaking your page in old browsers.

For the most recent tables regarding browser support, please see http://caniuse.com.

Exercise 9.1: Using the new input attributes

In this exercise, you learn some input tags you may already be familiar with as well as some new HTML5 attributes for these elements.

Objectives

After completing this exercise, you will be able to do the following:

- List the new type attributes for the `<input>` element.
- Describe how the new form types are presented by different browsers.
- Describe how the new form types behave in different browsers.
- Use the new input types.
- Determine which browsers support the new input types.

Along with the new `<input>` element, HTML5 provides new attributes that identify the input type, such as telephone numbers, URLs, and so on. Several browsers will not respond to this additional information, but the potential is now there to do so. Smart phones often use this information to display the proper alphabetic or numeric keypad as needed. In this exercise, you use the new `type` attribute of the `<input>` element.

The input-attributes-starter.html file as shown in Chrome.

Step 1   Open the file "input-attributes-starter.html" from the constraintValidation-API folder.

Step 2   Locate the form with the input fields. Locate the second input field with the `id` of userPhone.

Step 3   Replace the type attribute as shown:

```
<input type="tel" name="userPhone" id="userPhone">
```

Step 4   Locate the input field with the `id` of userWebsite and replace the `type` attribute:

```
<input type="url" name="userWebsite" id="userWebsite"
```

Step 5   Locate the input field with the `id` of userEmail and replace the type attribute:

```
<input type="email" name="userEmail" id="userEmail">
```

Step 6   Locate the input field with the `display:inline` property and add the following attributes:

```
<input type="range" max="10" min="0" step="0.5" value="0">
```

Step 7   Save and test the file in Firefox.

Step 8   Save and test the file in Chrome. Depending on the version of Chrome you are using, you may see the range field shown below. However, if you interact with the range control, the browser does not display the value.

> Email:
>
> [   ]
>
> Activity Level: ⬚   Level: 0
>
> Age:
> [18   ]

The HTML5 range control (next to Activity Level).

Step 9   Modify the range control to accommodate some JavaScript that you will write to display the range control value. The new code is shown below in bold:

```
<label for="activityLevel">Activity Level: </label>
<input type="range" max="10" min="0" step=".5"
        value="0" onChange="showActivityLevel(this.value)">
<span id="activityDisplay">Level 0</span>
```

Step 10   Write the following JavaScript in the `<head>` section to display the range control value:

```
<script>
function showActivityLevel(newVal) {
        document.getElementById("activityDisplay").innerHTML=" Level: " +
newVal;
}
</script>
```

Step 11   Save and test the file in Chrome or Safari. You should see the value of the range control to the right of the control.

> Activity Level: ⬚   Level: 4

The HTML5 range control functioning with the additional JavaScript.

Step 12   Save and test the file in a browser that does not support the range control (e.g., Internet Explorer 9.0). Use the http://caniuse.com website to see which browsers support HTML5 form attributes.

Activity Level: 0

Typical output from a browser that does not support the HTML5 range control.

Step 13   Locate the age input field and set the new HTML5 attributes:

```
<input name="age" id="age" type="number" max="100" min="18" step="1" val-
ue="18">
```

Step 14   Locate the input field with the id of color and set the type to "color" as shown below in bold:

```
<input type="color" name="color" id="color">
```

Step 15   Save and test the file in a browser that does not support the color attribute.

Step 16   Save and test the file in a browser that does support the color attribute.

Change the Default color of your Food Plate:

#000000

Other...

The new HTML5 input type color.

Note   Possible fallback solutions for the range control's lack of feedback may be found here:

http://demo.tutorialzine.com/2011/12/what-you-need-to-know-html5-range-input/ which includes a corresponding demo found here: http://demo.tutorialzine.com/2011/12/what-you-need-to-know-html5-range-input/

Step 17   Locate the Date field and add the type attribute:

```
<label for="joinDate">
        Date you would like to join:
</label>
        <input id="joinDate" type="date">
```

Step 18   Save and test the file in the Chrome browser.

Date you would like to join: 2011-08-24

The new HTML5 input type date.

Step 19   Save and test the file in the Opera 11.5 browser.

Step 20   Change the type attribute of the date input field to the other options listed below and test in the browser.

datetime-local (removed from the spec February 10, 2014, see:
            https://github.com/w3c/html/commit/3e5df1ee1aebed37571a23c9b62adc74a92a04b9)

time
date
week
month

Step 21   You may now close all files.

Step 22   Use your mobile device to see how these form controls are rendered by visiting http://www.kevinruse.com/forms.html.

Exercise summary

In this exercise, you learned some of the new attributes of HTML5 `<form>` elements. You should now have an idea of how these attributes are rendered in the most modern web browsers.

Exercise 9.2: Using the new form attributes

In this exercise, you learn some new attributes for HTML <form> attributes.

Objectives

After completing this exercise, you will be able to do the following:

- List the new `<form>` attributes.
- Use the new `<form>` attributes.
- Determine which browsers support the new `<form>` attributes.

Along with the new `<input>` element attributes, HTML5 provides a new set of attributes that apply to both old and new `<form>` elements. Like the new `<input>` attributes, these new `<form>` attributes will be ignored by browsers that do not support them.

The `placeholder` attribute

This attribute can be used to provide hints or default input. It is not intended to be the form control label.

Step 1   Open the file "form-attributes-starter.html" from the constraintValidation-API folder.

Step 2   Locate the user name input field and add the new `placeholder` attribute as shown:

`<input type="text" name="userName" id="userName" placeholder="First name only.">`

Step 3   Save and test the file in all browsers.

User Name
First name only.

Text-input element with the placeholder text visible in the text field.

Step 4   Remove the comments in the <style> block and rerun the file in a web browser. Note the change in placeholder text style. This code should work in Firefox, Chrome, and Internet Explorer.

The `autocomplete` attribute

This attribute is used to protect user-entered sensitive information from being stored in the local browser file.

The following chart describes the behavior of the autocomplete attribute.

Value	Behavior
on	The field is not secure; the data is not particularly sensitive and its value can be saved and restored.
off	The field is secure; it's data is sensitive and its value will not be saved.
unspecified	Defaults to the setting on the parent for; if there is no parent form, or no value is set on the parent form, then the behavior is the same as on.

The `autofocus` attribute

This attribute can be used give an element focus. It should only be used on one element on the page.

Step 5   Locate the user name input field and add the new autofocus attribute as shown:

```
<input type="text" name="userName" id="userName" placeholder="First name
only." autofocus>
```

Step 6   Save and test the file in the browser. The cursor should be placed in the userName field at load time.

The `list` attribute and the `<datalist>` element

Step 7   Add the `<input>` element with the list attribute shown below:

```
<p>I am also interested in tracking the following:</p>
<input type="text" id="categoryList" list="categories">
```

Step 8   Add the `<datalist>` element:

```
<datalist id="categories">
        <option value="Vitamins" label="Vitamins">
        <option value="Minerals" label="Minerals">
        <option value="Cholesterol" label="Cholesterol">
        <option value="Lipids" label="Lipids">
        <option value="Fiber" label="Fiber">
</datalist>
```

The `spellcheck` attribute

This attribute is used on input controls that accept text input. It indicates to the browser whether or not it should provide spelling feedback. Most browsers default to leaving the spellcheck function on.

Value	Behavior
spellcheck="true"	Suggests that the browser provide spelling feedback
spellcheck="false"	Suggests that the browser does not provide spelling feedback

Step 9   Add the spellcheck attribute on the textarea and test in several browsers.

Step 10   You may now close all files.

Note that the `<datalist>` element could be dynamically created at runtime with an AJAX request or server-side code.

To test this file on your mobile device, go to www.kevinruse.com/speech

Exercise summary

In this exercise, you learned some new attributes for both new and existing HTML <form> elements. You were also introduced to the new <datalist> element and its associated attributes.

HTML5 form validation

The HTML5 <form> elements and attributes include a JavaScript API that can help in the form validation process. The ConstraintValidation API includes properties and methods that take advantage of the new input types from the previous exercises. HTML5 form validation now occurs automatically on the client during submit.

Preventing default validation from occurring

The Form object includes a novalidate attribute that will prevent the default form validation. You can also add the form novalidate attribute to the Submit button to prevent default validation.

ConstraintValidation API

The form controls now have a new API. The tables below describe the form control properties, methods, and events.

Form properties

Property	Description
willValidate	Returns "true" if an element can be validated

Form control methods

Method	Description
checkValidity()	May also be used on the entire form (as well as individual form controls) to manually invoke the browser's validation checks; returns "true" or "false" depending on the success or failure of the check
setCustomValidity(message)	Sets a custom error message or pass in a custom error or an empty string to clear the error message

Form controls validity and validityState

All form controls now contain a validity property, which returns a ValidityState object. This object represents the <form> element's current validity state through a number of Boolean attributes, as shown in the chart below.

Validity State	Description
valueMissing	True if a required element is missing
typeMismatch	True if the input value does not match the type attribute
patternMismatch	True if the input value does not match the pattern attribute
tooLong	True if the element value exceeds the max length
rangeUnderflow	True if the element value is below the min value
rangeOverflow	True if the element value is above the max value
stepMismatch	True, if the element value does not fit the step attribute
valid	True if all of the above attributes are false

Exercise 9.3: Form validation

In this exercise, you control when form validation takes place and use the ConstraintValidation API to locate form input errors and create custom error messages.

Objectives

After completing this exercise, you will be able to do the following:

- Use the new required attribute on `<form>` elements.
- Understand and use the new validity and validity state attribute and value.
- Create custom error messages.

HTML5 validation is now automatic, although it can be turned off. Each `<form>` element now includes a `validity` attribute that holds the validity state of the element. In this exercise, you validate fields that are required for the user and locate form input errors such as missing or incorrect values.

Step 1   Open the file "form-validation-starter.html" from the constraint-validation-API folder.

Step 2   Examine the form on the page and locate the input elements for the user name and email address.

Step 3   Make these input fields required. In other words, the form should not validate unless the user enters input values into these two fields. The `required` attribute is shown for both fields in bold below:
```
<input type="text" name="User Name" id="userName"
    placeholder="First name only." required>
<input type="email" name="User Email" id="userEmail" required>
```

Step 4   Save the file and run it in a web browser. Click the Submit button without filling out the two text-input fields.

Step 5   Create a `<script>` block in the `<head>` section.
```
<script>
</script>
```

Once the page loads, start listening for invalid events dispatched by the form controls. You will add an event listener to the onload event that will call a function that will listen for invalid events dispatched by the form.

Step 6   Inside the <script> block you wrote in step 5, add the following listener:

```
window.addEventListener("load", startValidating, false);
```

Step 7   Now add the event handler function called startValidating.

```
function startValidating() {
    // Register an event listener for "invalid" events
    document.join_form.addEventListener("invalid", invalidHandler, true);
}
```

This event listener calls the event handler function called invalidHandler, which you will write next.

Step 8   Now add the event handler function called invalidHandler.

```
function invalidHandler(event) {
        var valState = event.target.validity;
        if (valState.valueMissing) {
                alert("You must complete the entire form. You did not com-
plete the " + event.target.name);
        }
    if (valState.typeMismatch) {
        alert("You must enter a valid value for " + event.target.name);
    }
    event.preventDefault()
    return false;
}
```

This function locates the elements passed in as an argument with `validity` attribute (or validity state) that is either `valueMissing` or `typeMismatch`, and then creates an appropriate error message. It also prevents the browser's default behavior for handling these events based on the fact that one form input type is email and they both contain the `required` attribute.

Step 9   Save the file and run the page in a web browser. You can test the code by submitting the form without filling out the required fields. You may now close all files. Open the finished file, which uses the invalid event's `preventDefault()` method to prevent the default browser validation.

Exercise outcome

The result of this exercise is the appearance of an alert box, driven by the code you wrote in steps 6–8, as well as the built-in form validation in the web browser.

Exercise summary

In this exercise, you learned more about both built-in and custom HTML5 validation techniques.

Resources

http://www.wufoo.com/html5/

http://www.html5pattern.com/

Challenge exercise

1. Using your IDE, open the file "constraintValidation-challenge-starter.html" from the challenge subdirectory.

2. Run the file in a web browser.

3. Your job is to use the constraintValidation API to make the following form modifications:

   a. The "Unit of Measurement" section is required.

   b. The "Height/Weight" section is required.

   c. The Height and Weight fields must contain only numbers.

   d. The "Contact Info" section is required.

   e. The Email field must contain a valid email address.

4. If you get stuck, "constraint-validation-challenge-finished.html" is a possible solution.

Chapter summary

This chapter introduced you to HTML5 forms, which include new type attributes, new <form> attributes, new control attributes, and a rich API for scripting forms.

Chapter 10

WebStorage API

In this chapter, you learn about the WebStorage API that stores session data that is accessible throughout the user's web session and local storage data which survives after the web page or even the entire browser is closed. This API has several advantages over the older method of storing data known as cookies.

The WebStorage API (first edition) API became a Candidate Recommendation on July 30, 2013. The WebStorage (second edition) API became a Candidate Recommendation on June 9, 2015.

Objectives

- ❏ Describe the WebStorage API.

- ❏ Explain use cases for the WebStorage API.

- ❏ Describe the advantages and disadvantages of using WebStorageAPIs.

- ❏ Detect browser support for web storage.

- ❏ List the two types of web storage.

- ❏ Use the new WebStorage API to store data on the client.

Introduction

Web storage is used to save data for the web application to use at a later time. The data can be saved for the duration of the browser session (i.e., until the user closes the browser, browser window, or tab running the application) or persisted beyond the browser session so that it will continue to be available to the user even after he or she closes the browser window or tab and then reopens it for a second session. Web storage may be used as a replacement for cookies. See "Cookies vs. session storage vs. local storage" below for an explanation of the advantages and disadvantages of each technique.

Browser support for the Storage object

For the most recent tables regarding browser support, please see http://caniuse.com.

The WebStorage API

The Storage object

"Each `Storage` object provides access to a list of key/value pairs, which are sometimes called items. Keys are strings. Any string (including an empty string) is a valid key. Values are similarly strings.

Each `Storage` object is associated with a list of key/value pairs when it is created, as defined in the sections on the sessionStorage and localStorage attributes. Multiple separate objects implementing the storage interface can all be associated with the same list of key/value pairs simultaneously."[1]

The WebStorage API recommends an arbitrary limit of five megabytes per origin. However the web browser may allow the user to increase or decrease this amount.

Storage object properties

Property	Description
`length`	Returns the number of key/value pairs currently present in the list associated with the `Storage` object
`sessionStorage`	Represents the set of storage areas specific to the current top-level browsing context
`localStorage`	Provides a `Storage` object for an origin

Each top-level browsing context has a unique set of session storage areas, one for each origin.

User agents should not expire data from a browsing context's session storage areas but may do so when the user requests that such data be deleted. Data can also be deleted when the user agent detects that it has limited storage space, or for security reasons. User agents should always avoid deleting data while a script that could access that data is running. When a top-level browsing context is destroyed (and therefore permanently inaccessible to the user), the data stored in its session storage areas can be discarded with it, as the API described in this specification provides no way for that data to ever be subsequently retrieved.

User agents must have a set of local storage areas, one for each origin.

---

1   http://www.w3.org/TR/webstorage/

User agents should expire data from the local storage areas only for security reasons or when requested to do so by the user. User agents should always avoid deleting data while a script that could access that data is running. [2]

Storage object methods

Method	Description
key(n)	Returns the name of the *n*th key in the list associated with the Storage object
getItem(key)	Returns the current value associated with the key argument provided
setItem(key,value)	Checks to see if a key/value pair exists that matches the key/value arguments provided. If not, a new key/value pair is added to the list associated with the Storage object using the given key argument with its value set to the value argument provided.
removeItem(key)	Causes the key/value pair with the given key argument to be removed from the list associated with the Storage object, if it exists. If no item with that key exists, the method will do nothing.
clear()	Deletes all of the key/value pairs in WebStorage for the entire domain at once

Storage object events

Method	Description
storage event	The storage event is fired when a storage area changes. This event fires only when a second browser window is running the same application and it is dispatched from the second browser window.

Storage event object properties

Property	Description
key	Returns the value that the key was initialized to; represents the value being changed
oldValue	Returns the value it was initialized to; represents the old value of the key being changed
newValue	Returns the value it was initialized to; represents the new value of the key being changed
url	Returns the value it was initialized to; represents the address of the document the key of which was changed
storageArea	Returns the value it was initialized to; represents the Storage object that was affected

When to use the WebStorage API

LocalStorage may be used in place of cookies. The larger storage size and the fact that the data stored is retrieved programmatically and not with every http request, often makes localStorage a better choice then cookies. Some use cases for localStorage include:

- Store user preferences

---

2 http://dev.w3.org/html5/webstorage/#the-storage-interface

- Store useful (but not sensitive) information, for example, the user's zip code but not the user's social security number
- Store the state of a game
- Store the state of a form (for later completion by the user)

When not to use the WebStorage API

Sometimes web applications allow users a variety of pathnames that lead to a single domain (some of these applications include blog sites, build-your-own-website sites, hosting services, etc.). This can lead to different users using different pathnames on a single domain. Since the domain is the same, they can access the storage area of the whole origin and therefore each other's data. For example, users of services with paths like freeblogs.org/user1/ and freeblogs.org/user2/ should not use web storage. Another valid reason to avoid client-side storage via web storage is its location in the browser cache: when the user empties their cache, they lose the data and, therefore, data critical to the application is vulnerable.

Cookies vs. session storage vs. local storage

The ability to store information on the client-side is not new and has been achieved with somewhat lengthy JavaScript in the past, which works quite well. It does however, have some drawbacks. For example, there is a 4KB limit within which to store the data, and because a cookie is requested with every HTTP "get" request, the traffic from client to server increases for every web page that contains cookies. Cookies do have advantages, including sharing data between client and server for such purposes as maintaining state.

A new HTML5 alternative to cookies is local and session storage, both of which store data on the client in the form of key/value pairs that are tied to a specific domain. Local storage will persist beyond the browser session. In other words, the user can close the browser tab or window or even the browser itself and upon revisiting the site can still obtain the data in the keys. Session storage on the other hand is erased as soon as the browser window, tab, or the browser itself is closed. Local storage makes it possible to store information on the client side so that a web application can still be used even if the user is offline.

Exercise 10.1: Detecting browser support for the WebStorage API

In this exercise, you check to determine if the user's browser will support the new WebStorage API.

Objectives

After completing this exercise, you will be able to do the following:

- Use JavaScript to determine if the browser supports the new `LocalStorage` object.

Step 1   Open the file "webStorage-support-starter.html" from the localStorage-API folder.

Step 2   Create a `<script>` block and write the following JavaScript:

```
<script>
    function checkStorageSupport() {
    if(window.localStorage) {
        console.log("This browser supports local storage.");
```

```
            }
      else {
            console.log("This browser does NOT support local storage.")
      }
};
</script>
```

Step 3   Save the file and test the page in all web browsers. You may now close all files.

Exercise outcome

This exercise results in a log statement to the console indicating support or lack of support for the WebStorage API.

Exercise summary

In this exercise, you learned one technique for testing browser support for local storage or session storage. An alert box was used to show support or lack of support. In the next exercise, you will write the programming logic to store session data *only* if the browser supports session storage.

Exercise 10.2: Storing and retrieving data

In this exercise, you save data for the user that may be accessed during their current session and will persist after the web page or even the browser is closed.

Objectives

After completing this exercise, you will be able to do the following:

- Use JavaScript to create a localStorage object.
- Use the LocalStorage API to save data from the web page that persists beyond the browser session (using the setItem() method).
- Use JavaScript to retrieve the stored data (using the getItem() method).

Step 1   Open the file "storing-data-starter.html" from the localStorage-API folder.

Step 2   Notice the two text-input fields for the user to enter their first name and title. Below these input fields are two buttons that you use to store and retrieve the data.

Step 3   In the <script> block, write the following function that checks for browser support before saving the user's input (first name and title).

```
function saveLocal() {
      if (window.localStorage) {
      var firstname = document.getElementById("firstname").value;
      var title = document.getElementById("title").value;
      var person = {"firstname":firstname,"title":title};
      localStorage.setItem("person",JSON.stringify(person));
       }
```

```
    else { console.log("Your Browser does not support Local Storage."); }
}
```

The "if" block checks for browser support and if "true" creates three variables. The first variable, "first-Name," stores the value of the input field with the `id` of "firstName." The second variable stores the value of the input field with the `id` of "title." Both variable declarations are set using the (web) `Document` object method `getElementByID()` to retrieve a node within the DOM. The third variable, "person," uses a JavaScript shorthand technique to create a `Person` object with two properties: firstname and title. The values for these two properties are set using the first two variables. Finally, the `localStorage` object's `setItem()` method is used to store the data into session storage. The data is being stored with JavaScript Object Notation (JSON). The `JSON.stringify()` method accepts a JavaScript object and returns its JSON equivalent. The "else" block will wite a message to the console if the user's browser does not support session storage.

Step 4 Call the `saveLocal()` function from the onclick event of the "saveBtn" <input> element.

```
<input id="saveBtn" type="button" value="Save Values" onclick="saveLocal()"/>
```

Step 5 Write the function to retrieve the stored local data from localStorage.

```
function readLocal(){
    if (window.localStorage) {
        //Get the Person object
        var person = localStorage.getItem("person");
        person = JSON.parse(person);
        alert(person.firstname + " is a " + person.title + ".");
        }
}
```

As with the saveLocal function, we first check for browser support of localStorage. If "true," a variable called "person" is declared and the value is set to the `localStorage` object's `getItem()` method, which returns the value of the session variable "person." Remember that the person variable is a JSON object, so the `JSON.parse()` method is used when assigning the value of the person variable. The `JSON.parse()` method parses a JSON string, reconstructing the original JavaScript object.

Step 6 Call the `readLocal()` method from the onclick event of the readBtn <input> element.

```
<input id="readBtn" type="button" value="Read Values" onclick="readLocal()"/>
```

Step 7 Save the file and preview the web page in Chrome. Type a first name and title and click the Save Values button. Then click the Read Values button. After testing in Chrome, try other web browsers.

Step 8 Close the web page and reopen it. Click the Read Values button and you should still see the values saved from step 7.

Step 9 Close the web browser and reopen the browser and the web page. Click the Read Values button and you should still see the values saved from step 7.

Note To test this file in Internet Explorer, it must be saved and run from the localhost server. Launch WAMP and then set the browser address to http://localhost. From the localhost directory, navigate to this chapter's folder and locate this exercise file and run it in the browser. The localStorage should work in Internet Explorer 8.0 and higher.

Step 10 Open the file called "Demo-unobtrusive.html" and the associated JavaScript file to see the same functionality written in jQuery as unobtrusive JavaScript.

Step 11 Review "Accessing storage with JavaScript expandos and Arrays" on the following page and try replacing the local storage code using Associative Array Notation or JavaScript expandos.

Step 12   You may now close all files.

Regarding quotes on JSON object keys or "Do I need quotes on keys?"

Douglas Crockford explained: "That was when we discovered the unquoted name problem. It turns out ECMA Script 3 has a whack reserved word policy. Reserved words must be quoted in the key position, which is really a nuisance. When I got around to formulizing this into a standard, I didn't want to have to put all of the reserved words in the standard, because it would look really stupid.

At the time, I was trying to convince people: yeah, you can write applications in JavaScript; it's actually going to work and it's a good language. I didn't want to say, then, at the same time: and look at this really stupid thing they did! So I decided, instead, let's just quote the keys.

That way, we don't have to tell anybody about how whack it is.

That's why, to this day, keys are quoted in JSON."

The presentation in which this statement was made: http://yuilibrary.com/theater/?start=41.

Accessing storage with JavaScript expandos and Arrays

You can use the following methods to write and read to local storage with JavaScript:

1. Associate array notation:
    ```
    localStorage['firstName'] = "Kevin";
    var firstName = localStorage['firstName'];
    ```

2. JavaScript expando:
    ```
    localStorage.firstName = "Kevin"
    var firstName = localStorage.firstName;
    ```

Exercise summary

In this exercise, you saved data locally and retrieved that data even after the browser was closed.

Exercise 10.3: Using sessionStorage

In this exercise, you save data for the user for the duration of their browser session.

Objectives

After completing this exercise, you will be able to do the following:

- Use JavaScript to create a `SessionStorage` object.
- Use the SessionStorage API.
- Use JavaScript to retrieve the stored data.

Step 1   Open the file "session-storage-starter.html" from the localStorage-API folder.

Step 2   Notice the two text-input fields where user can enter their first name and title. Below these input fields are two buttons that are used to store and retrieve the data.

Step 3   In the `<script>` block below the `checkStorageSupport()` function, write the following function that checks for browser support before saving the users input (first name and title).

```
function saveLocal() {
if (window.sessionStorage) {
      var firstname = document.getElementById("firstname").value;
      var title = document.getElementById("title").value;
      var person = {"firstname":firstname,"title":title};
      sessionStorage.setItem("person",JSON.stringify(person));
}
 else {
      console.log("Your Browser does not support Session Storage.");
      }
}
```

The "if" block checks for browser support and if "true" creates three variables. The first variable, "firstname," stores the value of the input field with the id of "firstname." The second variable stores the value of the input field with the id of "title." Both variable declarations are set using the `Document` object method `getElementByID()` to retrieve a node within the DOM. The third variable, "person," uses a JavaScript shorthand technique to create a `Person` object with two properties: firstname and title. The values for these two properties are set using the first two variables. Finally, the `sessionStorage` object's `setItem()` method is used to store the data to the session storage. The data is being stored with JavaScript Object Notation (JSON). The `JSON.stringify()` method accepts a JavaScript object and returns its JSON equivalent. The "else" block will log a message to the console if the user's browser does not support session storage.

Step 4   Call the `saveLocal()` function from the onclick event of the "loadBtn" `<input>` element.

```
<input id="saveBtn" type="button" value="Save Values" onclick="saveLocal()"/>
```

Step 5   Write the function to retrieve the stored session data from sessionStorage.

```
function readLocal() {
        if (window.sessionStorage) {
            //Get the Person object
            var person = sessionStorage.getItem("person");
            person = JSON.parse(person);
            alert(person.firstname + " is a " + person.title + ".");
        }
}
```

As with the saveLocal function, first check for browser support of sessionStorage. If "true," a variable called "person" is declared and the value is set to the `sessionStorage` object's `getItem()` method, which returns the value of the session variable "person." Remember that the person variable is a JSON object, so the `JSON.parse()` method is used when assigning the value of the person variable. The `JSON.parse()` method parses a JSON string, reconstructing the original JavaScript object.

Step 6   Call the `readLocal()` method from the onclick event of the readBtn `<input>` element.

```
<input id="readBtn" type="button" value="Read Values" onclick="readLocal()"/>
```

Step 7   Save the file and preview the web page in Chrome. Type a first name and title and click the Save Values button. Then click the Read Values button.

Step 8   Close the browser window or tab. Then test the page again and click the Read Values button. Because the session was terminated, you should no longer see a `Person` object. After testing in Chrome, try other web browsers. You may now close all open files.

Exercise outcome

This exercise results in the initial browser check saving the data to local storage, allowing you to click the Read Values button to see the stored data. After closing the browser window, however, you should no longer be able to retrieve the data.

Exercise summary

In this exercise, you saved web-page data on the client that was erased after the browser session ended.

Exercise 10.4: Responding to the storage event

In this exercise, you respond to changes in stored data using the `StorageEvent` object and its properties.

Objectives

After completing this exercise, you will be able to do the following:

- Understand what the storage event is and when it is dispatched.
- Listen for the storage event.
- Respond to the storage event.

Step 1   Open the file "storage-event-starter.html" from the webStorage-API folder.

If the browser supports local storage, you'll add an event listener for the storage event. Call the `addEventListener()` method of the `Window` object and pass three arguments. First, the name of the event you want to respond to is "storage." Next comes the name of the event handler function that you want to execute when the "storage" event is dispatched. The name of this function is `handleStorage()`. The final argument is a Boolean that states whether the event handler should be executed in the capturing or in the bubbling phase. If the last argument is set to "true," the event handler is set for the capturing phase; if it is set to "false," the event handler is set for the bubbling phase.

Step 2   Write the event listener for the storage event as shown in bold:

```
function checkStorageSupport(){
if(window.localStorage){
        console.log("This browser supports local storage.");
        window.addEventListener("storage", storageHandler, false);
        }
    else {
        console.log("This browser does NOT support local storage.");
        }
}
```

Now write the event handler function that will execute when the storage event is dispatched by the browser.

Step 3   Below the previous function, write the following handleStorage event handler:

```
function storageHandler(evt) {
        alert("You stored a value. Key = " + evt.key + " old value: " +
        evt.oldValue + " new value: " + evt.newValue + " at " +        evt.
storageArea.person);
}
```

Step 4   Open two browsers' windows and arrange them side by side. In each browser window, open the file "storage-event-starter.html."

Step 5   In one browser window, enter a first name and title, and then click the Save Values button.

This triggers the dispatching of the storage event. Because our event listener is listening for this storage event, the handleStorage event handler is invoked, which creates the alert box and access properties of the storage event, including the StorageEvent object properties: key, oldValue, newValue and storageArea.

Step 6   You may now close all open files.

Exercise summary

In this exercise, you learned how to respond to storage events. This knowledge might be helpful to let users know that local data storage has changed, for example. This can be accomplished because the storage event contains properties to store the old and new values (oldValue and newValue) as well as the storage area (storageArea). In this exercise, you learned how and where the StorageEvent is dispatched. You learned the StorageEvent objects' properties and how to access them.

Resources

Clearing Cache vs. clearing cookies: http://sharonminsuk.com/blog/2011/03/21/clearing-cache-has-no-effect-on-html5-localstorage-or-sessionstorage/

Storing images in LocalStorage: https://www.ibm.com/developerworks/mydeveloperworks/blogs/boble-ah/resource/hero-graphic.html?lang=en

StorageEvent demo: http://html5demos.com/storage-events

WebStorage specification (2nd edition): https://w3c.github.io/webstorage/

Challenge exercise

1. Using your IDE, open the file "localStorage-challenge-starter.html" from the challenge subdirectory.

2. Run the file in a web browser.

3. Your job is to store the following information (derived from the user's input on the form):

   a. A "user" object with the following properties:

      i. firstName

      ii. gender

      iii. ageGroup

4. You can confirm your answer, by checking the Resources tab on the Developer Tools (Chrome). After completing and submitting the form, you should see the Resources tab as shown below.

5. If you get stuck, "localStorage-challenge-finished.html" is a possible solution.

Chapter summary

In this chapter, you learned how to store data from your web page that the user can recall before a browser session ends with sessionStorage. You also learned how to store data from the web page that the user can recall after the browser session ends and even after the browser itself has been closed. You learned how to respond to the storage event that is dispatched whenever stored data has been changed.

Chapter 11

WebMessaging API

In this chapter, you send and receive messages from web pages, including web pages from a different domain. You learn how websites originating from different domains can use the origin property to establish trust before sending messages.

The WebMessaging API became a W3C Candidate Recommendation on May 19, 2015.

Objectives

- ❑ Describe the WebMessaging API.

- ❑ Send messages to another page with the `postMessage()` method.

- ❑ Send messages to a page in a different domain.

Introduction

Communicating by sending messages between documents with different origins is generally prohibited by a browser for security and privacy reasons. However, it can be incredibly useful to allow such communication. Take mashups, for example, where content from a content-driven page, such as financial or stock market information, is used in another domain, such as a portal or aggregator. The postMessage() method allows this type of communication to take place as well as allowing communication between pages with the same origin.

> "Web browsers, for security and privacy reasons, prevent documents in different domains from affecting each other; that is, cross-site scripting is disallowed.

> While this is an important security feature, it prevents pages from different domains from communicating even when those pages are not hostile. This section introduces a messaging system that allows documents to communicate with each other regardless of their source domain. They do so in a way designed not to enable cross-site scripting attacks.

> Authors should check the origin attribute to ensure that messages are only accepted from domains from which they expect to receive messages. Otherwise, bugs in the author's message-handling code could be exploited by hostile sites.

> Furthermore, even after checking the origin attribute, authors should also check that the data in question is of the expected format. Otherwise, if the source of the event has been attacked using a cross-site scripting flaw, further unchecked processing of information sent using the `postMessage()` method could result in the attack being propagated into the receiver."[1]

Web messaging's postMessage() method

The `postMessage()` method is a method of the `Windows` object.

```
postMessage(message, targetOrigin, [ports])
```

This method takes two arguments. The first argument is the message that you are sending, and the second argument is the target origin. A third, optional argument is an array of ports. If no ports argument is provided, the new ports array will be empty.

```
window.postMessage("Hi There", "http://www.yourwebsite.com");
```

The specification indicates that `postMessage()` may send any object, but at the time of this publication, `postMessage()` sends only strings. JSON (JavaScript Object Notation) may be used to parse objects into strings and back again with `stringify()` and `parse()` methods.

You can send messages to a target regardless of origin by setting the `targetOrigin` argument to "*". It is not advisable to send confidential messages with the * targetOrigin argument. You can also restrict your messages to same-origin targets only by setting the targetOrigin argument to "/".

Establishing trust between domains

---

1   Ian Hickson (editor), "HTML5 Web Messaging" W3C Recommendation 19 May 2015, http://www.w3.org/TR/webmessaging/

Web messaging between domains is made possible by first establishing trust between the domains. Domain A agrees to accept messages from domain B. After the message from domain A is received by domain B, domain B checks where the message originated. This information is provided by the web browser and is found in the header request. While web browsers sometimes send the "Referrer," the WebMessaging API now requires the browser to send the "origin" (which cannot be spoofed). The origin represents the domain making the request. Domain B should also check the datatype of the incoming message as a further safety check before accepting the message. When using `postMessage()`, the target origin must match the domain of the target document window or the postMessage call fails with a security error.

The origin

The origin is composed of a subset of a URL address and is designed to establish trust relationships on the Web. The origin consists of a scheme, a host, and a port. For example, in "http://www.kevinruse.com:8080" the scheme is "http," the host is "kevinruse.com," and the port is "8080." So an origin of https://www.kevinruse.com:8080 will not match the an origin of http://www.kevinruse.com:8080 because the schemes—"http" and "https"— do not match. The notion of the origin is used in cross-document messaging and XMLHttpRequest APIs.

What is cross-origin resource sharing?

Cross-origin resource sharing (CORS) is a browser technology specification. It specifies ways for a web service to provide APIs for scripts that come from different domains. Custom HTTP headers are used to tell the browser how to communicate with the server. Remember the scenario where domain A sends a message to domain B? If domain B accepts the message, the HTTP header includes the following message in its response: "Access-Control-Allow-Origin"; that returns the same origin, unless it is a public resource, in which case it returns the targetOrigin.

CORS support and the server

CORS is made possible by communication handled between the browser and the server. The browser adds extra header information and sometimes makes additional requests during a CORS request on behalf of the client. The HTTP response includes the following CORS-specific information:

```
Access-Control-Allow-Origin: http://www.kevinruse.com
Access-Control-Allow-Credentials: true
Access-Control-Expose-Headers: FooBar
```

Notice that the CORS-related headers are prefixed with "Access-Control-"; these are described in a CORS tutorial:

- **Access-Control-Allow-Origin (required):** This header must be included in all valid CORS responses; omitting the header will cause the CORS request to fail. The value of the header can either echo the origin request header (as in the example above) or be a '*' to allow requests from any origin. If you'd like any site to be able to access your data, using '*' is fine. But if you'd like finer control over who can access your data, use an actual value in the header.

- **Access-Control-Allow-Credentials (optional):** By default, cookies are not included in CORS requests. Use this header to indicate that cookies should be included in CORS requests. The only valid value for this header is "true" (all lowercase). If you don't need cookies, don't include this header (rather than setting its value to "false").

The Access-Control-Allow-Credentials header works in conjunction with the withCredentials property on the `XmlHttpRequest2` object. Both these properties must be set to "true" in order for the CORS request to succeed. If withCredentials is true, but there is no Access-Control-Allow-Credentials header, the request will fail (and vice versa).

It's recommended that you don't set this header unless you are sure you want cookies to be included in CORS requests.

- **Access-Control-Expose-Headers (optional):** The `XmlHttpRequest2` object has a `getResponseHeader()` method that returns the value of a particular response header. During a CORS request, the `getResponseHeader()` method can only access simple response headers. Simple response headers are defined as follows:

```
Cache-Control
Content-Language
Content-Type
Expires
Last-Modified
Pragma
```

If you want clients to be able to access other headers, you have to use the Access-Control-Expose-Headers header. The value of this header is a comma-delimited list of response headers you want to expose to the client.

As of this writing, all browsers have buggy `getRequestHeader()` implementations, so the headers may not be accessible to clients even after you set the Access-Control-Expose-Headers header.[2]

Ports and channel messaging

The following information comes from the editor's specification.

Independent pieces of code (e.g., running in different browsing contexts) can communicate directly using channel messaging. Channel Messaging uses two-way pipes with a port at each end. Messages are sent in one port and delivered asynchronous (as DOM events) at the other port, and vice versa. Message Channels are created as shown below:

```
var myChannel = new MessageChannel();
```

The `Channel` object has two properties: port1 (the first message port) and port2 (the second message port).

MessagePort methods

Properties	Description
postMessage()	Used to send messages to optional MessagePortArray ports
start()	Begins dispatching messages received on the port
close()	Disconnects the port so that it is no longer active

2 Monsur Hossain, "Using CORS," http://www.html5rocks.com/en/tutorials/cors/ (November 29, 2012)

The MessageEvent object properties

Properties	Description
`data`	Returns the data of the message
`origin`	Returns the origin of the message for server-sent events and cross-document messaging.
`close()`	Disconnects the port so that it is no longer active
`source`	Returns the windowProxy of the source window for cross-document messaging
`ports`	Returns the MessagePortArray sent with the message for cross-document messaging.
`lastEventId`	Returns the last event `id` for server-sent events[3]

[3] Ian Hickson (editor), "HTML5 Web Messaging (2ed.)," W3C Editor's Draft, 10 March 2015, http://dev.w3.org/html5/postmsg/#channel-messaging

Note To test cross-document web messaging, each page must be served from a different domain.

Exercise 11.1: Browser support

In this exercise, you check for browser support for cross-document messaging.

Objectives

After completing this exercise, you will be able to do the following:

- Check if the browser supports the `postMessage()` method.

Step 1 Open the file "webMessage-support-starter.html" from the webMessaging-API folder.

Step 2 Create a `<script>` block and add the following function:

```
<script>
    function checkPostMessage() {
        if(typeof window.postMessage !== 'undefined')
        console.log("postMessage API is supported in the browser.");
    }
</script>
```

Step 3 Call the `checkPostMessage()` function from the onload event.

```
<body onLoad="checkPostMessage();">
```

Step 4 Save the page and run it in all web browsers. Be sure to view the developer tools console so you can see the console log statement, which indicates whether or not the browser supports the PostMessage API.

Step 5 You may now close all open files and web browsers.

Exercise outcome

This exercise results in the appearance of a log statement in the Developer Tools' console that indicates support or lack of support for the PostMessage API.

Exercise summary

In this exercise, you determined if the web browser supports the postMessage API. Specifically, you checked for support of the postMessage method of the browser Window object.

Exercise 11.2: Send cross-document messages

In this exercise, you can execute cross-document messaging with the `postMessage` *method. You are also able to respond to message events.*

Objectives

After completing this exercise, you will be able to do the following:

- Use `postMessage()` to send messages to a web page with a different domain.
- Receive messages using the message event.

Step 1   Open the file "postMessage-starter.html" from the webMessaging-API folder.

Step 2   Locate line 18 and create an iframe below the comment that points to a web page whose scheme is "http" and whose host is "kevinruse.com."

```
<iframe id="iframe" src="http://www.kevinruse.com/KRA-HTML_FoodPlate/tips.
html"></iframe>
```

Step 3   Launch the Firefox web browser and go to http://www.kevinruse.com/KRA-HTML_FoodPlate/tips.html.

Note   Be sure to start WAMP before executing step 4.

Step 4   Save and run "postMessage-starter.html" from the Firefox web browser using the URL http://www.foodPlate.local/postMessage-starter.html.

Step 5   Enter a number between 1 and 10 in the text field at the top of the page and click the Get Food Tip button. You should get no response.

You will have the web page submit a message after clicking the Submit button, which will also dispatch a submit event.

Step 6   Add the event listener for the submit event in a `<script>` block below the `</form>` element.

```
addEventListener("submit", function(evt) {
}
```

Next you declare a global variable that stores the location of the iframe's contentWindow property. "The contentWindow property returns the `Window` object generated by a frame or iframe element (through the `Window` object, you can access the `Document` object and then any one of the document's elements)." [4]

Step 7   Declare a variable called "win" to store the reference to the iframe's contentWindow property as shown in bold below:

```
var win = document.getElementById("iframe").contentWindow;
addEventListener("submit", function(evt) {
}
```

---

[4] "IFrame contentWindow Property," http://www.w3schools.com/jsref/prop_frame_contentwindow.asp

Next you invoke the `postMessage()` method to send a message to the iframe page at http://www.kevinruse.com. The message contains the number between 1 and 10 that the user entered into the text-input field (the value property of the input element the id of which is "message."

Step 8   Send the message from the window as shown in bold below:

```
var win = document.getElementById("iframe").contentWindow;
addEventListener("submit", function(evt) {
        win.postMessage(
            document.getElementById("message").value,
            "http://www.kevinruse.com"
        );
}
```

Step 9   Type the remaining code shown below in bold, which prevents the iframe page from reloading and allows the message sent from kevinruse.com to persist in the iframe.

```
addEventListener("submit", function(evt) {
    win.postMessage(
        document.getElementById("message").value,
        "http://www.kevinruse.com"
    )
    if (evt.preventDefault) {
        evt.preventDefault();
    //otherwise set the returnValue of the original event to false (IE)
        }
        evt.returnValue = false;
    }
})
```

Note   You can eliminate the need for `preventDefault()` by using a type "button" instead of a type "submit."

Now it's time to see how to respond to the message event. This event will be dispatched when the iframe page at http://www.kevinruse.com receives the message sent by the `postMessage()` method written in step 8. The iframe page responds by sending its own message back to the page at www.FoodPlate.local.

Step 10   View the source code of the iframe page http://www.kevinruse.com/KRA-HTML_FoodPlate/tips.html and examine the code in the `<script>` block at the bottom of the page (shown below).

```
window.onmessage = function(evt){
  if ( evt.origin !== "http://www.foodplate.local" ) {
    return;
  }
var tip = $('#healthTip' + evt.data).text();
var origin = evt.origin;
document.getElementById("tipGoesHere").textContent = origin + ": " + tip;
}
```

The first line of code adds an event handler function to the window's message event. An "if" condition tests if the `MessageEvent` object's origin property is not equal to http://www.FoodPlate.local and exits the function if it is not. Otherwise a variable is declared that holds the text of a div (see the source code for a series of `<div>` elements) the id of which is equal to the string "#healthTip" followed by a number between 1 and 10. A second variable is declared called "origin" that holds the `Event` objects origin property. Finally, the last line of code gets an empty `<div>` element with the id "tipGoesHere" and sets the div element's textContent property to a string that begins with the Event object's origin followed by a colon and a space bar and then the value of the tip variable.

Note   You may use "innerHTML" to replace the "textContent" property, however the innerHTML property is not the best choice for security reasons. The received message may be a malicious JavaScript that could then be injected and executed immediately through innerHTML. It is recommended that you use the textContent property instead.

Step 11   Run "postMessage-starter.html" from the browser.

Note   Be sure to start WAMP and then launch the page from www.FoodPlate.local using the Firefox Web browser.

Step 12   Fill out the form and click the Submit button.

You should now see a food tip appear in the iframe. After pressing the Submit button, a different tip appears for each number you enter in the text-input field.

Step 13   You may now close all open files.

Exercise outcome

This exercise results in a "Food tip of the day" paragraph displaying inside the iframe after a number between 1 and 10 is entered in the form and the Submit button is clicked. A unique food tip should appear for each number entered into the form.

Additional security checks

It is best to check not only for origin but also for the event data's datatype, format, and so on.

Exercise summary

In this exercise, you learned about web messaging and the postMessage() method. After learning how to send a message, you explored how to respond to the message from the receiving page.

Resources

HTML5 Web Messaging specification: http://www.w3.org/TR/webmessaging/

lastEventId property demo: http://help.dottoro.com/ljakhoda.php

Introduction to WebMessaging article: https://dev.opera.com/articles/window-postmessage-messagechannel/

How to enable CORS on your server: http://enable-cors.org/

Challenge exercise

1. Using your IDE, open the file "webMessaging-challenge-starter.html" from the Sites/LocalSite folder.

2. Confirm that you have started the WAMP server.

3. Direct your web browser to the url: http://www.foodplate.local and then click on the "challenge" directory. Open the file "webMessaging-challenge-starter.html."

4. Your job is to use the postMessage() method of the WebMessaging API to send a random number between 0 and 4 to "http://www.kevinruse.com." The message should be sent after the user clicks the "Food Group of the Day?" button.

5. The code on the "kevinruse.com" page looks like this:

```
<script>
window.onmessage = function(evt){
  if (evt.origin !== "http://www.foodplate.local") {
    return;
  }
    var foodGroups = ['fruit', 'vegetable', 'dairy', 'protein', 'grain']
    var foodGroupOfTheDay = foodGroups[evt.data];
    document.getElementById("foodGroup").textContent = foodGroupOfTheDay;
}
</script>
```

6. If you get stuck, "webMessaging-challenge-finished.html" is a possible solution. Be sure to run both the starter and finished files from "http://www.foodplate.local".

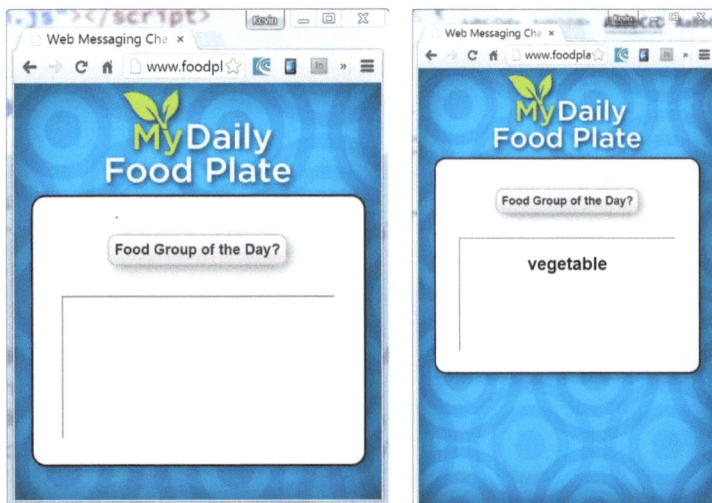

Before clicking the button.   After clicking the button a random food group should appear.

Chapter summary

In this chapter, you learned why you might want to send messages to other domains and why the browser prohibits this kind of communication (cross-site scripting attacks). You learned about message channels and ports for controlling the mechanisms used to create and send messages. You also learned how the origin property can be used as a method of establishing trust between domains so that messages can be communicated back and forth.

Chapter 12

Dataset API

In this chapter, you associate HTML elements with data. You learn the new HTML attribute known as the data-* attribute and use the dataset API to both set and retrieve the data on the HTML element.

The dataset API was introduced in the HTML 5 vocabulary and associated APIs on August 28 2014.

Objectives

❑ Describe and use the data-* attribute.

❑ Associate custom data attributes with HTML elements.

❑ Set and get custom data-* attributes.

Introduction

Many web applications benefit from the use of metadata within HTML elements. For example, a list of employees are returned via AJAX from a server-side database; the application logic depends on knowing whether or not employees on the list are part time or full time. Perhaps a table or unordered list will be created from this data. In a case like this, the following form might be helpful:
`<li emp-status="part-time">`. Now, the `<li>` element has metadata associated with its contents. HTML elements can carry custom data attributes in the following form:
`<element data-customname = "value">`

data-* syntax rules

These custom attributes, also known as the data-* attributes, allow developers to associate data with HTML attributes. The data-* attribute must follow certain rules.

data-* attribute rule	Example
Must begin with data-	`<h1 data-`
Must contain only letters, numbers	`<h1 data-status>` `<p data-rule-1>`

May contain these symbols: dash (-), dot (.), colon (:), underscore (_)	`<li data-account-number>`
	`<li data-code.rule>`
	
	`<li data-employee:code>`
	
	`<li data-employee_record>`

Should not contain ASCII capital letters (A–Z).	

The data- attribute name is transformed into a `DOMStringMap` object. A `DOMstringmap` is defined by the W3C HTML specification (at http://www.w3.org/TR/html5/infrastructure.html#domstringmap-0) as follows:

- The `DOMStringMap` interface represents a set of name-value pairs. It exposes these using the scripting language's native mechanisms for property access.

- When a `DOMStringMap` object is instantiated, it is associated with three algorithms, one for getting the list of name-value pairs, one for setting names to certain values, and one for deleting names.

The transformed data- attribute name (the DOMStringMap) follows the rules shown below.

Attribute to DOMStringMap rules	
1	The data- prefix is removed (including the dash (-).
2	For any dash in the attribute that is followed by an ASCII lowercase letter (a–z), the dash is removed and the letter is changed to uppercase.
3	All other characters, including dashes are left unchanged.

The transformed data- attribute name (the `DOMStringMap`) follows the rules shown below.

DOMStringMap key to attribute rules	
1	A data- prefix is added (including the dash [-]). RESTRICTION: A dash must not be immediately followed by an ASCII lowercase letter (a–z) before the transformation.
2	Any ASCII uppercase letter (A–Z) is changed into a dash followed by its lowercase equivalent.
3	All other characters are left unchanged.

Here is an example transformation (from data-attribute to DOMString):

`<li data-employee-status>` becomes the key `employeeStatus`.

The dataset API

The dataset API provides access to data- attributes. It does so by providing an HTML attribute called "`dataset`." The dataset attribute contains the `DOMStringMap` object. The `DOMStringMap`'s key contains the name of the data attribute without the data- prefix (and subject to the rules in the "Attribute to DOMStringMap" rules table above).

Without the dataset API, the dataset attribute could be accessed via the standard HTML getters and setters for attributes, including `setAttribute()`, `getAttribute()`, and `removeAttribute()`. You can compare the performance with and without the dataset API at jsperf.com using the test found at http://jsperf.com/dataset-vs-attributes-loop/3.

The dataset API can be used any time metadata needs to be added to DOM elements. However, you may get better performance when accessing the data- attributes with standard DOM scripting.

Dataset API	
To set values	`document.getElementById("tag").dataset.status="fulltime";`
To get values	`var data=document.getElementById("tag").dataset.status`
To remove values	`delete document.getElementById("tag").dataset.status;`

Exercise 12.1: Setting dataset attributes

In this exercise, you add metadata to HTML <li> elements using the data- attribute.

Objectives

After completing this exercise, you will be able to do the following:

- Use the dataset API to set data- attributes.

The ability to dynamically add metadata to HTML elements can help when applying dynamic styles and facilitation business logic at runtime.

In this exercise, you add additional information to `<li>` elements. The example list below contains grains. Using JavaScript and the dataset API, you specify whether the grain is a whole grain or a refined grain.

Step 1   Open the file "dataset-setdata-starter.html" from the dataset-API folder.

Step 2   Run the file in the browser and examine the source code from the browser by doing one of the following:

- Right-click the page and choose the option: "View page source."
- Press Control + u on your keyboard.

Step 3   Notice the code that makes the unordered list. It should appear as shown below.

```
<ul>
    <li>Amaranth</li>
    <li>Cornbread</li>
    <li>Millet</li>
    <li>Noodles</li>
    <li>Pasta</li>
    <li>Popcorn</li>
</ul>
```

Step 4   Create a `<script>` block above the closing `</body>` element.

Step 5   Create a variable call `liElems` that holds all of the `<li>` elements.

```
var liElems = document.querySelectorAll('li');
```

Step 6   Add an event listener to the `setData` button.

```
document.getElementById('setData').addEventListener('click', setData);
```

Step 7   Write the `setData` event handler function to loop through the `<li>` elements and assign the proper grain type to each grain on the list via a `data-` custom attribute.

```
function setData() {
        for (var i = 0; i < liElems.length; i++) {
            if (liElems[i].innerHTML === "Amaranth") {
                liElems[i].dataset.grain = "whole grain";
            }
            else if (liElems[i].innerHTML === "Cornbread") {
                liElems[i].dataset.grain = "refined grain";
            }
            else if (liElems[i].innerHTML === "Millet") {
                liElems[i].dataset.grain = "whole grain";
            }
            else if (liElems[i].innerHTML === "Noodles") {
                liElems[i].dataset.grain = "refined grain";
```

```
            }

            else if (liElems[i].innerHTML === "Pasta") {

                liElems[i].dataset.grain = "refined grain";

            }

            else if (liElems[i].innerHTML === "Popcorn") {

                liElems[i].dataset.grain = "whole grain";

            }

        }

    }
```

Step 8   Save the file and run it in a Web browser with the console open and the Elements tab active. See the Chrome screenshot below.

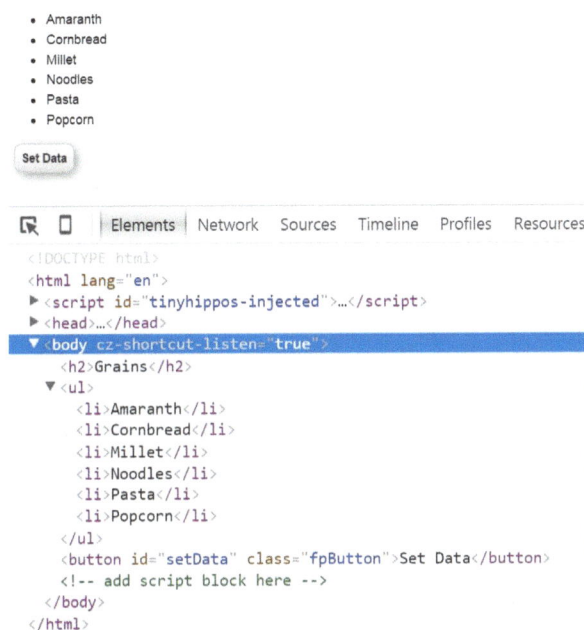

Step 9   In the Web browser, click the Set Data button and examine the Elements tab of the console. It should look like this.

Grains

- Amaranth
- Cornbread
- Millet
- Noodles
- Pasta
- Popcorn

Set Data

```
🔍 📱 | Elements | Network   Sources   Timeline   Profiles   Resources
<!DOCTYPE html>
<html lang="en">
▶ <script id="tinyhippos-injected">…</script>
▶ <head>…</head>
▼ <body cz-shortcut-listen="true">
    <h2>Grains</h2>
  ▼ <ul>
      <li data-grain="whole grain">Amaranth</li>
      <li data-grain="refined grain">Cornbread</li>
      <li data-grain="whole grain">Millet</li>
      <li data-grain="refined grain">Noodles</li>
      <li data-grain="refined grain">Pasta</li>
      <li data-grain="whole grain">Popcorn</li>
    </ul>
    <button id="setData" class="fpButton">Set Data</button>
  ▶ <script>…</script>
  </body>
</html>
```

Exercise summary

In this exercise, you used the dataset API to set the values associated with data- attributes.

Exercise 12.2: Getting dataset attributes

In this exercise, you access metadata that has been added to HTML <li> elements using the data-attribute.

Objectives

After completing this exercise, you will be able to do the following:

- Use the dataset API to get data- attributes.

The ability to dynamically add metadata to HTML elements can help when applying dynamic styles and facilitation business logic at runtime.

In this exercise, you use the additional information that has been added to `<li>` elements. As above, the example list below contains grains. Using JavaScript and the dataset API, you indicate via background colors whether the grain is a whole grain or a refined grain.

Step 1   Open the file "dataset-getdata-starter.html" from the dataset-API folder.

Step 2   Run the file in the browser.

Step 3   Create a `<script>` block above the closing `</body>` element.

Step 4   Create a variable call `liElems` that holds all of the `<li>` elements.

```
var liElems = document.querySelectorAll('li');
```

Step 5   Add an event listener to the `wholeGrains` button.

```
document.getElementById('wholeGrains').addEventListener('click', function()
{

});
```

Step 6   Write the anonymous function, shown below in bold.

```
document.getElementById('wholeGrains').addEventListener('click', function()
{

        for (var i = 0; i < liElems.length; i++) {

        if (liElems[i].dataset.grain === "whole grain") {

                liElems[i].style.backgroundColor = '#00ff00';

        }

    }

});
```

Step 7   Write the event listener for the `refinedGrains` button.

```
document.getElementById('refinedGrains').addEventListener('click', function()
{

    for (var i = 0; i < liElems.length; i++) {

        if (liElems[i].dataset.grain === "refined grain") {

                //console.log(liElems[i] + " is a whole grain.");

                liElems[i].style.backgroundColor = '#ffff00';

        }

    }

});
```

Step 8   Save the file and run it in a Web browser. Click each button and confirm the response with the screen shots below.

After clicking the Whole Grains button: After clicking the Refined Grains button

Exercise summary

In this exercise, you used the dataset API to get the values associated with data- attributes.

Resources

HTML5 W3C Candidate Recommendation Dataset specification: http://www.w3.org/TR/html5/dom. html#dom-dataset

Comparison of DOM methods vs. dataset API method: http://jsperf.com/dataset-vs-attributes-loop/3.

HTML5 Living Standard specification: https://html.spec.whatwg.org/multipage/dom.html#dom-dataset

HTML5.1 Working Draft specification: http://www.w3.org/html/wg/drafts/html/master/dom.html#dom-dataset

Chapter summary

This chapter looked at the need to add metadata to DOM elements. The dataset API provides that capability through the creation of data- custom attributes, and the API provides access to these attribute values. The details of getting and setting data- attributes were examined, and the rules governing the use of the HTML dataset property were explained.

Chapter 13

Drag and Drop API

In this chapter, you make any object on the web page draggable. You also implement the Drag and Drop API and compare and contrast the HTML5 Drag and Drop API to a jQuerya approach.

The drag and drop API was introduced in the HTML 5.1 Nightly W3C Editor's Draft on August 28 2015.

Objectives

❑   Describe the Drag and Drop API.

❑   Implement drag and drop.

❑   Make objects on your web page draggable.

❑   List the events associated with drag and drop.

Introduction

Dragging and dropping is familiar to most PC users and has been in use on the desktop for a very long time. The notion of dragging and dropping components was arguably pioneered by Apple, for their groundbreaking early home computers. Dragging and dropping has become popular for web applications as well and may be appropriate for many desktop web applications. Work-arounds are required to implement drag and drop on mobile devices because they have default navigation behavior that is based on drag events that supersede any drag-and-drop code the developer creates.

What is drag and drop used for?

You can use drag and drop whenever it would appear intuitive for the user to manipulate or move objects in the browser with a mouse. Many learning portals use drag and drop in their learning modules. For example, a student may be looking at an image of an engine and off to the side are a series of images that represent parts of the engine. It's the student's job to drag the appropriate part to its corresponding location on the engine. Other uses for drag and drop include shopping carts, diagramming tools, simple file management applications, and games.

Browser support for drag and drop

At the time of publication, drag and drop is supported by all browsers, with Internet Explorer having partial support. See http://caniuse.com for up-to-date verification of drag-and-drop browser support.

Understanding drag and drop

It is simple to make an element draggable: give the element a draggable attribute and set an event listener for any of the drag events, such as dragstart, to which you wish to respond.

The event handler typically needs to check that it's not a text selection that is being dragged. It then needs to store data in the `DataTransfer` object and set the allowed effects (copy, move, link, or some combination).

The draggable attribute

The following is excerpted from the HTML5 Living Standard.

> All HTML elements may have the draggable content attribute set. The draggable attribute is an enumerated attribute. It has three states. The first state is true and it has the keyword true. The second state is false and it has the keyword false. The third state is auto; it has no keywords but it is the missing value default.
>
> The true state means the element is draggable; the false state means that it is not. The auto state uses the default behavior of the user agent."[1]

---

1 "6.7 Drag and Drop," HTML Living Standard, updated August 27, 2015, http://www.whatwg.org/specs/web-apps/current-work/multipage/dnd.html

Drag and drop with a data "payload"

The Drag and Drop API specifies the ability of the dragged object to carry a data "payload." For a complete definition of the drag data store and its related properties and events, see http://www.whatwg.org/specs/web-apps/current-work/multipage/dnd.html.

Exercise 13.1: Checking drag and drop support

In this exercise, you check for the "draggable" property of any HTML element. You'll create a `<span>` *element for this browser test.*

Objectives

After completing this exercise, you will be able to do the following:

- Determine if the web browser supports the `draggable` property.

As with most HTML5-related APIs, it's best to check for browser support before coding functionality that may not work in some browsers. The Drag and Drop API is widely supported. In the past, you tested for browser support of various APIs by calling the property of a known object in the API and, if the property existed, you could expect browser support for the given object of the API. However, the typical means for browser checking that you have used so far in this course will not work for drag and drop with Internet Explorer 6.0 or higher.

In this exercise, you create a `<span>` element with JavaScript, and then test for the draggable property.

Step 1   Open the file "dragDrop-support-starter.html" from the dragAndDrop-API folder.

Step 2   Create a `<script>` block in the `<head>` section and write a function called "`dragDropSupportCheck()`."

```
function dragDropSupportCheck() {
    var dragDropSupport;
    if ('draggable' in document.createElement('span')) {
        dragDropSupport = true;
        console.log("Drag drop support is " + dragDropSupport);
    }
}
```

Step 3   Call the function from the onload event of the `<body>` element, as shown below.

```
<body onload="dragDropSupportCheck()">
```

Next create a `<span>` element and then check for the existence of a "draggable" property. If you find a "draggable" property, the function returns "true," indicating drag and drop support.

Despite being the initial contributor of drag and drop, Microsoft implements it somewhat differently than the specification, so this specification will not work in some versions of Internet Explorer. Therefore, you will write an Internet Explorer detection block next.

Note   Optional test for Internet Explorer 9 is shown below:

```
//additional check for IE9
else if (navigator.appName === 'Microsoft Internet Explorer') {
```

```
var ua = navigator.userAgent;
var re = new RegExp("MSIE([0-9]{1,}[\.0-9]{0,})");
dragDropSupport = false;
if (re.exec(ua) !== null) {
    var rv = parseFloat(RegExp.$1);
    if (rv >= 6.0) {
        dragDropSupport = true;
    }
}
```

Step 4   Save and test the file in all browsers using the URL. Be sure to have each browsers' developer tools open to the console so that you can see the log statements.

Step 5   You may now close all open files.

Exercise outcome

This exercise results in the appearance of a log statement in the Developer Tools' console that indicates support or lack of support for the Drag and Drop API.

Exercise summary

In this exercise, you learned how to detect browser support for drag and drop and what is required to perform this check with Internet Explorer. In addition, you learned that to make an element draggable you simply add the "draggable" attribute to the HTML element and set the value to "true," for example, as here:

```
<div draggable="true">
```

Drag and Drop API

The Drag and Drop API allows elements with the "draggable" property set to respond to the following events, some of which require a drop zone.

Drag events

Drag Event	Description
dragstart	Dispatched when the user starts dragging an object
dragenter	Dispatched when the mouse is initially moved over the target element while a drag is occurring. A listener for this event could indicate whether a drop is allowed over the current location.
dragover	Dispatched when the mouse is moved over an element while a drag is occurring
dragleave	Dispatched when the mouse leaves an element while a drag is occurring
drag	Dispatched every time the mouse is moved while the object is being dragged
dragend	Dispatched when the user releases the mouse button while dragging an object

Exercise 13.2: Respond to drag events

The drag and drop API includes events related to the act of both dragging and dropping. This exercise focuses on the drag events.

Objectives

After completing this exercise, you will be able to do the following:

- Describe the drag events and when they are dispatched.
- Respond to the different drag events.

Step 1   Open the file "dragEvents-starter.html" from the dragAndDrop-API folder.

         To keep the file small and focused on drag events, the browser support script has been removed.

Step 2   View the page in the browser. It should appear as shown below.

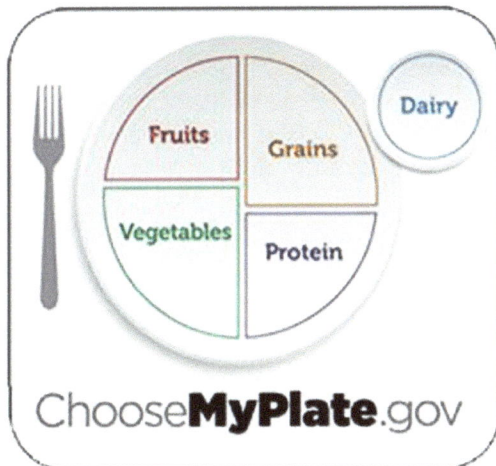

The dragEvents-starter.html file as shown in Chrome.

The first step in making an element draggable is to add the draggable attribute to the element.

Step 3   Locate the apple image and add the `draggable` attribute as shown below in bold:

```
<img src="assets/addFoodPage/images/fruit_sm.gif"
     alt="apple" name="fruitIcon"
     width="35" height="42"
     id="fruitIcon" draggable="true">
```

Step 4   Set the remaining graphics' draggable properties to false.

Remember, your goal in this exercise is to get familiar with the drag events. To begin the drag and drop, you need a draggable object and a drop zone. The draggable object is the image with the `id` of `fruitIcon`, and the drop zone is the image in the upper-left side of the plate with the `id` of `fruitempty`.

Next, you'll write some simple JavaScript that creates variables to store these two elements.

Step 5   Create a `<script>` block and write a function called `init()`.

Step 6   Create two variables called "fruitImg" and "fruitPlate" that reference the two image elements. Remember that fruitImg is the draggable element and fruitPlate is the drop zone.

```
function init(){
        var fruitImg = document.getElementById('fruitIcon');
        var fruitPlate = document.getElementById('fruitempty');
}
```

The first event to listen for is the one that occurs when the user begins to drag an element. This event is known as the startdrag event.

Step 7   Add an event listener to the fruitImg object and listen for the dragstart event, as shown in bold below. The event handler function is called `dragEventHandler()`, and you will not use the capture phase to listen for the event.

```
function init(){
    var fruitImg = document.getElementById('fruitIcon');
    var fruitPlate = document.getElementById('fruitempty');
    fruitImg.addEventListener('dragstart', dragEventHandler, false);
}
```

Step 8   Invoke the `init()` function from the onload event of the `<body>` tag.

```
<body onload="init()">
```

Now, write the event handler function dragEventHandler.

Step 9   Write the `dragEventHandler()` function. Use the jQuery method to obtain the div with the `id` of "status" to which you invoke the jQuery `text()` method to set the text of the div to read, "You started dragging the ."

```
function dragEventHandler(evt) {
 $('#status').text("You started dragging the " + evt.target.id );
}
```

Step 10   Save the file and test in several browsers. Your screen should look similar to the image below.

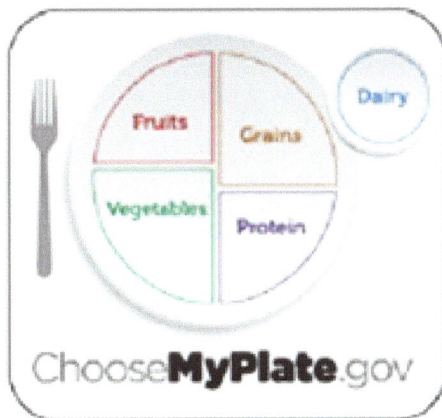

You started dragging thefruitIcon

The dragEvents-starter.html file after the dragstart event has been dispatched.

The dragstart event is dispatched once the mouse is pressed down on a draggable element, but only until the mouse has then moved, even one pixel.

The next event you learn is the drag event, and this behaves very differently. The drag event is continuously dispatched as long as the user's mouse is pressed down on a draggable element and subsequently moved. Unlike the dragstart event, the drag event continues to dispatch the event while the mouse is down, after moving one pixel or more.

Step 11   Comment the last event listener you wrote and add the following event listener as shown in bold below:

```
function init(){
        var fruitImg = document.getElementById('fruitIcon');
        var fruitPlate = document.getElementById('fruitempty');
        //fruitImg.addEventListener('dragstart', dragEventHandler, false);
        fruitImg.addEventListener('drag', watchMeDrag, false);
}
```

Step 12   Declare a variable called "dragTracker" and initialize it at 1. Then write the event handler called watchMeDrag(). The variable is used to track the number of times the drag event is dispatched.

```
var dragTracker = 1;
function watchMeDrag(evt) {
            $('#status').text("I'm dragging this many times: " + dragTracker++);
}
```

Step 13   Save and test the file in a drag-and-drop supported browser. Test the page in the following manner:

    1.   Press the mouse down on the apple and wait two seconds.

2. Drag the apple to a different location, while keeping the mouse down.

3. Hold the mouse down for two seconds.

Your screen should look similar to the screen shot below.

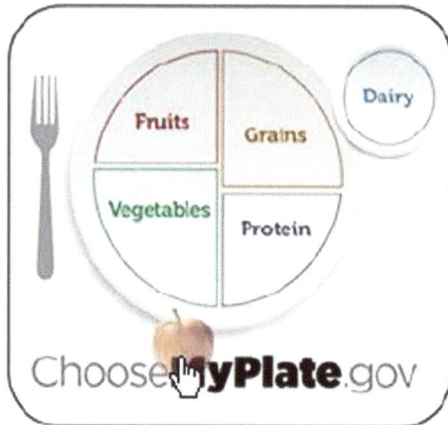

I'm dragging this many times: 680

The dragEvents-starter.html file during a drag event.

Step 14 Comment the last event listener you wrote and add the following event listener as shown in bold below:

```
function init(){
        var fruitImg = document.getElementById('fruitIcon');
        var fruitPlate = document.getElementById('fruitempty');
        //fruitImg.addEventListener('dragstart',
        handleFruitDragStart, false);
        //fruitImg.addEventListener('drag', watchMeDrag, false);
        fruitImg.addEventListener('dragend', watchMeDrag, false);
}
```

Step 15 Save and test the file in a drag-and-drop supported browser. Drag the apple and drop it on different parts of the plate. Try dragging the apple and dropping it off the plate. Notice that the counter now counts only the end of the drag, which is dispatched when the mouse is released.

Step 16 Comment the last event listener you wrote and add the following event listener as shown in bold below:

```
function init(){
        var fruitImg = document.getElementById('fruitIcon');
        var fruitPlate = document.getElementById('fruitempty');
        //fruitImg.addEventListener('dragstart', handleFruitDragStart,
false);
        //fruitImg.addEventListener('drag',  watchMeDrag, false);
        //fruitImg.addEventListener('dragend',  watchMeDrag, false);
```

```
            fruitPlate.addEventListener('dragenter', watchMeDrag, false);
}
```

Notice that this event listener is added to the drop zone: the fruitPlate image. Therefore, it is this element (the fruitPlate image) that responds to the `dragenter` event.

Step 17   Save and test the file in a drag-and-drop supported browser. Drag the apple and drop it on different parts of the plate, avoiding the fruit section. Next drop the apple on the fruit portion of the plate and note the counter variable. Try this several times. Notice that the mouse pointer must enter the perimeter of the drop zone in order for the event to be dispatched.

Step 18   Comment the last event listener you wrote and add the following event listener as shown in bold below:

```
function init(){
            var fruitImg = document.getElementById('fruitIcon');
            var fruitPlate = document.getElementById('fruitempty');
            //fruitImg.addEventListener('dragstart', handleFruitDragStart,
false);
            //fruitImg.addEventListener('drag',  watchMeDrag, false);
            //fruitImg.addEventListener('dragend',  watchMeDrag, false);
            //fruitPlate.addEventListener('dragenter', watchMeDrag, false);
            fruitPlate.addEventListener('dragleave', watchMeDrag, false);
}
```

This event is also added to the fruit plate image and is dispatched under the following conditions:

1.   When the mouse is released above the fruit portion of the plate

2.   When the mouse is dragged over the food plate and then dragged out while the mouse is down the entire time.

3.   During subsequent drag over and drag outs

Step 19   Comment the last event listener you wrote and add the following event listener as shown in bold below:

```
function init(){
            var fruitImg = document.getElementById('fruitIcon');
            var fruitPlate = document.getElementById('fruitempty');
            //fruitImg.addEventListener('dragstart', handleFruitDragStart,
false);
            //fruitImg.addEventListener('drag',  watchMeDrag, false);
            //fruitImg.addEventListener('dragend',  watchMeDrag, false);
            //fruitPlate.addEventListener('dragenter', watchMeDrag, false);
            //fruitPlate.addEventListener('dragleave', watchMeDrag, false);
            fruitPlate.addEventListener('dragover', watchMeDrag, false);
}
```

Step 20   Save and test the file in a drag-and-drop supported browser. Test the page as follows:

1.   Mouse down on the apple and drag it over the fruit portion of the plate.

2.   Leave the mouse down over the fruit portion of the plate.

The dragover event is dispatched as long as a draggable object is over the object with the event listener. Your screen should look similar to the screen shot below.

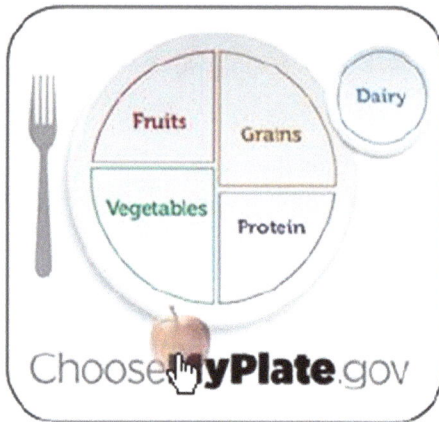

I'm dragging this many times: 680

Step 21   You may now close all open files.

To test this file on your mobile device, go to www.kevinruse.com/dragDrop

Exercise summary

In this exercise, you learned the drag and drop's drag events, including dragstart, dragenter, dragover, dragleave, and drag. You learned when these events are dispatched and how often. You also learned how to respond to these events. In the next exercise, you learn the drop event.

Drop events

The Drag and Drop API allow elements with the "draggable" property to respond to the following event.

Drop Event	Description
drop	Dispatched on the element where the drop occurred at the end of the drag operation

Exercise 13.3: Respond to drop event

The drag and drop API includes events related to the acts of both dragging and dropping. This exercise focuses on the drop event.

Objectives

After completing this exercise, you will be able to do the following:

- Describe the drop event and when it is dispatched.
- Respond to the drop event.
- Understand the problems associated with the drop event.

Step 1   Open the file "dropEvent-starter.html" from the dragAndDrop-API folder.

Notice the draggable apple image at the bottom of the page.

Step 2   Create a `<script>` block in the `<head>` section and write a function called `init()` that declares a fruitPlate variable that stores the image with the `id` "foodPlate." Then add an event listener that listens for the drop event and invokes the dropHandler event handler function.

```
function init(){
        var foodPlate = document.getElementById('foodPlate');
        foodPlate.addEventListener('drop', dropHandler, false);
}
```

Step 3   Write the `dropHandler()` function that creates an alert box that reads: "You dropped me on the plate." Indicate the event type in the string as shown below:

```
function dropHandler(evt) {
        alert("You dropped me on the plate during a " + evt.type + "
event.");
evt.preventDefault();
}
```

Step 4   Save the file and run it in a browser. Notice that the alert box never opens.

There is a problem with the way that the drop event fires. This, among other reasons, has caused considerable controversy around the Drag and Drop API. You can find more information (including rants) at http://www.quirksmode.org/blog/archives/2009/09/the_html5_drag.html and http://www.useragentman.com/blog/2010/01/10/cross-browser-html5-drag-and-drop/. (Warning: Language may be offensive.)

The solution to the drop problem is to listen for the dragOver event and stop the browser from implementing the dragOver event's default behavior, which is the cause of the drop problem. In some cases, you may have to prevent the default behavior of the dragenter event as well.

Step 5   Add a listener for the dragover event and write the event handler function as shown in bold below.

```
function init(){
        var foodPlate = document.getElementById('foodPlate');
        foodPlate.addEventListener('dragover', dragOverHandler, false);
        foodPlate.addEventListener('drop', dropHandler, false);
}
function dragOverHandler(evt) {
        if(evt.preventDefault) {
                evt.preventDefault();
        }
        return false;
}
```

Step 6   Save the file and test it in the browser. You should see the alert pop up after the apple has been dragged and dropped over the plate. Your screen should look similar to the screen shot below.

Note   Notice the page changes to display the apple image. To prevent this you also need to invoke the `prevent-Default()` method on the drop event as well. You end this chapter by writing a snippet of CSS that changes the mouse cursor when the user hovers his or her mouse over the apple. The cursor will change from the standard pointer to the hand cursor.

Step 7   Create a `<style>` block in the `<head>` section and add the following CSS:

```
<style>
        #apple {
                cursor:pointer;
        }
</style>
```

Step 8   Save the file and test it. You may test this file on your mobile device at http://www.kevinruse.com/dragDrop

Step 9   You may now close all open files.

Exercise summary

In this exercise, you learned how to respond to the drop event.

Note   Regarding the Drop events data transfer property:

Demo 13.1: Drag and drop with a data payload

This demo file includes a drag and drop using the drop events data transfer property. The dragged object can exchange data with the object it is being dropped on using a property of the drag event called the dataTransfer property. At the time of publication, this feature is not widely supported and the support it currently has is inconsistent at best. You can learn more about the dataTransfer property of the drop event at http://www.whatwg.org/specs/web-apps/current-work/multipage/dnd.html.

Step 1   Open the "dragDrop-with-data.html file" from the dragDrop-with-data-demo subfolder in the dra-gAndDrop-API folder.

Step 2   Run the file in the Chrome web browser and interact with the application.

Step 3   Review the source code with your instructor and identify the lines of code responsible for the data transfer.

Demo 13.2: Drag and drop with jQuery

This demo file includes a drag and drop created with the jQuery library.

Step 1   Open the "index.html file" from the demo-jquery-dragDrop subfolder in the dragAndDrop-API folder.

Step 2   Run the file in the Chrome web browser and interact with the application.

Step 3   Review the source code with your instructor and identify the lines of jQuery code responsible for both the drag and the drop behaviors found in the application.

Resources

W3C Working Draft: http://www.w3.org/TR/2010/WD-html5-20101019/dnd.html

Drag and Drop Demo with Data: http://nettutsplus.s3.amazonaws.com/64_html5dragdrop/demo/index.html

Challenge exercise

1. Using your IDE, open the file "dragDrop-challenge-starter.html" from the challenge subdirectory.

2. Run the file in a web browser.

3. Your job is to allow the apple to be dragged and dropped onto the fruit portion of the plate. When the apple is dropped on the fruit portion of the plate, an alert message should pop up. If any other food icon is dropped on the fruit portion of the plate a different alert box pops up. See the screen shot below for the final results.

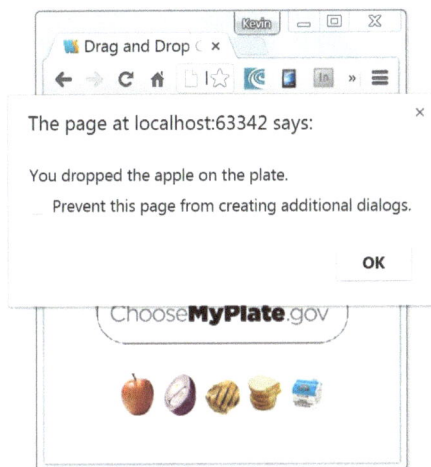

Result when the apple is dragged and dropped to the fruit portion of the plate.

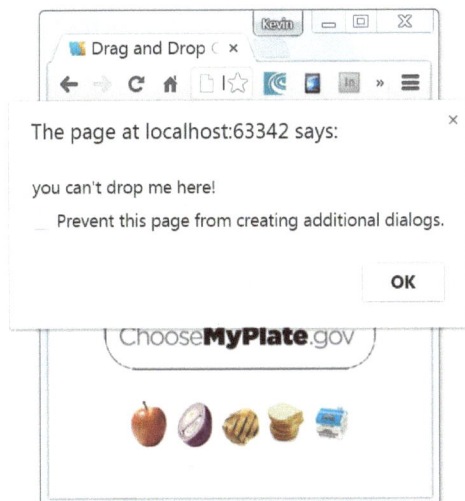

Result when a food icon other than the apple is dragged and dropped to the fruit portion of the plate.

4. If you get stuck, "dragDrop-challenge-finished.html" is a possible solution.

Chapter summary

In this chapter, you learned about the HTML5 Drag and Drop API. This is one area of the HTML5 group of specifications that receives a lot of attention, and not all of it is positive.

Chapter 14

Offline Applications API

In this chapter, you make your applications accessible both online and offline.

Offline Applications was published as a W3C Working Group Note on May 30, 2008.

Objectives

❑ Understand the browser cache.

❑ Understand the application cache.

❑ Create an application that displays when the user is offline.

❑ Determine if your application is offline.

❑ Understand the cache manifest file.

❑ Instruct the browser on how to cache files for offline use.

❑ Instruct the browser on how *not* to cache certain files.

❑ Create a manifest file.

❑ Instruct the browser to use alternative files when the user is offline.

❑ Associate the cache manifest file with a web page.

❑ Describe the cache events.

Introduction

Offline applications are web applications that are capable of being viewed and/or interacted with while the user is offline. A document known as a "cache manifest file" is loaded with the web page, and it tells the browser to cache the files necessary to run the application without Internet access. These files could be .html pages, stylesheets, and/or JavaScript.

HTML5 offers an offline application specification that is available at the World Wide Web Consortium website at http://dev.w3.org/html5/spec-author-view/offline.html

Why do we need offline applications?

The simple answer is that we do not always have Internet access. Many mobile devices are Wi-Fi only, so if the user is not near a Wi-Fi hot spot, he or she won't have Internet access. This is also true in remote areas as well as in some indoor areas. With offline applications, a user is still able to interact with an application even if he or she is offline.

Browser support for offline applications

For the most recent tables regarding browser support, please see http://caniuse.com.

Understanding the browser cache

The browser cache is an area within browsers in which images, scripts, and other parts of websites you encountered while browsing are temporarily stored. Browser caches can enhance both performance and load time because when a web page that has been cached is reloaded, the browser loads the page (if available) from its cache and not from the server. The good side of this is that the page loads much faster as do subsequent pages that have also been cached. The bad side is that there may be newer, more relevant information on the server page, but you are still being served the older cached version of the page.

Emptying the browser cache

Users may manually or automatically empty their cache files via a browser's built-in tools and plug-ins.

For example, you can empty the Firefox (Windows) browser cache this way: Choose Tools from the main menu bar, then Options, and click the Network tab. Locate the "Offline Storage" section and you can see that you can clear the cache by clicking the Clear Now button. You can also override the default cache file limit size and uncheck the option that automatically alerts the user if an application is attempting to store data for offline use.

- Firefox (OSX): Choose Menu: Preferences → Advanced → Network → Offline Storage
- Chrome (OSX): Use Developers Tools: Tools → Developers Tools → Resources Tab
- Opera (OSX): Choose Menu: Settings → Preferences → Advanced → Storage
- Safari (OSX): Use Developers Tools: Settings Menu → Preferences → Advanced → click Show Develop in the menu bar → Develop → Show Web Inspector → click Storage

Exercise 14.1: Understanding browser cache

In this exercise, you learn how to browse files stored in the browser's cache and view a summary of the browser cache. You'll see the size and contents of the browser cache.

Objectives

After completing this exercise, you will be able to do the following:

- Understand the browser cache.
- View the browser's cached files in Firefox.

Step 1   Open the Firefox browser and type "about:cache" in the address bar.

The web page you see allows you to view a summary of your browser cache and also allows you to browse the files stored in the cache. You can modify the command as shown below for more specific cache information.

This provides the size and contents of the data Firefox has saved to disk: (about:cache?device=disk)

This provides the size and contents of the data Firefox has saved in memory: (about:cache?device=memory)

The Chrome browser has a similar feature.

Step 2   Open the Chrome browser and type "chrome://appcache-internals" in the address bar.

Exercise summary

In this exercise, you used components of the Chrome and Firefox web browsers to examine the size and contents of the browser cache.

Understanding applicationCache

The `window.applicationCache` object is your programmatic access to the browser's application cache. Its status property is useful for checking the current state of the cache.

The applicationCache status property values

UNCACHED	No cache manifest file exists.
IDLE	All resources are up to date and stored in the cache.
CHECKING	The browser is reading the manifest.
DOWNLOADING	The browser is downloading new or updated resources.
UPDATEREADY	New/updated resources are now available in the cache.
OBSOLETE	There was a manifest file, but now it's missing.
UNKNOWN CACHE STATUS	

The chart below is taken from http://www.whatwg.org/specs/web-apps/current-work/multipage/offline.html.

UNCACHED (numeric value 0:

The ApplicationCache object's cache host is not associated with an application cache at this time.

IDLE (numeric value 1):

The ApplicationCache object's cache host is associated with an application cache whose application cache group's update status is idle, and that application cache is the newest cache in its application cache group, and the application cache group is not marked as obsolete.

CHECKING (numeric value 2):

The ApplicationCache object's cache host is associated with an application cache whose application cache group's update status is checking.

DOWNLOADING (numeric value 3):

The ApplicationCache object's cache host is associated with an application cache whose application cache group's update status is downloading.

UPDATEREADY (numeric value 4):

The ApplicationCache object's cache host is associated with an application cache whose application cache group's update status is idle, and whose application cache group is not marked as obsolete, but that application cache is not the newest cache in its group.

OBSOLETE (numeric value 5):

The ApplicationCache object's cache host is associated with an application cache whose application cache group is marked as obsolete.

Exercise 14.2: Checking browser support

In this exercise, you learn about the applicationCache property of the Window object. You write a simple JavaScript that will determine if the user's browser supports applicationCache.

Objectives

After completing this exercise, you will be able to do the following:

- Determine if the user is either online or on a network connection.

Step 1   Open the file "appCache-support-starter.html" from the appCache-API folder.

Step 2   Create a `<script>` block in the `<head>` section.

Step 3   Add the following code, which attempts to access the Window objects applicationCache property:

```
<script>

if (window.applicationCache){

        console.log("This browser supports Application Cache.");

}
```

```
else {

        console.log("This browser does NOT support Application Cache.");

}

</script>
```

Step 4   Save and test the file in all browsers. Internet Explorer 9.0 does **not** support application cache.

Exercise summary

In this exercise, you learned how to check for browser support for offline applications.

The navigator.online property

The `window.navigator.online` returns "false" if the user agent is definitely offline (disconnected from the network). It returns "true" if the user agent might be online.

The online and offline events are fired when the value of this attribute changes.

Note   This attribute is inherently unreliable. A computer can be connected to a local area network without having Internet access.[1]

Exercise 14.3: Determining offline status

In this exercise, you determine if the user is online or offline by checking the value of the online property of the Navigator object.

Objectives

After completing this exercise, you will be able to do the following:

- Determine if the browser supports application cache.

Step 1   Open the file "offline-starter.html" from the appCache-API folder.

Step 2   In the `<script>` block below the existing script, add the following function called checkStatus():

```
function checkStatus() {
    if (navigator.online){
        alert("Yep...You're Online");
    }
    else {
        alert("Nope...You're Not Online");
    }
}
```

Step 3   Locate the getStatus button at the bottom of the page and add the click event as shown in bold below:

---

1   "7.7 Offline Web applications," HTML Living Standards, updated August, 27, 2015,
    http://www.whatwg.org/specs/web-apps/current-work/multipage/offline.html

```
<input type="button" name="getStatus" id="getStatus" value="Get Online Status"
onClick="checkStatus()">
```

Step 4   Open in the browser while online. Internet Explorer, Opera, and Firefox have an offline mode.

Step 5   Use the browsers above (except Internet Explorer) and/or terminate your Internet connection.

Step 6   Test the file again when you are offline.

Exercise outcome

This exercise results in the appearance of an alert box that indicates if the web browser is currently on a network connection. If the `online` property of the `browser` object is true, it does not guarantee that the browser has Internet access, only that it is on a network.

Exercise summary

In this exercise, you learned the online property of the Window's `Navigator` object.

Understanding the cache manifest file

The cache manifest file is identified in the HTML element's manifest attribute as a URL, and it is fetched and processed during the application cache download process. It is written in plain text and has a MIME type of text/cache-manifest. The cache manifest file is stored on the server. You may have to add files to the server to ensure this MIME type can be fetched. For example, if you are using Apache, you would add an .htaccess file with this line:

```
AddType text/cache-manifest    .manifest
```

What is the cache manifest file, and when is it used?

The cache manifest file has a simple purpose: it tells the browser which files should be cached for offline access, which files must never be cached, and which files to use as a fallback file in the event that a file is unreachable.

The following rules must be followed when creating a cache manifest file:

- The file extension is typically .manifest or .appCache.
- The first line of code must read CACHE MANIFEST.
- Commented lines must be begin with #.
- Sites are limited to 5MB worth of cached data.
- If the manifest file or a resource specified in it fails to download, the entire cache update process fails.
- The browser will keep using the old application cache in the event of failure.
- The * may be used as wildcard in any of the cache manifest sections listed below.
- The encoding type must be UTF-8.

Manifest files consist of one or more of these three sections:

CACHE: Lists the files that must be cached (this is the default section if no sections are specified)

NETWORK: Lists the files that must *not* be cached

FALLBACK: Lists the files that will be used to replace resources that cannot be cached

Exercise 14.4: The cache manifest file

In this exercise, you learn the syntax and purpose of a cache manifest file. You'll see where the cache manifest file should be stored and how to implement it in a web page.

Objectives

After completing this exercise, you will be able to do the following:

- Describe the cache manifest file.
- Write a cache manifest file.
- Understand where to store the cache manifest file.
- Utilize a cache manifest file.

Step 1   Create a new file, name it "offline.manifest," and save it in the appCache-API folder.

Step 2   Type the first line:

```
CACHE MANIFEST
```

Step 3   Add a return and then type the first comment

```
# files to be cached
```

Step 4   The CACHE header is the default and may be omitted. For clarity, you will add the first section header indicating that all of the files below it are to be cached.

```
CACHE:

index.html
styles/foodPlate.css
scripts/index.js
scripts/addFood.js
scripts/register.js
scripts/jquery_1_6_1.js
scripts/jquery-ui-1.8.14.custom.min.js
html/register.html
html/addFood.html
images/foodDiaryPlate.png
images/favicon.png
images/foodItems/apple_sm.gif
images/foodItems/dairy_sm.png
images/foodItems/grain_sm.png
images/foodItems/protein_sm.png
images/foodItems/veg_sm.png
images/foodPlates/myPlate_empty_all.png
```

```
images/myPlate/background.png
images/myPlate/fruit.jpg
images/myPlate/fruitempty.png
images/myPlate/grain-dairy.jpg
images/myPlate/grain.jpg
images/myPlate/graindairyempty.png
images/myPlate/protein.jpg
images/myPlate/proteinempty.png
images/myPlate/text.jpg
images/myPlate/text.png
images/myPlate/vegempty.png
images/myPlate/vegetable.jpg
images/myPlate_full/text.jpg
```

Step 5   The NETWORK section is used to create a white list (an approved list of files for a particular purpose) for files that require network connectivity. Any request for pages in this white list will bypass the cache, even if the user is offline. Add a network section that points to a file (which is empty and only for demonstration purposes) as shown below:

```
# do NOT cache

NETWORK:

scripts/bogusScript.cgi
```

Step 6   The FALLBACK section is the last section and provides a fallback resource for files that cannot be fetched.

```
FALLBACK:

14.4_finished.html Fallback.html
```

This code causes the browser to load Fallback.html when it is unable to access 14.4_finished.html.

Associating the cache manifest with a web page

To associate the cache manifest file with a web page, add a manifest attribute to the HTML element and set the value to the URL of the cache manifest file.

Step 7   Open the file "appCache-events-starter.html" in your code editor and in the Chrome web browser. Do not close the browser after opening the file.

Step 8   Go back to your editor and add the following code to the HTML element (shown in bold) .

```
<!DOCTYPE HTML>
<html manifest="offline.manifest">
```

This HTML file would be implicitly included in the cache manifest file even if it is not mentioned specifically in the CACHE section. All pages with the "manifest" attribute are implicitly included in the cache manifest.

Step 9   Save the file and return to Chrome. Open the Chrome console and refresh the page. Examine the results of the console with your instructor.

Step 10   You may now close all open files.

Exercise summary

In this exercise, you learned how to write a cache manifest file and include it within your web application.

Understanding cache events

When a cache manifest file is implemented, the browser cache goes through a series of events relating to the caching of files. Here is an overview of the caching process and its associated events.

First the manifest file is found via the following code:

```
<html lang="en" manifest="offline.manifest">
```

Then the browser dispatches the "onchecking" event on the `ApplicationCache` object.

If the cache manifest file is being read for the first time, an "ondownloading" event is dispatched. This is followed by the downloading of all of the files specified in the cache manifest file. While this downloading is taking place, the browser periodically dispatches the "onprogress" event. This event contains information about the number of files that have been downloaded and how many are left to be downloaded.

Once all files have been successfully downloaded, the browser dispatches a final "oncached" event. This places your application in the "IDLE" state.

If the cache manifest file has already been read from another page, then all of the required resources will already be in the cache. At this point, however, the manifest file may have changed.

If the cache manifest file has not changed, the browser dispatches an "onupdate" event and the application is in the "IDLE" state.

If the cache manifest file has changed, an "ondownloading" event is dispatched and the resources are downloaded again. Providing version numbers to your cache manifest would indicate a change in the cache manifest file.

The onprogress and oncached events are dispatched as described earlier, and the process ends with an onupdateready event. However, although the cache has been updated, the new cache manifest will not be in use because you will have to reload the page to display the latest version.

Any errors in this process result in an onerror event, which essentially halts the caching process (examples of errors include changing the name of the cache manifest file, bad file paths and/or paths to files that don't exist).

You can force the browser to check the manifest file with the `applicationCache.update()` method. You can then force the switch to the new cache with the `applicationCache.swapCache()` method. The page will still need to be reloaded to use the new version.

The following two paragraphs and chart are taken from the W3C HTML5 Editors Draft August 22, 2012 (http://dev.w3.org/html5/spec-preview/offline.html):

"When the user visits a page that declares a manifest, the browser will try to update the cache. It does this by fetching a copy of the manifest and, if the manifest has changed since the user agent last saw it, redownloading all the resources it mentions and caching them anew.

As this is going on, a number of events get fired on the `ApplicationCache` object to keep the script updated as to the state of the cache update, so that the user can be notified appropriately.

The events are as follows.:

ApplicationCache Events

Event Name	Interface	Dispatched When . . .	Next Events
checking	Event	The user agent is checking for an update or attempting to download the manifest for the first time. This is always the first event in the sequence.	noupdate, downloading, obsolete, error
noupdate	Event	The manifest hadn't changed.	Last event in sequence.
downloading	Event	The user agent has found an update and is fetching it or is downloading the resources listed by the manifest for the first time.	progress, error, cached, updateready
progress	ProgressEvent	The user agent is downloading resources listed by the manifest.	progress, error, cached, updateready
cached	Event	The resources listed in the manifest have been downloaded, and the application is now cached.	Last event in sequence.
updateready	Event	The resources listed in the manifest have been newly redownloaded, and the script can use swap-Cache() to switch to the new cache.	Last event in sequence.
obsolete	Event	The manifest was found to have become a 404 or 410 page, so the application cache is being deleted.	Last event in sequence.
error	Event	The manifest was a 404 or 410 page, so the attempt to cache the application has been aborted.	Last event in sequence.
		The manifest hadn't changed, but the page referencing the manifest failed to download properly.	
		A fatal error occurred while fetching the resources listed in the manifest.	
		The manifest changed while the update was being run.	The user agent will try fetching the files again momentarily.

Exercise 14.5: Understanding cache events

In this exercise, you view a live application from kevinruse.com that uses applicationCache because testing application cache on localhost can be problematic.

Objectives

After completing this exercise, you will be able to do the following:

- Understand the caching process
- Understand cache events

Step 1   Open the Chrome web browser and launch the web developers' tools by using one of the two methods below.

    1.   Control + Shift + I
    2.   From the main menu bar, choose the Settings button (the button icon with three horizontal bars) →More Tools →Developer Tools.

Step 2   From the developer tools section, make sure the Console tab is active.

Testing pages that use applicationCache can sometimes be problematic on the localhost. Therefore in our next exercise, you will visit a page from www.kevinruse.com that includes a cache manifest. The browser's console will log statements in response to the applicationCache events.

Step 3   Start the Chrome browser and go to the following web page:
http://www.kevinruse.com/Lesson_11_Offline_Applications/index.html

Look at the developer tools; you should see several alert boxes similar to the one shown below.

Notice that the console reports the status of the caching as shown:

Step 4   Spend a few minutes viewing the source code.

Step 5   Now reload "http://www.kevinruse.com/Lesson_11_Offline_Applications/index.html" in the browser.

The page should have loaded quickly. Note on the console that it was loaded from the cache.

Now that the page has loaded, you will disconnect your Internet connection and continue to interact with the application.

Step 6   Disconnect your Internet connection.

Step 7   Click the Register button and continue the registration process.

Step 8   Reconnect your Internet connection.

Step 9   Revisit "http://www.kevinruse.com/Lesson_11_Offline_Applications/index.html."

You should now see the data you entered while offline.

Step 10   View the local file that handles applicationCache events called "14.4_appCache_events.html."

Step 11   You may now close all browser windows.

Exercise summary

In this exercise, you saw the caching process and followed the various cache events.

Resources

Offline Web Applications Working Group Note: http://www.w3.org/TR/offline-webapps/

Offline Web Applications WHATWG: https://html.spec.whatwg.org/multipage/browsers.html#offline

Offline Application JavaScript Library: http://github.hubspot.com/offline/docs/welcome/?utm_source=javascriptweekly&utm_medium=email

Offline Applications slideshow: http://www.slideshare.net/peterlubbers/using-html5-application-cache-to-create-offline-web-applications

Using Application Cache article from Mozilla: https://developer.mozilla.org/en-US/docs/Web/HTML/Using_the_application_cache

Chapter summary

In this chapter, you learned how to allow web applications to continue working even when the user is offline. You learned how to use a cache manifest file to instruct the browser to cache (or not cache) pages within the web application that subsequently allow the user to view and interact with the web pages when offline. Typical files to cache include stylesheets, HTML files, and JavaScript files. You also examined the caching process from a live application using Chrome.

Chapter 15

XMLHttpRequest Level 2 API

In this chapter, you use the new features of XMLHttpRequest (XHR) level 2, including authentication of the user with credentials and responding to the progress event.

XHR level 2 was published as a W3C Working Group Note on November 18, 2014.

Objectives

☐ Describe the XMLHttpRequest API.

☐ Understand the limitations of XHR level 1.

☐ Describe the new features of XHR level 2.

☐ Check for browser support of XHR level 2.

☐ Describe cross-origin resource sharing (CORS).

Introduction

In this chapter, you learn the API that made AJAX possible: the `XMLHttpRequest` (XHR) object. The XHR object makes it possible to send and receive data from a backend server. The developer typically sends and/or receives XML or text data. The `XHR` object can accept XML or any text-based format. One of the main benefits of XHR is the ability to retrieve data when the page loads, which allows the page to utilize that data in various ways while the user interacts with the web page—and without the need for repeated requests for data throughout the session.

XHR API

Creating an XHR request is as simple as:

```
var myrequest = new XMLHttpRequest();
```

You then open the connection and send the request with the following:

```
myrequest.open("GET","books.xml",false);

myrequest.send();
```

The `open()` method specifies the method (e.g., GET), the resource (e.g., books.xml), The third argument specifies that the request be handled asynchronously when set to "true."

The XML that is returned is then parsed with the help of the browser's built-in XML parser and some JavaScript. In the past, AJAX requests for external resources (i.e., XML, text) could be made only for resources on the same domain. Cross-domain requests are now allowed with XHR level 2 due to cross-origin resource sharing (CORS). **Note:** Your server must support CORS.

When a request is made by a web page for a resource, the browser creates an origin header that identifies the requestor. The resource file itself contains code that allows the requestor access to it by referencing its origin. See the code snippet below, which is part of an XML file that you will request in a subsequent exercise.

```
<?access-control allow="http://www.foodplate.local"?>
```

XHR supports requests made over both HTTP and HTTPS. Another advantage of XHR level 2 over its predecessor is its ability to respond to additional events beyond the single readystatechange event of XHR level 1. The additional XHR events in level 2 include the following: `loadstart`, `progress`, `abort`, `error`, `load`, and `loadend`.

What is XHR used for?

Anytime your page requires data from a page within or outside the host's domain, you can use XHR. The request both to and from may execute at load time and obtain the site's needed data without initiating subsequent requests that may slow the site down.

The XHR level 2 `send()` method can take a file or blob object as a parameter, which adds the possibility of uploading files. "A blob (alternately known as a binary large object, basic large object, BLOB, or BLOb) is a collection of binary data stored as a single entity in a database management system. Blobs are typically images, audio, or other multimedia objects, though sometimes binary executable code is stored as a blob. Database support for blobs is not universal."[1]

---

1   "Binary large object," Wikipedia, ttp://en.wikipedia.org/wiki/Binary_large_object

Benefits of XHR level 2

XHR level 2 has numerous benefits over the using the standard XMLHttpRequest object, including:

- Level 2 allows for cross-domain resource sharing (CORS).
- It supports numerous events including a progress event.
- The target server may serve secured content with appropriate users' credentials.

The XHR object: readyState property

The `XHR` object includes a readyState property that verifies the status of an object using a value of 0 to 4. The readyState property may have any of the following values:

Note   An entity-body is only present in a message when a message-body is present. The entity-body is obtained from the message-body by decoding any transfer-encoding that might have been applied to ensure safe and proper transfer of the message.

The XHR Object

The XHR object: Events

Unlike XHR level 1, XHR level 2 supports more than one event handler: `onloadstart`, `onprogress`, `onabort`, `onerror`, `onload`, `ontimeout`, `onloadend`, and `onreadystatechange`.

The XHR object: Methods

Method	Description
`open(method, URL, async, user, password)`	Opens the connection
`setRequestHeader(header, value)`	Appends a header to the list of headers
`send()`	Initiates and sends the request
`abort()`	Cancels any network activity; preventively terminates the HTTP request
`client.getResponseHeader(header)`	Returns the header field value from the header response of which the field name matches header, unless the field name is Set-Cookie or Set-Cookie2
`client.getAllResponseHeaders()`	Returns all headers from the response, with the exception of those for which the field name is Set-Cookie or Set-Cookie2
`client.overrideMimeType(mime)`	Sets the content-type header for the response to MIME

The XHR object: Properties

Property	Description
`client.timeout`	The number of milliseconds a request can take before being terminated (initially zero, which means there is no timeout)
`client.upload`	Returns the associated `XMLHttpRequestUpload` object
`client.status`	Returns the HTTP status code

`client.statusText`	Returns the HTTP status text
`client.responseType [ = value ]`	Returns the response type. (Can be set to change the response type. Values are the empty string [default], "arraybuffer," "blob," "document," "json," and "text.")
`client.response`	Returns the response entity body
`client.responseText`	Returns the text response entity body
`client.responseXML`	Returns the document response entity body
`client.withCredentials`	True when user credentials are to be included in a cross-origin request (initially false) False when they are to be excluded in a cross-origin request and when cookies are to be ignored in its response

Exercise 15.1: Checking for browser support

In this exercise, you check for browser support of XHR level 2.

Objectives

After completing this exercise, you will be able to do the following:

- Check for browser support by creating an XHR object.

- Use the withCredentials property of the XHR object.

Step 1   Open the file "xhr-support-starter.html" from the xhr-level2 folder.

Step 2   Create a script block above the closing `</body>` element and declare a global variable called "xhr" to store the new XHR object. Declare a variable reference to the `<p>` element with the `id` of "tipText."

```
<script>
        var tipText = document.getElementById('tipText');

        var xhr;

</script>
```

Step 3   You will use the withCredentials attribute to check for browser support. Modify the existing code as shown below in bold:

```
var tipText = document.getElementById('tipText');

var xhr = new XMLHttpRequest();

if(typeof xhr.withCredentials ===  "undefined") {
  tipText.innerHTML = "Your Browser does not support Cross-Origin
  XMLHttpRequest.";
      }
  else {
  tipText.innerHTML = "Your Browser does support Cross-Origin XMLHttpRequest.";
      }
```

Step 4   Save the file and test it in all browsers. Look for the text in the `<div>` to check for browser support.

Step 5   You may now close all open files.

Exercise outcome

This exercise results in the appearance of a paragraph within a div element that indicates support or lack of support for the XHR level 2 API.

Exercise summary

In this exercise, you learned how to check for browser support of XHR level 2 by creating a new XHR object and checking for the existence of the withCredentials property.

Exercise 15.2: Understanding the progress event

In this exercise, you learn about the XHR level 2 progress event and how to respond to it.

Objectives

After completing this exercise, you will be able to do the following:

- Understand the progress event.
- Respond to the progress event.
- Use properties of the progress event, including loaded and total.

Step 1   Open the file "xhr-progress-starter.html" from the xhr-level2-API folder.

Step 2   Create the following variable inside the `<script>` block, below the xhr variable.

```
var progressXHR = document.getElementById ('xhrProgress');
progressXHR.min = 0;
progressXHR.max = 100;
var xhrlocation = "http://www.kevinruse.com/KRA-HTML_FoodPlate/messages.xml";
```

Step 3   Below the last line you typed, invoke the `xhr open()` method. Pass the method "GET" followed by the xhr-Location and set the synchronous flag to "true" to fetch the resource synchronously.

```
xhr.open('GET', xhrlocation, true);
```

Step 4   On the next line, invoke the `xhr send()` method. Since you are not sending any data, you will pass a null value to the method.

```
xhr.send(null);
```

Step 5   Add the onprogress event handler function

```
xhr.onprogress = function(evt) {
}
```

Step 6   Inside the function, add a console log statement that indicates the bytes loaded and the total bytes.

```
console.log("Loaded " + evt.loaded + " of " + evt.total);
```

Step 7   Save this file into C:\foodPlate\Sites\LocalSite and test the file from the web browser using the URL http://www.foodPlate.local/xhr-progress-starter.html.

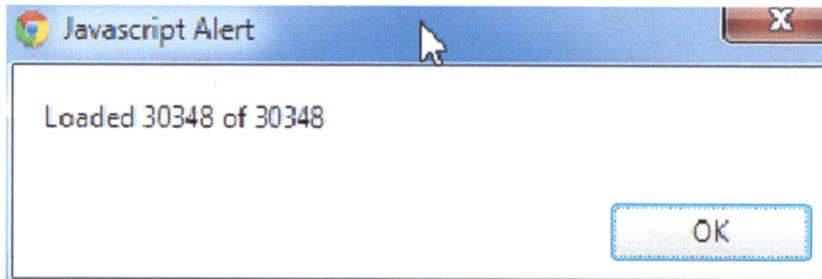

The file xhr-progress-starter.html showing the bytes loaded.

Note   Before running this file, be sure that you have started the WAMP server. If you are running the file through WebStorm, it will be sufficient to use the WebStorm-configured project server.

Step 8   Next you'll pass the bytes loaded and bytes total information to the progress bar on the page. Add the following code below the `console.log()` statement:

`progressXHR.value = (evt.loaded / evt.total) * 100;`

Step 9   Save and test the file in a web browser. Hold down the shift key and click the browser's Refresh button to see the progress bar move.

Step 10   You may now close all open files.

Exercise outcome

When viewed in a web browser, this exercise results in a progress bar that tracks the progress of the XHR request. You should see the green bar move from left to right as the download progresses.

Exercise summary

In this exercise, you learned how to respond to new events associated with XHR level 2, including the progress event. You learned some of the properties of this event including bytes loaded and bytes total.

Exercise 15.3: Understanding the onload event

In this exercise, you learn about the XHR level 2 load event and how to respond to it.

Objectives

After completing this exercise, you will be able to do the following:

- Understand the load event.
- Respond to the load event.

Step 1   Open the file "xhr-onLoad-starter.html" in the xhr-level2-API folder.

Step 2   Add the following code, shown below in bold, to the `<script>` block:

```
<script>
    var xhr = new XMLHttpRequest();
    var progressXHR = document.getElementById ('xhrProgress');
    progressXHR.min = 0;
    progressXHR.max = 100;
    var xhrlocation = "http://www.kevinruse.com/KRA-HTML_FoodPlate/messages.
xml";
    xhr.open('GET', xhrlocation, true);
    xhr.send(null);
    xhr.onload = function(evt) {
            document.getElementById('loadStatus').innerHTML = "Loading ...";
            }
    xhr.onloadend = function() {
            document.getElementById('loadStatus').innerHTML = "Finished";
            }
    xhr.onprogress = function(evt) {
            progressXHR.value = (evt.loaded / evt.total) * 100;
            document.getElementById('loadStatus').innerHTML = "Loading ...";
            document.getElementById('progProperties').innerHTML =
                evt.lengthComputable;
            document.getElementById('progBytesTotal').innerHTML = evt.total;
        }
    }
</script>
```

Step 3   Save this file into C:\foodPlate\Sites\LocalSite and test the file from the web browser using the URL http://www.foodPlate.local/xhr_onLoad_starter.html.

Note   Before running this file, be sure that you have started the WAMP server. If you are running the file through WebStorm, it will be sufficient to use the WebStorm-configured project server.

Step 4   Try holding the shift key down while refreshing the page in the browser. Do this more than once.

Step 5   You may now close all open files.

Exercise outcome

When viewed in a web browser, this exercise results in properties of the XHR object being displayed in the browser window in response to XHR level 2 events.

Exercise summary

In this exercise, you responded to the load event by adding event handlers for the initial XHR load event and the loadend event.

Exercise 15.4: Displaying XML returned from XHR

In this exercise, you use the data returned from an XHR request. You will be requesting an XML file called "message.xml," which contains various health tips. The goal is to pick a random health tip from the XML file and display it for the user in a predefined `<div>` element.

Objectives

After completing this exercise, you will be able to do the following:

- Make an XHR request.
- Use the returned data from an XHR request.

Step 1   Open the file "xhr-display-AJAX-starter.html" from the xhr-level2 folder.

Step 2   Create a `<script>` block before the closing `<body>` element.

Step 3   Declare these required variables.

```
var xhr;
var tipText = document.getElementById('tipText');
var xmlTips;
var tip;
```

Step 4   Write a function called `loadTip()`.

```
function loadTip() {
};
```

Step 5   Place a try/catch inside the function and add an alert box in the catch section to catch errors returned by the XHR object's `send()` method.

```
function loadTip() {
        try {
        }
        catch(err){
          alert('Try failed. Error occurred: ' + err);
        }
}
```

Step 6   Add the try logic to create an XHR object, open the connection, and send the request as shown below.

```
function loadTip() {
    try {
            xhr = new XMLHttpRequest();
            xhr.open('GET', 'http://www.kevinruse.com/KRA-HTML_Food
Plate/messages.xml', false);
            xhr.send(null);
    }
    catch(err){
            alert('Try failed. Error occurred: ' + err);
    }
}
```

Step 7   Set the variable to store the returned XML which is stored in the XHR objects' responseXML property. Then call the output function, which will output the results to the web page.

```
function loadTip() {
    try {
    xhr = new XMLHttpRequest();
    xhr.open('GET', 'http://www.kevinruse.com/KRA-HTML_FoodPlate/messages.
xml', false);
    xhr.send(null);
    xmlTips = xhr.responseXML;
    output();
            }
    catch(err){
            alert('Try failed. Error occurred: ' + err);
    }
```

Step 8   At the top of the script block, add the following event listener to call `loadTip()` at startup (shown in bold):

```
var xhr;
var tipText = document.getElementById('tipText');
var xmlTips;
var tip;
window.addEventListener('load', loadTip, false);
```

Step 9   Write the `output()` function.

```
function output() {
    var randomNumber=Math.floor(Math.random()*11);
        tip = xmlTips.getElementsByTagName("message")[randomNumber].child-
    Nodes[0].nodeValue;
    tipText.textContent = tip;
}
```

Step 10   Save and test in the browser. Be sure to use the browser's developer tools to locate the XHR response.

Note   Before running this file, be sure that you have started the WAMP server. If you are running the file through WebStorm, it will be sufficient to use the WebStorm-configured project server.

The finished file

```
<script>
    var xhr;
    var tipText = document.getElementById('tipText');
    var xmlTips;
    var tip;
    window.addEventListener('load', loadTip, false);

    function loadTip() {
        try {
            xhr = new XMLHttpRequest(),
            xhr.open('GET', 'http://www.kevinruse.com/KRA-HTML_Food
Plate/messages.xml', false);
            xhr.send(null);
```

```
                    xmlTips = xhr.responseXML;
                    output();
                    }
            catch(err){
                    alert('Try failed. Error occurred: ' + err);
            }

            function output() {
                    var randomNumber=Math.floor(Math.random()*11);
                    tip = xmlTips.getElementsByTagName("message")[randomNumber].
    childNodes[0].nodeValue;
                    tipText.textContent = tip;
            }
        }
        </script>
```

Step 11   Be sure to save all of the files into C:\FoodPlate\Sites\LocalSite and test the file using www.foodPlate.local.

Step 12   You may now close all open files.

Exercise outcome

This exercise results in the display on the web page of a random food tip of the day from the XML fetched via the XHR object. Each time you refresh the page in the browser, you should see a different food tip of the day displayed.

Exercise summary

In this exercise, you learned how to display the data returned from an XHR level 2 request. You used the data from the external XML file and displayed it to the user.

Resources

XHR Level 2 Working Group Note: http://www.w3.org/TR/XMLHttpRequest2/

XHR withCredentials articles from Opera: https://dev.opera.com/articles/xhr2/#xhrcredentials

Pure HTML5 file upload with XHR: https://www.script-tutorials.com/pure-html5-file-upload/

XHR demo: http://arunranga.com/examples/access-control/preflightInvocation.html

Chapter summary

In this chapter, you learned about the new features associated with making an XMLHttpRequest. You learned that the XHR object can request any text-based file or XML. You learned that there are many new events associated with XHR and that you can also make requests across domains using the cross-origin resource-sharing specification.

Chapter 16

Web Sockets API

In this chapter, you make full duplex connections from client to server with the WebSocket specification.

The WebSocket API became a W3C Candidate Recommendation on September 20, 2012.

Objectives

❑ Understand client/server communication over HTTP.

❑ Understand client/server communication over HTTP using WebSocket.

❑ Describe the WebSocket specification.

❑ Use the WebSocket specification.

Introduction

Currently when a browser visits a website, an HTTP request is made from the client computer's web browser to the web server hosting the website. The server acknowledges the request and sends back the requested web page. This request/response model takes some time depending on a variety of factors including network traffic, connection speed, and so on. Sometimes the data on the page may have changed in the time it took to serve the page.

Note about HTTP, in regard to Web Sockets, that the protocol is "stateless." In other words, there is no persistent connection between the client and server, but instead, a single request is made from the client and the server returns a single response. When a protocol is "stateful," then a sequence of commands can be treated as a single communication. A stateful protocol requires a persistent connection. HTTP clients and servers are not required to maintain state between transmitted commands or requests/responses. The lifetime of an HTTP 1.1 connection is limited to a single request-response exchange.

A number of methods have been used over the years to minimize the traffic required in the request/response model. One method involves frequently polling the server for updated information; other methods include server-side push technologies. With polling, the browser sends requests at specified intervals. However, it's possible that polling at a given time results in no new data, and at other times the polling interval is not frequent enough to catch all of the data changes. The end result: Connections are open and closed unnecessarily. Another solution is long polling, in which the request to the server is "parked" for a specified period of time. A notification is sent or not sent within that specified period of time. If the notification comes in within the time period, then a message is sent to the client. If not, the server sends a response to terminate the open or "parked" request. The end result may or may not provide any substantial performance gain.

What is a Web Socket?

The WebSocket specification is designed to open a real-time, two-way communication between a client and server, whereby the server can send data to the client as soon as it has new data without waiting for an HTTP request. The specification includes a simple API for scripting purposes. In addition, WebSocket allows cross-origin communication between the communicating parties with the server determining whether service is available to any participant or just a specific set of trusted domains.

WebSocket API properties

Property	Description	
url	Must return the result of resolving the URL that was passed to the constructor; it doesn't matter what it is resolved relative to, since you already know it is an absolute URL.	
readyState	Represents the state of the connection and can have the following values:	
	CONNECTING (numeric value 0)	The connection has not yet been established.
	CLOSING (numeric value 2)	The connection is going through the closing handshake.
	OPEN (numeric value 1)	The WebSocket connection is established, and communication is possible.
	CLOSED (numeric value 3)	The connection has been closed or could not be opened.

WebSocket API event handlers

Events	Description
onopen	The socket is open and can send messages.
onmessage	A message has been received.
onerror	There is an error in the message/socket.
onclose	The socket has been closed.

WebSocket methods

Methods	Description
send(data)	This method transmits data using the connection.
close()	*If the readyState attribute is in the CLOSING (2) or CLOSED (3) state,* do nothing.
	The connection is already closing or is already closed. If it has not already closed, a close event will eventually fire.
	If the WebSocket connection is not yet established, fail the WebSocket connection and set the readyState attribute's value to CLOSING (2).
	If the WebSocket closing handshake has not yet been started, start the WebSocket closing handshake and set the readyState attribute's value to CLOSING (2), *otherwise,* set the readyState attribute's value to CLOSING (2).

Using a WebSocket server with the WebSocket API

To use the WebSocket API, you must have a certain configuration setup on your server. Essentially, using the API requires a socket server capable of establishing a connection with the client. The socket server then waits for messages from the client and can also send messages to the client. There are several socket servers available including the following:

- phpwebsocket   PHP (http://code.google.com/p/phpwebsocket)
- jWebSocket   Java
- web-socket-ruby   Ruby
- Socket IO-node   node.js
- Kaazing WebSocket   Java-based WebSocket gateway
- mod_pyWebSocket   Python-based extension for the Apache HTTP server
- Netty   Java network framework
- websocket   Python
- wsproxy   WebSocket-to-generic-TCP-socket proxy

Exercise 16.1: WebSocket browser support

In this exercise, you check for browser support for WebSocket.

Objectives

After completing this exercise, you will be able to do the following:

- Understand how to check for WebSocket support.
- Know which browsers do and do not support WebSocket.

Step 1   Open the "webSocket-support-starter.html" in the webSocket-API folder.

Step 2   Add a `<script>` block and write the `CheckWebSocket()` function as shown below:

```
<script>
function checkWebSocket() {
        if("WebSocket" in window) {
            console.log("Web Socket is supported by your browser.");
        }
        else {
            console.log("Web Socket is NOT supported by your browser.");
        }
}
</script>
```

Step 3   Call the `checkWebSocket()` function from the onload event.

```
window.addEventListener('load', checkWebSocket);
```

Step 4   Save and test in the Chrome browser. Be sure to have the console open to view the log statements.

Step 5   You may now close all open files.

Exercise outcome

This exercise results in a console log statement that indicates support for the WebSocket API.

Exercise summary

In this exercise you determined browser support for the WebSocket API by checking for the existence of the `socket` property of the `Window` object.

Exercise 16.2: WebSocket handshake

In this exercise, you review the client/server process for initiating WebSocket communication over HTTP version 1.1.

Objectives

After completing this exercise, you will be able to do the following:

- Understand client/server communication over HTTP.
- Understand the WebSocket handshake.

Step 1   Open the Chrome web browser and go to http://www.websocket.org/echo.html.

Step 2   Turn on the Chrome Developer Tools with Control + Shift + I.

Step 3   Using the Network tab on the developer's tools. On the right side of the DevTools panel, locate the network-traced files (html, css, js, images, etc.) and click the "www.websocket.org/echo.html." Then click the Headers subtab. Be sure to click the View Source link, as shown below.

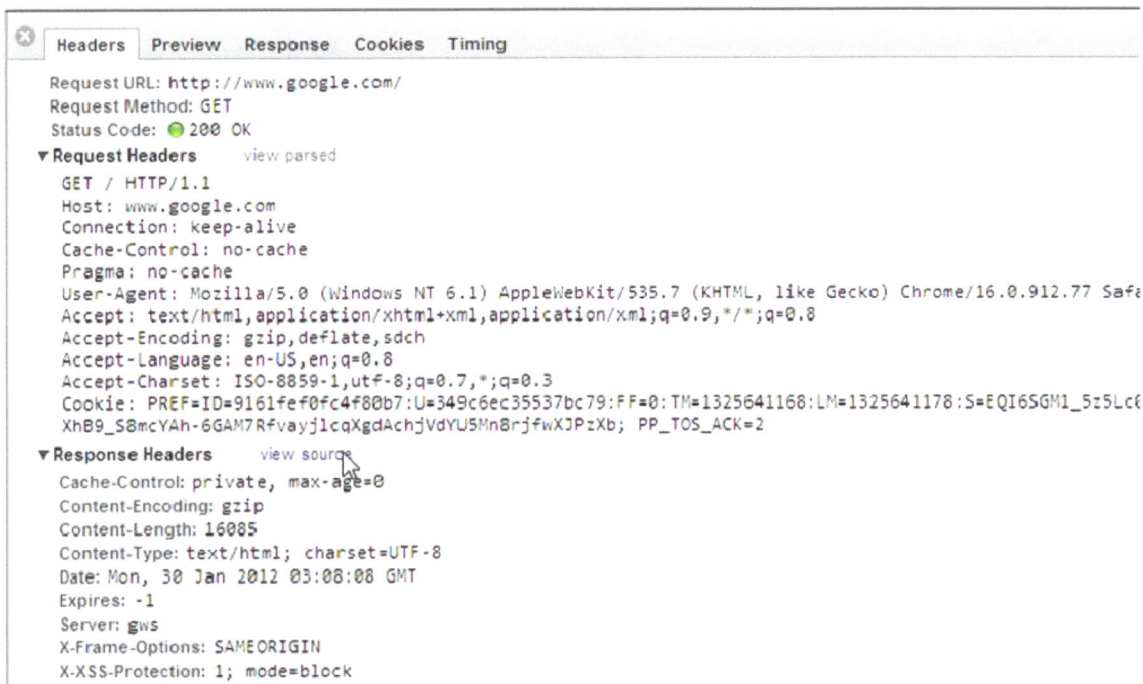

Step 4   Notice the simple HTTP 1.1 GET request headers. Review the response header as well.

Step 5   Now you'll open a page that uses WebSocket to review the handshake. You will, again, watch the http request. The difference this time is that you will see the upgrade from http to websocket.

To establish a WebSocket handshake, the client and server both make an upgrade from the HTTP protocol to the WebSocket protocol. This initial handshake is done via the HTTP headers.

Step 6   Open http://websocket.org/demos.html in Chrome. Feel free to examine some of the demos before moving on to the next step. Be sure you come back to the demo's page after viewing some of the demos.

Step 7   Click the first link under the Echo Test section at http://websocket.org/echo.html.

Step 8   Using the Chrome Developer Tools, click on the Network tab. Make sure that the All option is selected from the options at the bottom of the panel.

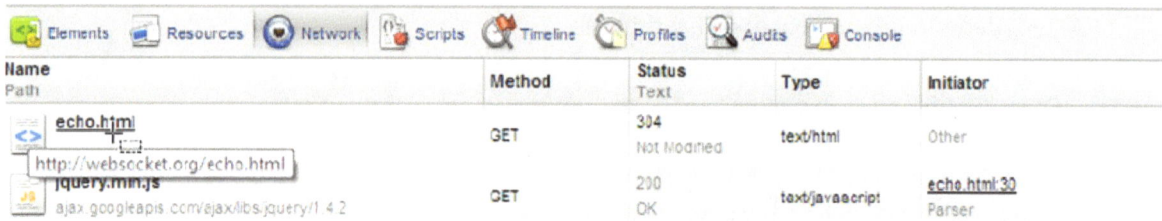

Step 9 Click on the echo.html file on the left.

Step 10 Review the request and response headers.

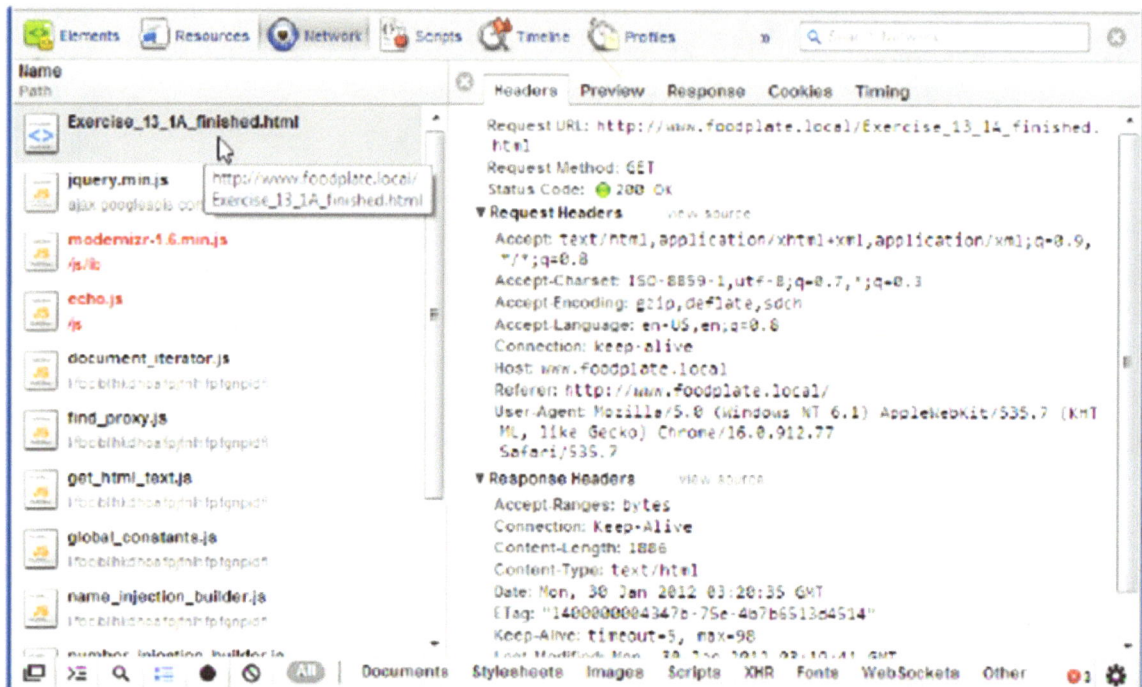

Step 11 Now click the Connect button on the web page.

Echo Test

The first section of this page will let you do an HTML5 WebSocket test against the echo server. The seco
walks you creating a WebSocket yourself.

Try it out

This browser supports WebSocket

Location:

ws://echo.websocket.org

☐ Use secure WebSocket (TLS)

[Connect] [Disconnect]

Message:

Rock it with HTML5 WebSocket

[Send]

Log:

Step 12 Click on the Web Sockets button on the Developer Tools panel.

Step 13 Click on the EchoWebsocket file on the left. If your screen shows "?encoding=text," you can hover over it with your mouse to confirm that it is, in fact, echo.websocket.org.

Elements   Resources   Network   Scrip

Name
Path

echo.websocket.org
echo.websocket.org

ws://echo.websocket.org/

Step 14 Examine the header request and note the handshake process and upgrade.

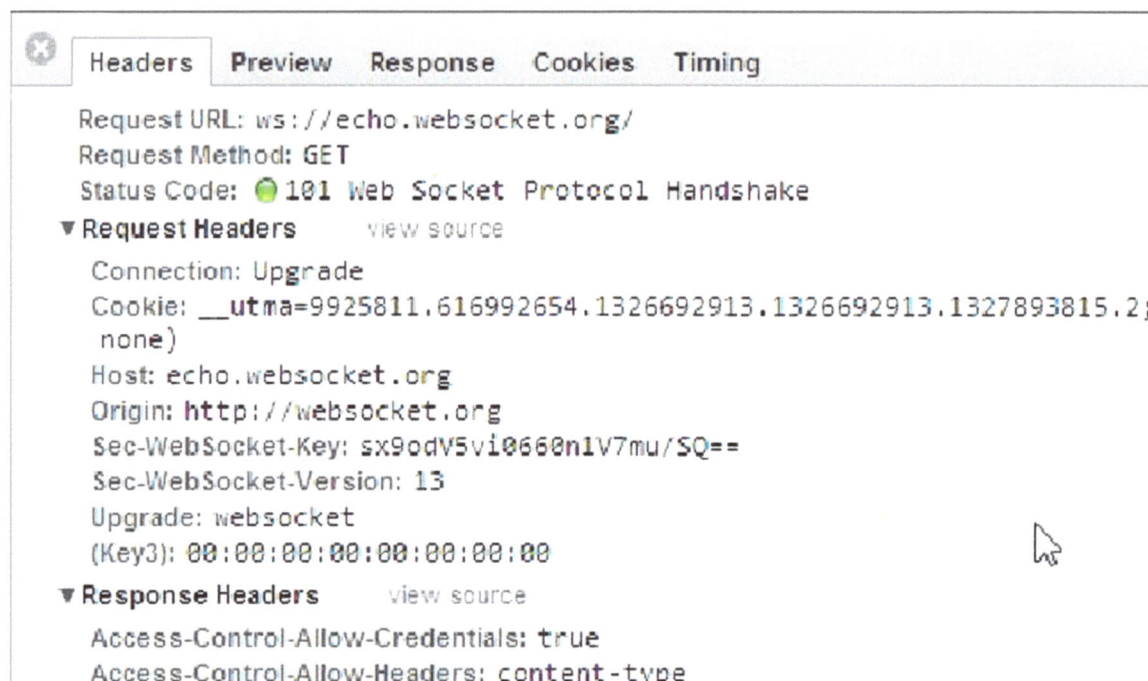

Step 15   You may now close the all browser windows as well as any open files.

Exercise summary

In this exercise, you learned the upgrade process used by the HTTP 1.1 protocol when a WebSocket is used. You watched the handshake process using Chrome Developer Tools.

Exercise 16.3: Using the WebSocket specification

In this exercise, you will implement the WebSocket API.

Objectives

After completing this exercise, you will be able to do the following:

- Describe the WebSocket specification.
- Use the WebSocket specification.

Step 1   Open the file "webSocket-finished.html" in the webSocket-API folder.

Step 2   Open the file "echo-finished.js" in the js folder inside the webSocket-API folder.

Step 3   Locate the lines of code that detect for browser support for the WebSocket.

Step 4   Locate the lines of code that provide the URL of the WebSocket.

Step 5   Locate the line of code that instantiates the WebSocket.

Step 6 Locate the event handlers for onopen, onclose, onmessage, and onerror.

Step 7 Locate the line of code that invokes the `WebSocket send()` method.

Review the code with your instructor.

Step 8 Locate the web socket constructor and pass the second optional argument: protocol using a value of SOAP, thereby indicating to the server that your application supports the Simple Object Access Protocol (SOAP). SOAP then becomes a protocol that the client can use to communicate with the server. The code to modify is shown below in bold.

```
websocket = new WebSocket(wsUri.value, 'SOAP');
```

The protocol argument may be either a single protocol name or an array of protocol names that the server will include in its response when establishing the web socket connection. This is the web socket protocol according to the Web Socket proposal at https://tools.ietf.org/html/rfc6455: "The server selects one or none of the acceptable protocols and echoes that value in its handshake to indicate that it has selected that protocol."

```
for example: Sec-WebSocket-Protocol: chat
```

There are currently three types of protocols that may be specified in the protocols array argument:

- Registered protocols that have been registered according to RFC 6455 (The WebSocket Protocol) as well as the Internet Assigned Numbers Authority (IANA). SOAP is an example of a registered protocol.

- Open protocols that have not been registered as official standard protocols.

- Custom protocols written by your organization.

Step 9 Save the file and run the web page in the Chrome Browser. Complete steps a–f.
   a. Be sure to press F12 to expose Chrome's Developer Tools.
   b. Press the Network tab to activate the network panel.
   c. Refresh the page.
   d. Press the Connect button on the web page.
   e. Using Chrome's Developer tools, press the 'WS' (WebSocket) button along the top of the Network panel.
   f. Click on "echo.websocket.org" on the left side of the Network Panel.

Step 10 Notice the new HTTP Header property: Sec-WebSocket-Protocol, which now has a value of SOAP. See the screenshot below.

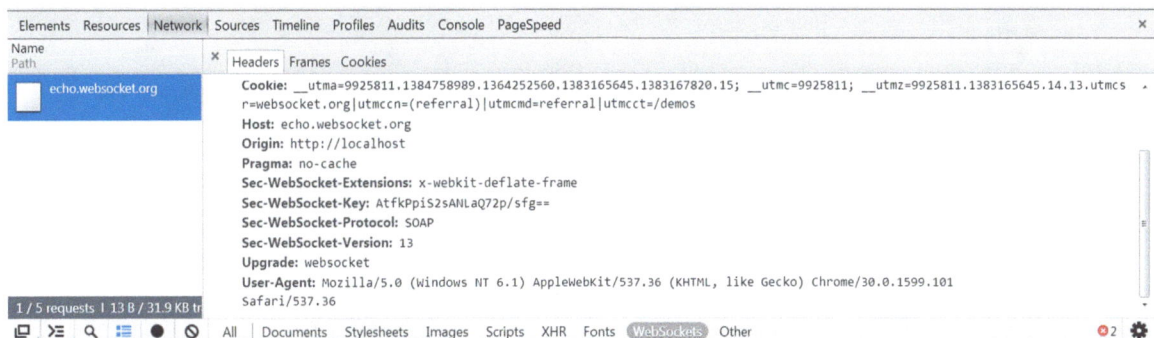

Note Custom protocols are also supported.

Step 11   Add the following code to the onClose eventhandler. The modified code is shown below in bold.

```
function onClose(evt)  {
        logToConsole("DISCONNECTED and wasClean = " + evt.wasClean);
        setGuiConnected(false);
}
```

Step 12   Save the file and run the web page in the Chrome Browser. Complete steps a–c.

    a.   Be sure to press F12 to expose Chrome's Developer Tools.

    b.   Press the Network tab to activate the network panel.

    c.   Refresh the web page.

    d.   Press the Connect button on the web page.

Step 13   Notice the message shown in the console of the web page. See the screenshot below (Chrome).

DEMO from http://websocket.org/demos.html

Echo Test

Location:

ws://echo.websocket.org

☐ Use secure WebSocket (TLS)

[Connect] [Disconnect]

Message:

Rock it with HTML5 WebSocket

[Send]

Log:

ERROR: undefined

DISCONNECTED and wasClean = false

[Clear log]

Note   The log section of the web page may also read:

```
"DISCONNECTED and wasClean=false. code=1006"
```

Step 14   Return to the code and remove the SOAP protocol.

Step 15   Save the file and run the web page in the Chrome Browser. Complete steps a–e.

    a.   Be sure to press F12 to expose Chrome's Developer Tools.

    b.   Press the Network tab to activate the network panel.

    c.   Press the Connect button on the web page.

    d.   Press the Send button to send a message.

    e.   Press the Disconnect button.

Step 16   Notice the message shown in the console of the web page. See the screenshot below.

DEMO from http://websocket.org/demos.html

Echo Test

Location:

ws://echo.websocket.org

☐ Use secure WebSocket (TLS)

[Connect] [Disconnect]

Message:

Rock it with HTML5 WebSocket

[Send]

Log:

CONNECTED

SENT: Rock it with HTML5 WebSocket

RESPONSE: Rock it with HTML5 WebSocket

DISCONNECTED and wasClean = true

[Clear log]

Step 17   Return to the code and add the SOAP protocol back to the constructor.

Step 18   Save the file and run the web page in the Chrome and Firefox Web Browsers. Complete steps a–c.
    a.   Be sure to press F12 to expose Chrome's Developer Tools.
    b.   Press the Network tab to activate the network panel.
    c.   Refresh the page.
    d.   Press the Connect button on the web page.

Step 19   Notice the message shown in the console of the web page.

Step 20   Return to the code and remove the SOAP protocol.

Step 21   You may now close all open files.

Exercise summary

In this exercise, you specified the "SOAP" protocol when implementing the socket. At publication time, this socket worked with SOAP in Firefox 40.0.3, but did not work in Chrome Version 45.0.2454.99 m (64-bit).

Resources

W3C specification: http://www.w3.org/TR/websockets/

Web Socket demos: http://jwebsocket.org/demos/fundamental

http://html5demos.com/web-socket

Web Socket cheat sheet: https://dzone.com/refcardz/html5-websocket?uid=900367&nid=111663&token=0900367052614a3c043a9#refcard-download-social-buttons-display

Web Socket tutorial: http://www.tutorialspoint.com/html5/html5_websocket.htm

Chapter summary

In this chapter, you learned about the WebSocket specification, which is designed to open a real-time, two-way communication between client and server, whereby the server can send data to the client as soon as it has new data without waiting for an HTTP request.

Chapter 17

Server-Sent Events API

In this chapter, you make single unidirectional channels between the server and the client that allow the server to push messages to the client.

Server-sent events became a W3C Candidate Recommendation on February 3, 2015.

Objectives

- ❏ Describe server-sent events.

- ❏ Understand the EventSource object.

- ❏ Describe the events associated with the EventSource object.

- ❏ Describe the advantages of server-sent events.

- ❏ Create a simple application that uses server-sent events.

Introduction

The server-sent events specification opens an HTTP connection that allows the server to push notifications to a client that has subscribed to messages in the form of DOM events. The `EventSource` object provides the means for this communication. An `EventSource` object is created that listens for message events from the server.

The server messages

The event source itself is typically a server-side script capable of pushing messages such as Common Gateway Interface (CGI) or PHP (Hypertext Preprocessor). The messages themselves are sent with a MIME type of text/event-stream and take the following format:

```
data: This is the first message. \n
data: This is the second message. It \n
data: has two lines. \n
data: This is the third message. \n\n
```

Each new line of the message begins with "data" followed by a colon, and the message ends with a single line break identifed by the "\n." The last line of the message ends with two line breaks identified by the "\n\n." Each consecutive line of data is treated as a single piece of data and fires a single message event. Nonconsecutive lines are considered separate messages.

Additionally, a streamed message event may optionally include a unique id, as in the following:

```
id: 123456789\n
data: some data here\n
data: more data\n\n
```

You may also add a "retry" with the message. The browser attempts to reconnect to the event source approximately three seconds after each connection is closed. You can change the default timeout by including a line beginning with `retry:` followed by the number of milliseconds to wait before trying to reconnect.

```
id: 123456789\n
retry: 5000\n
data: some data here\n
data: more data\n\n
```

Creating an EventSource

The EventSource constructor function takes two arguments. The first argument specifies the absolute URL to which to connect (e.g., the PHP). The second argument is optional settings such as the use of withCredentials.

```
var evtSrc = new EventSource('serversideScript.php');
```

The EventSource properties

Property	Description
readyState	This represents the state of the connection. It can have the following values:

	CONNECTING (numeric value 0) The connection has not yet been established, or it was closed and the user agent is reconnecting. OPEN (numeric value 1) The user agent has an open connection and is dispatching events as it receives them. CLOSED (numeric value 2) The connection is not open, and the user agent is not trying to reconnect. Either there was a fatal error, or the `close()` method was invoked.

The EventSource events

Events	Description
onopen	When a connection to the server is opened
onmessage	When a message is received
onerror	When an error occurs

The advantages of server-sent events

These are the advantages of server-sent events:

- Servers can push data to the client without requiring an initial HTTP request, thereby reducing network traffic.
- The client simply needs to listen for messages.
- There are many use cases for data pushes (e.g., status updates, stock quotes, database updates).
- No special protocol is required as the messages are sent via HTTP.
- They conserve more battery power in comparison to XMLHttpRequests.
- The browser on a mobile device tied to a specific carrier may offload the management of the connection to a proxy on the network, which could result in a reduction of the mobile device's data usage and result in power saving.

The disadvantages of server-sent events

- No cross-site communication is allowed.

Server-sent events summary

- Create an EventSource object passing in the event stream URL (the server-side code, e.g PHP).
- Register event listeners on the EventSource object.
- Send an event stream from the server.

Exercise 17.1: Using server-sent events

In this exercise, you respond to a server-sent event. The event message is sent via the server-side language PHP. You listen for the message from the server and then display the message.

Objectives

After completing this exercise, you will be able to do the following:

- Create an EventSource.
- Listen for messages from the server.
- Display messages received from the server.

Step 1   Open the file "SSEvents-starter.html" in the server-sent-events-API folder.

Step 2   Run the page in the browser.

Step 3   Return to your editor and create a `<div>` element below the last button with an `id` of "output." Leave the div empty of content.

```
<div id="output"></div>
```

Step 4   Add a `<script>` block in the `<body>` section just before the closing `<body>` element (`</body>`).

Step 5   Declare an EventSource by invoking the `EventSource` object's constructor function, and name the variable "evtSource."

Step 6   Pass to the EventSource constructor function the location of the server-side PHP script.

```
<script>
    var evtSource = new EventSource('http://localhost/scripts/time.php');
</script>
```

Step 7   After the last line of code, declare a variable called "output" that references the output `<div>` you created earlier. Add the connStatus variable referencing the paragraph with the id of "connStatus."

```
var output = document.getElementById('output');
var connStatus = document.getElementById('connStatus');
```

Step 8   Add an event listener to the EventSource that listens for the message event and calls onMsg. Pass "false" as the last argument to indicate that you do not wish to capture the event on the capture phase.

```
evtSource.addEventListener('message', messageHandler, false);
```

Step 9   Write the onMsg event handler function as shown in bold below:

```
<script>
    var evtSource = new EventSource('http://localhost/scripts/time.php');
    var output = document.getElementById('output');
    evtSource.addEventListener('message', messageHandler, false);
    function messageHandler(evt){
        output.innerHTML += evt.data + '<br>';
    }
</script>
```

Step 10   Add two more functions for the close and reopen events, as shown below in bold.

```
<script>
    var evtSource = new EventSource('http://localhost/scripts/time.php');
    var output = document.getElementById('output');
    evtSource.addEventListener('message', messageHandler, false);
    function messageHandler(evt){
        output.innerHTML += evt.data + '<br>';
```

```
        }
        function closeConnection(){
            evtSource.close();
                output.innerHTML += "The Connection was closed.<br>";
        }
        function reOpen(){
            evtSource =  new EventSource('http://localhost/scripts/time.php');
            output.innerHTML += "The Connection was reopened.<br>";
                evtSource.addEventListener('message', messageHandler, false);
        }
    </script>
```

Step 11 Add onclick handlers to the buttons, as shown below in bold:

```
<button type="button" onclick="closeConnection()">Close Connection</button>
<button type="button" onclick="reOpen()">Reopen Connection</button>
```

Step 12 Save and test the file in the browser using the URL http://localhost, and then locate this file in the directory shown in the web browser.

Step 13 Locate the "message" event handler and add an event handler for the "onopen" event as shown below:

```
evtSource.addEventListener('onopen', getStatus, false);
```

Step 14 Call the `getStatus()` method from the `messageHandler()` event handler as shown below in bold:

```
function messageHandler(evt){
        output.innerHTML += evt.data + '<br>';
        getStatus();
}
```

Step 15 Write the `getStatus()` method below the messageHandler function.

```
function getStatus(){
    if(evtSource.readyState == 0) {
    connStatus.innerHTML = "readyState = 0 CONNECTING The connection is being
established.";
    }
    else if(evtSource.readyState == 1) {
    connStatus.innerHTML = "readyState = 1 OPEN The connection is open and
dispatching events.";
    }
    else if(evtSource.readyState == 2) {
    connStatus.innerHTML = "readyState = 2 CLOSED The connection is not being
established, has been closed, or there was a fatal error.";
    }
}
```

Step 16 Save and test the file in the browser using the URL http://localhost, and then locate this file in the directory shown in the web browser.

Step 17 From the scripts directory of your data files, open the file "hot.txt" The text file contains only the number 1.

Step 18 Modify the file "SSEvents-starter.html" as shown below in bold and save the file.

```
var evtSource = new EventSource('http://localhost/scripts/time-conditional.
php');
```

Step 19   Save and test the file in the browser using the URL http://localhost, and then locate this file in the directory shown in the web browser.

Time Console:

readyState = 1 The connection is open and dispatching events.

[Close Connection] [Reopen Connection]
server time at hot data: 08:37:47
server time at hot data: 08:38:02
server time at hot data: 08:38:20
server time at hot data: 08:38:35
server time at hot data: 08:38:50

Note   The server should be serving the time to the client web browser as shown below.

Note   Be sure to have Chrome's Developer Tools open and trace the network traffic through the Network tab. You should no longer see periodic requests for the PHP file as the server-sent message is now dependent on the condition of the text in hot.txt.

Step 20   Now, using the "hot.txt" file, change the "1" to a "2", and save the file.

Step 21   Revisit the page in the browser; the server should now stop sending the message to the client.

Note: Once the value of hot.txt has changed to "2," you will begin to see periodic requests to time-conditional.php.

Step 22   Return the value of hot.txt to a value of "1" and save the file.

Step 23   Revisit the page in the browser, and the network traffic should reveal an end to repeated requests to time-conditional.php.

Step 24   You may now close all open files.

Exercise summary

In this exercise, you learned how to use server-sent events so that the client can receive periodic messages from the server.

Resources

W3C specification: http://www.w3.org/TR/eventsource/

Scaling Server-sent Events slideshow: http://www.slideshare.net/cdmalord/addressing-the-scalability-challenge-of-server-sent-events-presentation

Server-sent Events articles:

http://www.eriwen.com/javascript/server-sent-events/

http://www.sitepoint.com/server-sent-events/

Chapter summary

In this chapter, you learned the API responsible for providing server-side pushes of data from the server to the client. You learned the advantages and disadvantages of this technique. You learned the `EventSource` object and its properties, methods, and events.

Chapter 18

Canvas APIs

In this chapter, you will create a 2D drawing surface with the <canvas> element. You will programmatically "draw" on the canvas with JavaScript.

The Canvas 2D Context specification became a W3C Candidate Recommendation on July 2, 2015.

The WHATWG specification document:
https://html.spec.whatwg.org/multipage/scripting.html#the-canvas-element.

Objectives

❏   Describe the new <canvas> element and its attributes.

❏   Explain what the <canvas> element is used for.

❏   Understand when to use the new <canvas> element and attributes.

❏   Determine which browsers support the <canvas> element.

❏   Explain the canvas Application Programming Interface (API).

❏   Use the new <canvas> element.

❏   Draw with JavaScript using the canvas API.

❏   Determine browser support for the new <canvas> element.

Introduction

HTML5 introduces the `<canvas>` element that is used to create a 2D and 3D drawing surface. Currently the canvas supports only 2D drawing. The actual drawing is accomplished via JavaScript.

The `<canvas>` element provides scripts with a resolution-dependent bitmap canvas, which can be used for rendering charts and graphs, game graphics, or other visual images.

Developers should not use the `<canvas>` element in a document when a more suitable element is available. For example, it is inappropriate to use a `<canvas>` element to render a page heading. If the desired presentation of the heading is graphically intense, it should be marked up using appropriate elements (typically `<h1>`) and then styled using CSS and supporting technologies.[1]

What are the new elements?

Only one new element has been added: `<canvas>`.

The `<canvas>` element attributes

Attribute	Value	What it's used for
width	Valid non-negative integer	Defines the width of the canvas.
height	Valid non-negative integer	Defines the height of the canvas.

Why use the Canvas API?

The `<canvas>` element provides a drawing surface that is used to render graphics at runtime with JavaScript. Use cases for the `<canvas>` tag include dynamically generated charts and graphs and even logos and sketches if they are user-driven.

Canvas quick summary

- Artwork is rendered at runtime via JavaScript
- `<canvas>` element creates a 300 pixel wide by 150 pixel tall rectangular drawing surface
- Canvas includes an API for drawing
- Should not be used when another HTML element would suffice (ie. header, image, etc.)
- Includes a 2D and 3D context

Uses for the new <canvas> element

- Programmatically draw vector art on your web page
- Create user-driven artwork such as graphs and charts
- Dynamically change the vector art on your web page

For the most recent tables regarding browser support, please see http://caniuse.com.

---

1   http://www.w3.org/TR/html5/the-canvas-element.html#the-canvas-element

Exercise 18.1 Detecting browser support for `<canvas>`

In this exercise, you will determine if the user's browser will support the canvas API. You will use JavaScript to detect support for the HTML5 <canvas> element.

Objectives

After completing this exercise, you will be able to do the following:

- Use JavaScript to determine if the browser supports the new `<canvas>` element.

Step 1   Open the file "canvas-support-starter.html" from the canvas-API folder.

Step 2   Create a `<script>` block in the `<head>` section and write the following JavaScript:

```
<script>
        var testCanvas = document.createElement("canvas");
        var canvasCheck=(testCanvas.getContext)? true : false;
        console.log("Canvas support = " + canvasCheck);
</script>
```

The first line of JavaScript creates a sample `<canvas>` element. Line two checks if the canvas object supports the `getContext()` method which is a method of the `<canvas>` element. The last line creates a log statement that indicates "true" if the browser supports the `<canvas>` element.

Step 3   Save and test the file in a web browser. You may now close all files.

In a real-world application the canvas API's logic would only take place if the web browser supported the `<canvas>` element.

Exercise outcome

This exercise results in a log statement to the console indicating support or lack of support for the `<canvas>` element.

Exercise summary

In this exercise you used a JavaScript technique for determining if the end user's web browser supports the new HTML5 `<canvas>` element. After dynamically creating a `<canvas>` element, you determine browser support by checking for the existence of a property or method of the canvas API which in this case was the `getContext()` method.

Exercise 18.2 Resizing the canvas

In this exercise, you will resize and style the <canvas> element using JavaScript.

Objectives

After completing this exercise, you will be able to do the following:

- Style the canvas with CSS.
- Resize the canvas with JavaScript.

Step 1   Open the file "canvas-resize-starter.html" from the canvas-API folder.

Step 2   Change the `<canvas>` elements `width` and `height` properties to 200 pixels as shown below in bold.

```
<canvas id="myCanvas" width="200" height="200">
        <p>Your browser does not support the Canvas element.</p>
</canvas>
```

Step 3   Create a style block and style the new `<canvas>` element with an id selector as shown:

```
<style>
    #myCanvas  {
                 border: dashed 1px black;
            }
</style>
```

Step 4   Save and test the file. You should see a dashed, one-pixel, black border surrounding the perimeter of the `<canvas>` element.

Step 5   Note the "Resize Canvas" button and its onClick event handler.

Step 6   In the `<head>` section, create an onClick handler for the "Resize Canvas" button as shown.

```
<script>
    function resizeCanvas() {
            var myCanvas = document.getElementById('myCanvas')
            myCanvas.width = 400;
            myCanvas.height = 400;
            }
</script>
```

Step 7   Run the page in all web browsers and click the "Resize Canvas" button. Note the size change of the canvas. You may now close all files.

Exercise summary

In this exercise, you programmatically changed the height and width of the canvas using JavaScript.

Exercise 18.3 Drawing rectangles on `<canvas>`

In this exercise, you will programmatically draw a rectangle on the canvas using JavaScript.

Objectives

After completing this exercise, you will be able to do the following:

- Use JavaScript to draw a rectangle on the canvas.
- Fill a rectangular shape on the canvas.
- Place an outline (stroke) around a rectangular shape on the canvas.
- Clear a rectangular shape on the canvas.
- Set canvas properties.

Step 1   Open the file "rectangles-starter.html" from the canvas-API folder.

Step 2   Create a `<script>` block in the `<head>` section and write the following `drawOnCanvas()` function:

```
<script>
function drawOnCanvas() {
        var canvas = document.getElementById('myCanvas');
        var context = canvas.getContext('2d');
        context.strokeRect(0,0,canvas.width,canvas.height);
        context.fillRect(25, 25, 100, 50);
        context.clearRect(30, 30, 75, 25);
}
</script>
```

The first line of code obtains the `<canvas>` element with the id `myCanvas`. In order to "draw" on the canvas, the context must be obtained with the canvas API method called `getContext()`. The remaining lines of code perform the actual "drawing." The `strokeRect()` method draws a rectangular outline. The `fillRect()` method draws a filled rectangle and the `clearRect()` clears the specified area making it fully transparent.

`//fillRect(x,y,width,height)`   Draws a filled rectangle

`//strokeRect(x,y,width,height)` Draws a rectangular outline

`//clearRect(x,y,width,height)`   Clears the specified area and makes it fully transparent

Step 3   Call the function by adding an `onClick` handler to the button as shown below in bold.

```
<input type="button" id="drawCanvas" value="Draw on Canvas" onclick="drawOn-
Canvas()"/>
```

Step 4   Run the page in all web browsers and click the "Draw on Canvas" button. You should see three rectangles drawn inside of the canvas. You may now close all files.

Exercise summary

In this exercise, you used JavaScript to access the canvas API methods that allow you to draw, fill, clear and outline rectangles on the canvas.

Exercise 18.4 Drawing arcs on the `<canvas>`

In this exercise, you will draw an arc on the canvas using JavaScript.

Objectives

- After completing this exercise, you will be able to do the following:
- Use JavaScript to draw on the canvas
- Draw an arc on the canvas
- Stroke (outline) the arc

Step 1   Open the file "arcs-starter.html" from the canvas-API folder.

Step 2   Note the `<canvas>` element with the id `myCanvas` in the `<body>` section of the page.

Step 3   Inside the`<script>` block in the `<head>` section, modify the following `drawArc()` function as shown below in bold:

```
<script>
    function drawArc() {
        var canvas = document.getElementById('myCanvas');
        var context = canvas.getContext('2d');
        //arc(x, y, radius, startAngle, endAngle, anticlockwise)
        context.arc(75,75,35,0,Math.PI,false);
        context.stroke();
    }
</script>
```

As in previous exercises, the first line of JavaScript gains access to the canvas object storing it in the variable called "canvas." Line two gets the canvas context. Remember that at the time of publication only 2D canvases are supported. Next, the `arc()` method of the canvas object is called. Six parameters may be passed to this method. The x and y point at which to begin the arc, the radius of the arc, the start angle and the end angle followed by the direction of the arc, which is determined by passing true for anticlockwise and false (the default) for a clockwise direction. The last line renders an outline (stroke) to the arc.

Step 4   Call the `drawArc()` function from the onload event on the `<body>` element as shown in bold below:

```
<body onload="drawArc();">
```

Step 5   Save and test the file in a web browser. You should see an arc drawn on the canvas.

Step 6   Try changing some of the arguments passed into the arc method and view the results in the browser. You may now close all files.

Exercise summary

In this exercise, you used JavaScript to create an arc on the canvas. The canvas object's API method called was the `arc()` method and the arc was outlined with the `stroke()` method.

Exercise 18.5 Drawing quadratic curves

In this exercise, you will draw a quadratic curve on the canvas using JavaScript.

Objectives

After completing this exercise, you will be able to do the following:

- Use JavaScript to draw on the canvas.
- Draw a quadratic curve on the canvas.
- Outline the quadratic curve.

Step 1   Open the file "quad-curves-starter.html" from the canvas-API folder.

Step 2   Note the `<canvas>` element with the id "myCanvas" in the `<body>` section of the page.

Step 3   Inside the `<script>` block in the `<head>` section and modify the following `drawQuadCurve()` function as shown below in bold:

```
<script>
    function drawQuadCurve() {
        var canvas = document.getElementById('myCanvas');
        var context = canvas.getContext('2d');
        context.beginPath();
        context.moveTo(25,75);
        //quadraticCurveTo(cp1x, cp1y, x, y)
        context.quadraticCurveTo(135, 0, 275, 75);
        context.stroke();
    }
</script>
```

As in previous exercises, the first line of JavaScript gains access to the canvas object, storing it in the variable called "canvas." Line two gets the canvas context. Next, the `beginPath()` method of the canvas object is called. The `moveTo()` method sets the starting point of the curve. Imagine holding a pencil and moving your hand to the location where you wish to begin to draw. The `moveTo()` method takes two parameters which represent the x and y coordinate within the canvas where your vector shape will begin. Next, we call the `quadraticCurveTo()` method, passing to it four arguments. The first control point's x coordinate, the first control point's y coordinate, and the x and y coordinates of the curve itself. Finally the `stroke()` method applies the outline to the curve.

Step 4   Call the `drawQuadCurve()` function from the onload event on the `<body>` element as shown in bold below:

```
<body onload="drawQuadCurve();">
```

Step 5   Save and test the file in a web browser. You should see a quadratic curve drawn on the canvas.

Step 6   Try changing some of the arguments passed into the quadraticCurveTo() method and view the results in the browser. You may now close all files.

Exercise summary

In this exercise, you used JavaScript to create a quadratic curve on the canvas. The canvas object's API method called was the `quadraticCurveTo()` method and the arc was outlined with the `stroke()` method.

Exercise 18.6 Drawing Bézier curves on the `<canvas>`

In this exercise, you will draw a Bézier curve with JavaScript using two control points on the canvas.

Objectives

After completing this exercise, you will be able to do the following:

- Use JavaScript to draw on the canvas.
- Draw a Bézier curve on the canvas.
- Outline the Bézier curve.

Step 1   Open the file "bezier-curves-starter.html" from the canvas-API folder.

Step 2   Note the `<canvas>` element with the id "myCanvas" in the `<body>` section of the page.

Step 3   Inside the `<script>` block in the `<head>` section and modify the following **drawBezierCurve()** function as shown below in bold:

```
<script>
    function drawBezierCurve() {
        var canvas = document.getElementById('myCanvas');
        var context = canvas.getContext('2d');
        context.beginPath();
        context.moveTo(25,75);
        //bezierCurveTo(cp1x, cp1y, cp2x, cp2y, x, y)
        context.bezierCurveTo(75, 37, 70, 25, 50, 25);
        context.stroke();
    }
</script>
```

As in previous exercises, the first line of JavaScript gains access to the canvas object storing it in the variable called "canvas." Line two gets the canvas context. Next, the `beginPath()` method of the canvas object is called. The `moveTo()` method sets the starting point of the curve. Imagine holding a pencil and moving your hand to the location where you wish to begin to draw. The `moveTo()` method takes two parameters which represent the x and y coordinate within the canvas where your vector shape will begin. Next, we call the `bezierCurveTo()` method, passing to it six arguments: The first control point's x coordinate, the first control point's y coordinate, the second control point's x coordinate and the second control point's y coordinate followed by the x and y coordinates of the curve itself. Finally the `stroke()` methods applies the outline to the curve.

Step 4   Call the `drawBezierCurve ()` function from the onload event on the `<body>` element as shown in bold below:

```
<body onload="drawBezierCurve();">
```

Step 5   Save and test the file in a web browser. You should see a bezier curve on the canvas. You may now close all files.

Step 6   Try changing some of the arguments passed into the drawBezierCurve () method and view the results in the browser. You may now close all open files.

Exercise summary

In this exercise, you used JavaScript to create a Bézier curve on the canvas. The canvas object's API method called was the `bezierCurveTo()` method and the curve was outlined with the `stroke()` method.

Exercise 18.7 Creating a linear gradient

In this exercise, you will create a linear gradient on the canvas using JavaScript.

Objectives

After completing this exercise, you will be able to do the following:

- Use JavaScript to render a linear gradient.
- Draw a rectangle and fill it with a linear gradient.

Step 1   Open the file "linear-gradient-starter.html" from the canvas-API folder.

Step 2   Create a `<canvas>` element with the id "myCanvas" in the `<body>` section of the page as shown below:

```
<canvas id="myCanvas" width="600" height="100">
```

Step 3   Inside the `<script>` block above the closing `</body>` element modify the following JavaScript as shown below in bold.

```
<script>
    var canvas = document.getElementById("myCanvas");
    var context = canvas.getContext("2d");
    var grad = context.createLinearGradient(0,0,175,50);
    grad.addColorStop(0,"#FF0000");
    grad.addColorStop(1,"#00FF00");
    context.fillStyle = grad;
    context.fillRect(0,0,175,50);
</script>
```

As in previous exercises, the first line of JavaScript gains access to the canvas object storing it in the variable called "canvas." Line two gets the canvas context. The third line creates a variable called "grad" that creates the gradient. The `createLinearGradient()` method is passed to the beginning x and y coordinates followed by the end x and y coordinates. The colors of the gradient are created with the `addColorStop()` method, which accepts two arguments: the offset and the color value. The offset is measured with a number between 0 and 1. Finally the `fillStyle()` property of the context is set to the gradient and the `fillRect()` method is called to create the rectangle.

Step 4   Save and test the file in a web browser. You should see a linear gradient drawn on the canvas that gradiates from red to green changing colors at the 50% point.

Step 5   Try changing some of the color stops and view the results in the browser.

Step 6   Try adding some new color stops and view the results in the browser.

Step 7   You may now close all open files.

Exercise summary

In this exercise, you used JavaScript to create a linear gradient that was then applied as the fill style for a rectangle.

Exercise 18.8   Creating a pattern on the `<canvas>`

In this exercise, you will create a repeating pattern on the canvas using JavaScript.

Objectives

After completing this exercise, you will be able to do the following:

- Use JavaScript to render a pattern on the canvas.
- Create an image object to use for the pattern.

Step 1   Open the file "pattern-starter.html" from the canvas-API folder.

Step 2   Create a `<canvas>` element with the id "myCanvas" in the `<body>` section of the page with a width of 1024 pixels and a height of 200 pixels.

Step 3   Inside the `<script>` block in the `<head>` section modify the following JavaScript as shown in bold below:

```
<script>
    window.onload = function() {
        var canvas = document.getElementById("myCanvas");
        var context = canvas.getContext("2d");
        var imageObj = new Image();
        imageObj.onload = function()
          {
            var pattern = context.createPattern(imageObj, "repeat-x");
            context.rect(10, 10, canvas.width - 20, canvas.height - 20);
            context.fillStyle = pattern;
            context.fill();
          };
        imageObj.src = "images/samplePNG.png";
    };
</script>
```

As in previous exercises, the first line of JavaScript gains access to the canvas object storing it in the variable called "canvas." Line two gets the canvas context. The third line creates a new image object. The next line responds to the loading of the image by executing the function, which creates a pattern out of the image and repeats the image along the x axis of its painted area. A rectangle is created which will be filled with the pattern created. Finally the source of the image object is set to the image "samplePNG. png."

Step 4   Save and test the file in a web browser. You should see several images of dice repeated across the canvas from left to right.

Step 5   Try changing some of the arguments passed to the createPattern method and view the results in the browser. You may now close all files.

Exercise summary

In this exercise, you used JavaScript to create a pattern that was then applied as the fill style for a rectangle.

Exercise 18.9 Canvas Demos

In this exercise, you will review some demo files to better understand the capabilities of the `<canvas>` element and drawing API.

Objectives

After completing this exercise, you will be able to do the following:

- Use JavaScript to render a simple pie chart.
- Use JavaScript to create a more sophisticated pie chart.
- Understand the globalCompositeOperation property to create overlapping shape effects.
- Render text on the canvas.

Step 1   Open the Demo files in this chapters' demos folder and review the code with your instructor.

Step 2   Visit the following sites to view excellent examples of the new HTML5 Canvas:

- http://ie.microsoft.com/testdrive/Graphics/WorkerFountains/Default.html
- http://williancarvalho.com/catcher/
- http://gyu.que.jp/jscloth/
- http://andrew-hoyer.com/experiments/cloth/
- http://experiments.lionel.me/blocs/
- http://davidwalsh.name/canvas-demos
- http://webdev.stephband.info/parallax_demos.html
- http://www.effectgames.com/demos/canvascycle/
- http://www.paulbrunt.co.uk/bert/
- http://www.mrspeaker.net/dev/parcycle/

Step 3   Compare programmatic drawing on the canvas with the Scalable Vector Graphics demos found in the SVG folder in the canvas-API directory.

Challenge Exercise 19A: Build a canvas page

Step 1   Open the file called "canvas-challenge-starter.html" from the challenge subdirectory inside of the canvas-API folder.

Step 2   Use a canvas element and JavaScript to create the basic structure for the following screen.

Chapter summary

In this chapter, you were introduced to the HTML5 canvas and its associated API. You created the canvas and then programmatically drew on the canvas with JavaScript. There is much more to this powerful drawing API and you can find more information in the resources section for this chapter.

Chapter 19

Geolocation APIs

In this chapter, you will use geolocation information provided to the web browser by the device running the browser. This information is used by the geolocation API and may include the position coordinates: latitude and longitude, the accuracy of the position, altitude and altitude accuracy.

The Geolcation API specification became a W3C Candidate Recommendation on October 24, 2013.

Objectives

- ☐ Describe the geolocation API.

- ☐ Understand the geolocation object.

- ☐ List the geolocation objects' methods.

- ☐ Understand the position object.

- ☐ Understand the position interface attributes.

- ☐ Check for browser support of geolocation.

- ☐ Find the user's location.

- ☐ Use the user's location to create a Google map.

Introduction

Geolocation is a feature of many mobile devices including smart phones that provide the user with their current geographic location based on latitude and longitude. Geolocation is an API that allows the programmer to utilize the mechanism within a device to determine its geographic location. Handheld devices, such as smart phones use a variety of methods to ascertain their location including built-in GPS as well as several methods of triangulation that involve the use of nearby cell phone towers or hot-spots such as WiFi with MAC (media access control) addresses from either RFID (radio frequency identification), Wi-Fi or Bluetooth. Some older devices also use the Global System for Mobile Communications (GSM) or Code Division Multiple Access (CDM) identifications. CDM is a competing cell phone service technology to GSM.

What is the geolocation API used for?

Any time your application would benefit from knowing the user's location, you can use the geolocation API. You should bear in mind, however, that not all of the methods used by the device have a high degree of accuracy, so as with all things web related, you will need to determine if geolocation is appropriate for your project.

Browser Support for geolocation

For the most recent tables regarding browsers support please see http://caniuse.com.

The Geolocation API

"The Geolocation object is used by scripts to programmatically determine the location information associated with the hosting device. The location information is acquired by applying a user-agent specific algorithm, creating a Position object, and populating that object with appropriate data accordingly.

Objects implementing the Navigator interface (e.g., the window.navigator object) must also implement the NavigatorGeolocation interface [NAVIGATOR]. An instance of NavigatorGeolocation would be then obtained by using binding-specific casting methods on an instance of Navigator." [1]

The geolocation object is a property of the navigator object. If the object exists, geolocation services are available on the device. No method of the geolocation object may be invoked until the user provides permission to share their location.

---

1   http://dev.w3.org/geo/api/spec-source.html

The Geolocation object methods

Method	Description
getCurrentPosition()	Returns the current location (single fixed location) of the device (web browser, cell phone, etc.)
	Arguments: 1. Callback function to be executed if position is determined. 2. Callback function to be executed if device fails to determine position. 3. Options: maximum age of the position returned and the time to wait for a request
watchPosition()	Returns the current location of the device and provides a mechanism for responding to updated position data.
	Arguments: 1. Callback function to be executed once after the position is initially determined, and optionally multiple times thereafter if the position data has changed. 2. Callback function to be executed if device fails to determine position. 3. Options: maximum age of the position returned and the time to wait for a request.
clearWatch()	Checks the value of its watchID argument. If it is a valid and previously started watch process it stops the watch process preventing any further callbacks from being invoked.
	Arguments: 1. WatchID

The position options object properties

Properties	Description
enableHighAccuracy	The enableHighAccuracy attribute provides a hint that the application would like to receive the best possible results. This may result in slower response times or increased power consumption. The user might also deny this capability, or the device might not be able to provide more accurate results than if the flag wasn't specified. The intended purpose of this attribute is to allow applications to inform the implementation that they do not require high accuracy geolocation fixes and, therefore, the implementation can avoid using geolocation providers that consume a significant amount of power (e.g., GPS). This is especially useful for applications running on battery-powered devices, such as mobile phones. [1]
timeout	The timeout attribute denotes the maximum length of time (expressed in milliseconds) that is allowed to pass from the call to getCurrentPosition() or watchPosition() until the corresponding successCallback is invoked. If the implementation is unable to successfully acquire a new position before the given timeout elapses, and no other errors have occurred in this interval, then the corresponding errorCallback must be invoked with a PositionError object whose code attribute is set to TIMEOUT. Note that the time that is spent obtaining the user permission is not included in the period covered by the timeout attribute. The timeout attribute only applies to the location acquisition operation. [14]
maximumAge	The maximumAge attribute indicates that the application is willing to accept a cached position whose age is no greater than the specified time in milliseconds. If maximumAge is set to zero, the implementation must immediately attempt to acquire a new position object. Setting the maximumAge to infinity must determine the implementation to return a cached position regardless of its age. If an implementation does not have a cached position available whose age is no greater than the specified maximumAge, then it must acquire a new position object. In case of a watchPosition(), the maximumAge refers to the first position object returned by the implementation.

The position interface

The position interface is the container for the geolocation information returned by this API. This version of the specification allows one attribute of type coordinates and a timestamp. Future versions of the API may allow additional attributes that provide other information about this position (e.g. street addresses). The timestamp attribute represents the time when the position object was acquired in the form of a DOMTimeStamp which represents a number of milliseconds.

The position interface attributes

Properties	Description
latitude longitude	Geographic coordinates specified in decimal degrees.
altitude	Denotes the height of the position, specified in meters above the [WGS84] ellipsoid. If the implementation cannot provide altitude information, the value of the attribute must be null.
accuracy	Denotes the accuracy level of the latitude and longitude coordinates. It is specified in meters and must be supported by all implementations. The value of the accuracy attribute must be a non-negative real number.
altitudeAccuracy	The attribute is specified in meters. If the implementation cannot provide altitude information, the value of this attribute must be null. Otherwise, the value of the altitudeAccuracy attribute must be a non-negative real number.
The accuracy and altitudeAccuracy values returned by an implementation should correspond to a 95% confidence level. meaning that 95% of reported positions fall within the radius of the accuracy amount (meters)	
heading	The attribute denotes the direction of travel of the hosting device and is specified in degrees, where 0° ≤ heading < 360°, counting clockwise relative to true north. If the implementation cannot provide heading information, the value of this attribute must be null. If the hosting device is stationary (i.e., the value of the speed attribute is 0), then the value of the heading attribute must be NaN.
speed	Denotes the magnitude of the horizontal component of the hosting device's current velocity and is specified in meters per second. If the implementation cannot provide speed information, the value of this attribute must be null. Otherwise, the value of the speed attribute must be a non-negative real number. [2]
timestamp	Property returns the time when the position location was obtained as a DOMTimestamp. A DOMTimeStamp represents a number of milliseconds.

Exercise 19.1 Checking for geolocation support

In this exercise, you will check for browser support for the geolocation API.

Objectives

After completing this exercise, you will be able to do the following:

- Use JavaScript to test for browser support of geolocation.

Step 1   Open the file "geolocation-support-starter.html" in the geolocation-API folder.

Step 2   Notice the `<div>` element that follows the `<h1>` below the `<body>` element.

You will use this div tag to let the user know if their browser supports the geolocation API. The `<div>` tag contains a `<p>` or paragraph element with an id of "status." The paragraph contains the sentence "HTML5 Geolocation is not supported in your browser." You will write a JavaScript that determines if the browser supports geolocation, and if it does, you will dynamically change the contents of that paragraph to read "HTML5 Geolocation is supported in your browser," and then you will determine the browsers location and display longitude and latitude coordinates.

Step 3   Create a script block inside the `<head>` element and write the following JavaScript:

```
<script type="text/javascript">
    function loadGeoData() {
        if(navigator.geolocation) {
            document.getElementById("status").innerHTML = "HTML5 Geolocation is
supported in your browser.";
        }
        else {
            document.getElementById("status").innerHTML = "HTML5 Geolocation is
not supported in your browser.";
        }
    }
</script>
```

The function `loadGeoData()` determines browser support of geolocation by placing the navigator's geolocation property within an if block. If the property exists, the browsers supports geolocation and returns "true"; if the navigator object does not have a geolocation property, then the browser does not support geolocation and the if condition returns "false."

Should the if block return true, the document object's `getElementById()` method is invoked and passes the argument "status" which is the id property of the `<div>` element. After obtaining the `<div>` element, the inner HTML code is replaced with the string "HTML5 Geolocation is supported in your browser."

Step 4   Call the `loadGeoData()` method from the onload event of the `<body>` element as shown below in bold:

`<body onload="loadGeoData()">`

Step 5   Save and test the file in all web browsers.

Step 6   You many now close the file.

Exercise outcome

This exercise results in the appearance of a paragraph in the web browser that indicates support or lack of support for the geolocation API.

Exercise summary

In this exercise, you learned how to use JavaScript to test for browser support of geolocation.

Exercise 19.2 Finding the user's location

In this exercise, you acquire the location of the end user's device.

Objectives

After completing this exercise, you will be able to do the following:

- Use JavaScript to find the user's position.
- Use the `getCurrentPosition()` method of the geolocation object.
- Understand the properties of the position object including the `coords` property which contains latitude and longitude properties.

Step 1   Open the file "geolocation-starter.html" in the geolocation-API folder.

Step 2   Locate the `loadGeoData` function and call the `getCurrentPosition()` method of the geolocation object which is property of the navigator object. You will pass one argument to the method: the `updateLocation` function. This is the callback function to be executed if the position coordinates are returned by the web browser. This line of code is shown below in bold.

```
function loadGeoData() {
        if(navigator.geolocation) {
        document.getElementById("status").innerHTML = "HTML5 Geolocation is
supported in your browser.";
        navigator.geolocation.getCurrentPosition(updateLocation);
          }
  }
```

Note   It is a best practice to include an error handler in the call to `getCurrentPosition()`.

Step 3   Below the `loadGeoData()` function, write the `updateLocation()` method that will be invoked when the `getCurrentPosition()` method returns a position.

```
function updateLocation(position) {
        var latitude = position.coords.latitude;
        var longitude = position.coords.longitude;
        if (!latitude || !longitude) {
          document.getElementById("status").innerHTML = "HTML5 Geolocation
is supported in your browser, but your location is currently not available.";
          return;
        }
    document.getElementById('atitude').innerHTML = latitude;
    document.getElementById('longitude').innerHTML = longitude;
      }
```

The `updateLocation` function is passed the position returned by the `getCurrentPosition` method. Two variables are created called `latitude` and `longitude`, and their values are set by the position object's coords property which itself has the properties: latitude and longitude. If either of these values don't exist, then the status span element's innerHTML is set to: "HTML5 Geolocation is supported in your browser, but location is currently not available." Should the if block returns "false," the code below the if block is executed. These two lines of code get the latitude and longitude elements and set their innerHTML to the value of the variables of the same name that are storing the latitude and longitude from the position object.

Step 4   Save and test the file in all web browsers.

Step 5   Within the web page you should see a latitude and longitude value appear in the table. You may now close the file.

Step 6   The code used in this exercise if available online.

If you have a smart phone, try going to the following URL:

http://www.kevinruse.com/geo.html

Step 7   Write down the latitude and longitude returned and compare it with others in the class.

Step 8   You may now close all open files.

Exercise summary

In this exercise, you located the user's latitude and longitude coordinates and tested your code on both your desktop web browser and mobile device.

Optional exercise: Unobtrusive JavaScript and jQuery

Step 1   Rename "geolocation-starter.html" to "geolocation-A.html"

Step 2   Modify the file to reference an external JavaScript named "geolocation_unobtrusive.js"

Step 3   Move the JavaScript from the HTML file to the new JavaScript file and edit the JavaScript to use jQuery.

Step 4   Save and test the new HTML file that now uses unobtrusive JavaScript. If you get stuck, the finished file is located in the scripts folder of this chapter's data files.

Exercise 19.3   Display location with Google Maps

In this exercise, you will acquire the location of the end user's device and display it in the browser with Google Maps. The Google Maps JavaScript API lets you embed Google Maps in your web pages. The Google Maps API is beyond the scope of this course but you can learn more about writing JavaScript to access Google Maps at http://code.google. com/apis/maps/documentation/javascript/tutorial.html, and the documentation may be found at https://developers. google.com/maps/documentation/javascript/reference.

Objectives

After completing this exercise, you will be able to do the following:

- Obtain the Google Maps JavaScript library.
- Write a function that uses the position properties to create a Google map.
- Display the Google map with a marker on the user's location.

Step 1 Open the file "google-map-starter.html" in the geolocation-API folder.

Step 2 Create a script tag to access the Google Maps JavaScript:

```
<script src="http://maps.google.com/maps/api/js?sensor=false"></script>
```

Remember from the previous exercises that the getCurrentPosition() method accepts two parameters that are callback functions: one is invoked when a position is successfully returned and the other is invoked when the getCurrentPosition() method fails to return a position. In the next step you will write these two functions which we will call success() and error().

Step 3 Create a <script> block below the first script element and write the following two functions (don't forget to pass the position parameter):

```
function success(position) {
}
function error() {
}
```

We'll begin with the "success" function, which will notify the user that their position has been found, and we will create and display a Google map with a marker indicating the user's location. The JavaScript will accomplish this by doing the following:

1. Locate the <span> element with the id of "status."
2. Do nothing if the classname associated with status is equal to "success."
3. Set the innerHTML of the status span to read: "The browser has found your location."
4. Create a <div> element to store the map.
5. Set the id, height and width properties of the new <div>.
6. Locate the <article> element and add the new <div> as a child of the <article> element.
7. Create a variable to store the Google app information which is obtained via the Google Maps LatLng()
   method and passing to it the position from getCurrentPosition().
8. Set the Google Maps options.
9. Create a map object.
10. Create a map marker and set its options.

Step 4 Complete the following success() function:

```
function success(position)  {
        var status = document.querySelector('#status');
        if (status.className == 'success') {
            return;
        }
        status.innerHTML = "The browser has found your location.";
        status.className = 'Success';
        var mapcanvas = document.createElement('div');
        mapcanvas.id = 'mapcanvas';
        mapcanvas.style.height = '400px';
        mapcanvas.style.width = '560px';
        document.querySelector('div').appendChild(mapcanvas);
        var latlng = new google.maps.LatLng(position.coords.latitude,
        position.coords.longitude);
```

```
            var myOptions = {
                zoom: 15,
                center: latlng,
                mapTypeControl: false,
                navigationControlOptions: {style:
                        google.maps.NavigationControlStyle.SMALL},
                        mapTypeId: google.maps.MapTypeId.ROADMAP
            };
            var map = new  google.maps.Map(document.getElementById("mapcanvas"),
        myOptions);
            var marker = new google.maps.Marker({
            position: latlng,
            map: map,
            title:"You are here!"
            });
    }
```

The error() method will notify the user of their status by setting the status <span> elements class to "fail."

Step 5   Write the error() function and pass in a msg argument.

```
function error(msg) {
        var status = document.querySelector('#status');
        status.innerHTML = typeof msg === 'string' ? msg : "failed";
        status.className = 'fail';
}
```

You may have noticed that we have not yet called the geolocation's getCurrentPosition() method. You will do that now.

Step 6   Write an "if" block to test for browser support and invoke the getCurrentPosition() method. If the browser does not support geolocation invoke the error() method and pass "not supported" as the msg argument. This code should go below the error() function (but not inside the function).

```
if (navigator.geolocation){
        navigator.geolocation.getCurrentPosition(success, error);
    } else {
            error('not supported');
    }
```

Step 7   Save and test the file in all web browsers. You should see a Google Map in the web browser showing a marker that indicates your position on the map.

Close the file.

The code used in this exercise if available online.

If you have a smart phone, try going to the following URL:

http://www.kevinruse.com/geoMap.html

Step 10   Compare the Google map with others in the class.

Exercise summary

In this exercise, you created a Google map that marked the user's location.

Exercise 19.4 Obtaining position information

In this exercise, you acquire additional information about the user's position.

Objectives

After completing this exercise, you will be able to do the following:

- Read properties of the position object including altitude, accuracy, timestamp and altitudeAccuracy.

Step 1   Open the file "position-starter.html" in the geolocation-API folder.

Step 2   Locate the four buttons below the table and add event handlers as shown in bold below:

```
<input type="button" name="getAccuracy" id="getAccuracy" value="Get Accuracy"
onclick="getAccuracy();">
    <input type="button" name="getTimeStamp" id="getTimeStamp" value="Get
Time" onclick="getTimeStamp();">
    <input type="button" name="getAltitude" id="getAltitude" value="Get Alti-
tude" onclick="getAltitude();">
    <input type="button" name="getAltitudeAccuracy" id="getAltitudeAccuracy"
value="Get Altitude Accuracy" onclick="getAltitudeAccuracy();">
```

Step 3   Just below the `<script>` tag, declare four global variables to store the accuracy, altitude, timestamp and altitude accuracy.

```
<script>
var accuracy;
var timestamp;
var altitude;
var altitudeAccuracy;
```

Step 4   In the `updateLocation()` function (after latitude and longitude are declared) assign the values of the four variables declared in step 5. Add a date object, which will be used to convert the timestamp from milliseconds to a date.

```
accuracy = position.coords.accuracy;
timestamp = position.timestamp;
altitude = position.coords.altitude;
altitudeAccuracy = position.coords.altitudeAccuracy;
date = new Date(timestamp);
```

Step 5   Write four event handler functions that create alert boxes that display the accuracy, timestamp, altitude and altitude accuracy.

```
function getTimeStamp(){
        alert("Time position was acquired: " + date.toLocaleString());
    }
    function getAccuracy(){
```

```
        alert("Position was acquired with an accuracy of: " +  accuracy + "
meters");
    }
    function getAltitude(){
        alert("Position altitude is: " +  altitude + " meters");
    }
    function getAltitudeAccuracy(){
        alert("Positions Altitude Accuracy is: " + altitudeAccuracy);
    }
```

Step 6   Save and test the file in all web browsers. Click the four buttons and see if the information is returned.

Step 7   Close the file.

Step 8   The code used in this exercise if available online.

If you have a smart phone, try going to the following URL:

http://www.kevinruse.com/geoAccuracy.html

Step 9   Compare the results of clicking the buttons with others in the class.

Step 10   You may now close all open files.

Exercise summary

In this exercise, you read some of the properties of the position object to obtain further information such as the accuracy of the position in meters, the altitude, the accuracy of the altitude and the time the position was acquired in milliseconds.

Demo 19.1 Google Maps Demo

In this demonstration, you will examine the Google Maps API and locate where the geolocation API calls are made.

Step 1   Using your IDE, open the file google-map-demo.html from the geolocation-API folder and test the file in a web browsers.

Step 2   Examine the file in the Web browser, and return to your IDE.

Step 3   Locate the line of code with the call to the geolocation method used in this file.

Step 4   Locate the line of code that uses the coords property and its' properties.

Step 5   Locate the line of code where the Google Map object is instantiated.

Step 6   Locate the line of code where the Google Marker object is instantiated.

Step 7   Review the remaining code with your instructor and close all open files.

Chapter summary

In this chapter, you learned how to use the geolocation API. You learned the properties of the position object and how it is obtained via the device that runs the web page (i.e., tablet or smartphone). You learned how to pass geolocation position information to other APIs including Google Maps.

Chapter 20

Web Workers API

Web workers run JavaScript on a separate thread and therefore do not interfere or slow down any other scripts or interactivity on your web page. In this chapter, you will learn two different types of web workers used to boost the performance of your web pages.

The Web Workers API specification became a W3C Candidate Recommendation on May 1, 2012.

Objectives

❑ Understand the need for web workers.

❑ Describe what web workers can and cannot do.

❑ Create a web worker.

❑ Use a web worker.

❑ Understand how web workers communicate with the web page.

❑ Terminate a web worker.

❑ List the two types of web workers.

Introduction

"This specification defines an API for running scripts in the background independently of any user interface scripts.

This allows for long-running scripts that are not interrupted by scripts that respond to clicks or other user interactions, and allows long tasks to be executed without yielding to keep the page responsive.

Workers (as these background scripts are called herein) are relatively heavy-weight, and are not intended to be used in large numbers. For example, it would be inappropriate to launch one worker for each pixel of a four megapixel image.

Generally, workers are expected to be long-lived, have a high start-up performance cost, and a high per-instance memory cost." [1]

Note   You use a worker by communicating with it using messages. All browsers support passing in a string message (Firefox 3.5 also supports passing in JSON-compatible objects). This message will be communicated to the worker (the worker can also communicate messages back to the parent page). This is the extent to which communication can occur.

Features available to workers

Due to their multi-threaded behavior, web workers only have access to a subset of JavaScript features:
- The navigator object
- The location object (read-only)
- XMLHttpRequest
- setTimeout()/clearTimeout() and setInterval()/clearInterval()
- The Application cache
- Importing external scripts using the importScripts() method
- Spawning other web workers

Web workers do NOT have access to
- The DOM (it's not thread-safe)
- The window object
- The document object
- The parent object

Why use Web Workers?

Have you ever seen an "Unresponsive JavaScript" alert box? This occurs because a long-running JavaScript is running very slow and, while it is trying to run, it halts all other user activity, such as clicking on buttons, dynamically changing CSS, etc. The browser intervenes to ask if you would like to halt the execution of this slow running script. To solve this problem the Web Worker API allows scripts to run independently of any other user-interface script.

---

1   http://www.whatwg.org/specs/web-apps/current-work/multipage/workers.html#introduction-9

Part of the problem is the fact that the web browser provides a single thread of execution visible to scripts and is sometimes said to be "single-threaded." Although this might not be technically accurate among all web browsers, the fact remains the tasks allotted to JavaScript by developers are visible as single threads.

"In computer science, a thread of execution is the smallest unit of processing that can be scheduled by an operating system. The implementation of threads and processes differs from one operating system to another, but in most cases, a thread is contained inside a process. Multiple threads can exist within the same process and share resources such as memory, while different processes do not share these resources. In particular, the threads of a process share the latter's instructions (its code) and its context (the values that its variables reference at any given moment). To give an analogy, multiple threads in a process are like multiple cooks reading off the same cook book and following its instructions, not necessarily from the same page." [2]

To present another analogy, it's like going to the pharmacist to order medication and all the work is done by the pharmacist himself. The pharmacist takes in your prescription, logs it into the computer, goes in the back and creates the medication, bottles and labels the medication and is also responsible for calling your physician and then delivering the medication. In a busy pharmacy this would obviously be very time consuming because he or she could not fulfill a new order until they were done with the current order. Instead pharmacies employ various workers who handle different part of the process. Web workers perform tasks in a similar fashion.

When should web workers be used?

Web workers may be used for computationally demanding work that you want to perform on the client, not on the server. The threads started by web workers are memory intensive and should be used accordingly. Common use cases for web workers include the sometimes extensive JavaScript required to control the canvas element, including processing images and video. Game developers can take advantage of both artificial intelligence libraries as well as physics engines without freezing the UI by using web workers. Manipulating data-centric application data on the client may be labor-intensive based on the volume of data, in which case, web workers could help. Check out http://ie.microsoft.com/testdrive/Graphics/WorkerFountains/Default.html for an example of web workers used with the canvas element.

How do Web Workers work?

When a web worker is created via the code: `worker = new Worker("scripts/myJS.js")` "The browser resolves the script's URL ("scripts/myJS.js"). If it cannot resolve the URL path the browsers should throw a SyntaxError exception. If the URL's origin is not the same as the origin of the page that contains the worker, the browser should throw a SecurityError exception. If neither exception is thrown, the browser then creates a DedicatedWorkerGlobalScope object, known as the worker global scope object. Immediately after this a new worker object is created and known as the "worker." A message port is created for communication between the page that spawned the worker and the worker and is known as the "outside port." The "outside port" is associated with the worker and is "owned" by the global object of the script that created the worker. Another message port is created that is owned by "worker global scope" and is known as the "inside port." The "inside port" is associated with the "worker global scope."[2]

---

2   http://en.wikipedia.org/wiki/Thread_%28computing%29

The Web Worker API

The `Worker()` constructor call creates a worker and returns a worker object representing that worker, which is used to communicate with the worker. That object's `onmessage` event handler allows the code to receive messages from the worker. [3]

The worker object implements the AbstractWorker interface. This interface includes the following methods:

The AbstractWorker interface methods

Method	Description
`terminate()`	This effectively terminates the worker from executing its code. See the close() method below for a closer examination of how terminate works.
`postMessage()`	This method is used to send messages back and forth. Dedicated workers use MessagePort objects behind the scenes and therefore support all the same features, such as sending structured data, transferring binary data, and transferring other ports.

The WorkerGlobalScope object

The global scope is the "inside" of a worker.

WorkerGlobalScope object properties

The WorkerGlobalScope object is used to reference the global scope within the workers and includes the following properties:

Properties	Description
`self`	This returns the WorkerGlobalScope object itself. The global scope represents the "inside" of the worker i.e. the JavaScript file that the worker executes.
`location`	This returns the WorkerLocation object, which is created for the worker global scope at the time the worker was created. The WorkerLocation object represents an absolute URL set at the worker's creation.

WorkerGlobalScope object methods

Method	Description
`close()`	When this method is called, the browser must discard any tasks that have been added to the event loops task queues as well as prevent any further tasks from being added to the queue. This is done by setting the WorkerGlobalScope object's closing flag to "true."

---

3   http://dev.w3.org/html5/workers/#dedicatedworkerglobalscope

WorkerGlobalScope events

The WorkerGlobalScope object can respond to the following events:

- `onerror`
- `onoffline`
- `ononline`

Browser support for web workers

For the most recent tables regarding browsers support please see http://caniuse.com.

Types of Web Workers

There are two types of web workers: dedicated and shared.

Dedicated

These are linked to the page that created them in a one to one relationship (meaning one web worker per parent document.

Shared

These are named workers that can be accessed from any page in the same origin.

Exercise 20.1 Checking for web worker support

In this exercise, you will determine if the web browser supports web workers.

Objectives

After completing this exercise you will be able to do the following:

- Use the JavaScript typeof() method to determine if the browsers supports web workers.

Step 1   Open the file "webWorker-support-starter.html" from the webWorkers-API folder.

Step 2   Create a `<script>` block in the `<head>` section of the web page.

Step 3   Create an if block that uses the JavaScript typeof() method to return the window object's global worker property. If the browser does not support web workers this property will be "undefined."

```
<script>
if(typeof(window.Worker)){
    console.log("Your browser supports Web Workers");
}
else {
    console.log("Your browser DOES NOT support Web Workers");
};
</script>
```

Step 4   Save and test the file in all browsers.

Step 5   Open the file "web-worker-support-a-finished.html" and review another technique for checking browser support of web workers.

Step 6   Test the file in all web browser.

Exercise outcome

This exercise results in the appearance of a log statement in the Developer Tools' console that indicates support or lack of support for the web worker API.

Exercise summary

In this exercise, you learned how to check for browser support of web workers by attempting to obtain the window object's global worker property.

Exercise 20.2 Creating a web worker

In this exercise, you will create a web worker to execute JavaScript to perform a background process that does not interfere with or slow down the main page. While this exercise will use a simple JavaScript, remember that the best use case for web workers is CPU-intensive long-running calculations. In this way you can take advantage of machines running multi-core CPUs.

This exercise implements a basic form that determines the user's Body Mass Index or BMI. The user supplies their weight and height using either centimeters and kilograms or inches and pounds and the calculator performs the math that determines their BMI. The JavaScript that performs the math is called from a web worker and it is the web worker that returns the BMI calculation. Remember that calculating a person's BMI is a trivial JavaScript task and is used here to demonstrate the Web Worker API. It is not a good reason to use a Web Worker because the use case for a worker is a long-running, complex JavaScript.

Objectives

After completing this exercise, you will be able to do the following:

- Create a web worker.
- Tell the web worker what to do.
- Describe how the web worker sends the results of its work to the page that called it.
- Listen for incoming messages from the web worker.

We will perform the following basic tasks:

1. Create a web worker object.

2. Pass the web worker a JavaScript file to be executed.

3. From the web page which created the web worker, add an event listener to listen for incoming messages from the web worker.

4. Pass information from the web page to the worker.

5. Add listeners inside the web worker to listen for incoming messages from the web page.

Step 1 Open the file "webWorker-starter.html" from the webWorker-API folder and run it in a web browser.

Step 2 Notice the BMI calculator and interact with it. It does not calculate the BMI. We will assign a web worker to that task.

Step 3 Locate the `<script>` block above the closing `</body>` tag.

First, you will declare variables for the information we will need to pass to the web worker, including the unit of measurement chosen by the user, the user's height and weight, the "Calculate" button and the worker itself.

Step 4 In the existing `<script>` block, declare the following variables: `calcBMI_btn`, `units`, `height`, `weight` and `worker`.

```
<script>
    <!-- add variables here -->
    var units;
    var height;
    var weight;
    var worker;
```

Step 5 Locate the `document.ready()` function.

Step 6 Locate the check for web worker support. Add this code inside the `document ready()` function.

Now its time to create the web worker.

Step 7 Inside the if block create the web worker as shown in bold below:

```
if(typeof(Worker) !== "undefined"){
        worker = new Worker("scripts/bmi.js");
        console.log("Your browser supports Web Workers");
    }
    else {
      console.log("Your browser DOES NOT support Web Workers");
      }
});
```

Now you will listen for messages sent by the worker script ("bmi.js"). You will use the addEventListener method and pass to it the event you want to listen for: "message," and the callback function to be executed when the event is dispatched: "messageHandler." The last argument indicates that you will not listen for this message in the capture phase of event bubbling.

Step 8 Add the event listener as shown in bold below:

```
if(typeof(Worker) != "undefined"){
        worker = new Worker("bmi.js");
        worker.addEventListener("message", messageHandler, true);
        console.log("Your browser supports Web Workers");
    }
    else {
      console.log("Your browser DOES NOT support Web Workers");
            }
});
```

You also have to code the "Calculate BMI" button to respond to the click event, and in so doing we will provide the values the user entered to their corresponding variables i.e., height, weight, etc. Notice that for lesson brevity we are not validating the form, which is something that should be done on the client to ensure that the user has in fact entered a height and a weight and used the correct format (i.e., integers) and that they have selected a radio button choice.

You will activate the button from inside the document ready() function, so add the following jQuery to select the button and respond to the click.

Step 9   Add the calcBMI_btn event handler for the click event. Add this code below the last code block you wrote in step 8:

```
$('#calcBMI_btn').click(function() {
        units = $('[name="units"]:radio:checked').val();
        height = $('#h').val();
        weight = $('#w').val();
});
```

In step 9, you responded to the click event of the calcBMI_btn by assigning values to the variables: units, height and weight. The unit's buttons value was obtained via a jQuery selector that locates the value (val()) of an element with the name "units" ([name="units"]) that is a radio button that has been selected (:radio:checked).

The next step is to post a message to the web worker. The message will tell the worker what the user chose for units of measurement as well as their height and weight. Notice the curly brace notation inside the postMessage() methods parentheses in step 10.

Step 10   Add the postMessage() method as shown below in bold:

```
$('#calcBMI_btn').click(function() {
    units = $('[name="units"]:radio:checked').val();
    height = $('#h').val();
    weight = $('#w').val();
    worker.postMessage( {"units" : units,
                         "height" : height,
                         "weight" : weight});
});
```

Now, remember that in step 8 you added an event handler function to respond to the message event. However, we did not yet write that function. You will do that next.

Step 11   Write the messageHandler() function below the code you wrote in step 10 as shown below:

```
function messageHandler(evt) {
        $('#bmi').val(evt.data)
        //alert(evt.data);
    }
```

Step 12   Keep this file open.

Notice that the function accepts a single argument which is the message event object. Next the input field with the id of "bmi" is located with $('#bmi') and its value is set with the val() method. The value passed to this method is the message event object's data property, which is the data sent by the web worker. We have not written the web worker yet, but it will execute a postMessage() of its own and it will send the calculated BMI value via this method. The message event's data property will hold this data. Lastly and optionally, we execute an alert method to test the function. This line is currently commented, however you can uncomment it and test it after we have written the web worker.

Exercise summary

In this exercise, you learned how to create a web worker, post a message to the web worker and write an event handler to handle the web worker's response. You cannot test this file because we have not yet created the JavaScript that is associated with this web worker. You will do that in the next exercise.

Exercise 20.3 The Web Workers JavaScript

In this exercise, you will finish the work begun in exercise 20.2 by writing the JavaScript that has been associated with the web worker you created in the previous exercise. This JavaScript will perform the calculations that calculate the userss BMI.

Objectives

After completing this exercise, you will be able to do the following:

- Listen for a message to the web worker from the page that spawned the worker.
- Write a messageHandler() function.
- Obtain data from the message sent by the web page to the worker.
- Send data back from the worker to the page that spawned the worker.
- Test web workers.

Step 1   Create a new JavaScript file, called "bmi.js" and save it in the scripts folder inside of webWorkers-API folder.

First, you will add an event listener and listen for the message event from the page you created in the previous exercise.

Step 2   Add the following event listener for the message event:

```
self.addEventListener("message", messageHandler, true);
```

Step 3   Write the messageHandler() function. Be sure to pass in the "evt" parameter that represents the message event object and declare the variables to store (height, weight and bmi) as follows:

```
function messageHandler(evt) {
        var weight;
        var height;
        var bmi;
}
```

Step 4   Using the "data" property of the message event, determine if the user has chosen "metric" or "English" values for their unit of measurement:

```
function messageHandler(evt) {
        var weight;
        var height;
        var bmi;
        if(evt.data.units == "en"){
        }
```

```
            else if(evt.data.units == "metric") {
            }
      }
```

Step 5   Assign values to height and weight according to the user's unit of measurement choice:

```
function messageHandler(evt) {
      var weight;
      var height;
      var bmi;
      if(evt.data.units == "en") {
        weight = evt.data.weight;
        height = evt.data.height;
      }
      else if(evt.data.units == "metric") {
        weight = evt.data.weight * 2.20462262;
        height = evt.data.height * 0.393700787;
      }
}
```

Step 6   Calculate the BMI using the formula below and assign the results to the "bmi" variable. Be sure to use the toFixed() JavaScript method before returning the BMI value. The toFixed() method formats a number to use as a specified number of trailing decimals. The number is rounded up, and nulls are added after the decimal point (if needed), to create the desired decimal length. [4]

```
function messageHandler(evt) {
      var weight;
      var height;
      var bmi;
        if(evt.data.units == "en"){
        weight = evt.data.weight;
        height = evt.data.height;
  }
      else if(evt.data.units == "metric"){
            weight = evt.data.weight * 2.20462262;
            height = evt.data.height * 0.393700787;
      }
      bmi = weight * 703 / (height * height);
      bmi = bmi.toFixed(3);
      }
```

Step 7   Lastly, use the postMessage() method to send the BMI to the web page you created in the previous exercise.

```
function messageHandler(evt) {
      var weight;
      var height;
      var bmi;
```

---

4 http://www.w3schools.com/jsref/jsref_tofixed.asp

```
                    if(evt.data.units == "en"){
                       weight = evt.data.weight;
                       height = evt.data.height;
                    }
                    else if(evt.data.units == "metric"){
                       weight = evt.data.weight * 2.20462262;
                       height = evt.data.height * 0.393700787;
                    }
                    bmi = weight * 703 / (height * height);
                    bmi = bmi.toFixed(3);
                    postMessage(bmi);
                 }
```

Note   To test these files you must use a web server. You will test the files "bmi.js" and "webWorker-starter.html." You will need to test these files through a server, so you will test them through localhost, the WAMP server.

Step 8   Launch any web browser that supports web workers.

Step 9   Type: "http://localhost" in the address bar and you should see the contents of the foodPlate directory.

Step 10   Click the "web-worker-starter.html" page and interact with the form, entering a unit of measurement choice and a height and weight. Click the "Calculate" button and the web page should send the information to the web worker and the web worker should respond by calculating and returning the BMI, which the web page will enter into the text input field.

Step 11   You may now close all open files.

Exercise outcome

This exercise when viewed in the web browser should display a simple calculator that returns a BMI value after the form has been filled out and the form's "Calculate" button has been clicked.

Exercise summary

In this exercise, you learned how to create a JavaScript that was used by a web worker. You wrote the code that performed the communication between the web worker and the page that spawned the worker.

Exercise 20.4 Terminating a web worker

In this exercise, you terminate a web worker and effectively stop it from executing any of its code.

Objectives

After completing this exercise, you will be able to do the following:

- Stop a web worker.
- Write and call the terminate() method.

Step 1   Open the file "terminating-starter.html" from the webWorkers-API folder and run it in a web browser. Be sure to interact with the form.

Step 2   Locate the `messageHandler()` function at the bottom of the `<script>` block and add a click event handler for the "Terminate" button.

```
function messageHandler(evt) {
        $('#bmi').val(evt.data);
        //alert(evt.data);
}
$('#terminate').click(function() {
        worker.terminate();
});
```

In this code you use the following jQuery to access the element with the id of "terminate":

```
<input type="button" name="terminate" id="terminate" value="Terminate Worker">
```

Then a click handler function is added that calls the worker object's terminate() method.

Step 3   Save the file and retest it in the browser. Be sure to test the file from http://localhost.

Step 4   Calculate your BMI by filling out the form. After you click the "Calculate" button try changing some numbers
and then click the "Calculate" button again.

Step 5   Now click the "Terminate" button and try calculating BMI with new numbers for height and width. The calculator should no longer work and the current BMI should not change.

Step 6   You may now close all open files.

Exercise outcome

This exercise when viewed in the web browser should display a simple calculator that returns a BMI value after
the form has been filled out and the forms' button has been clicked. If you then, change any values on the form
and click the "Calculate" button a second time, the forms BMI field should NOT update.

Terminating the worker from the worker script

If you wish for the worker to terminate itself, use the following method:

```
this.close()
```

Exercise summary

In this exercise, you learned how terminate a web worker with the terminate() method of the worker object.

Exercise 20.4-a Web worker error event

*Unhandled errors within a web worker JavaScript file will fire error events on the worker object. The main page that
spawned the worker can listen for these events and respond accordingly. Logging these errors can be facilitated by the
properties of the event object, including: the filename, lineno and message. In this exercise you will reference a web
worker JavaScript that contains an error. You will listen for the error event and respond by logging the error event
properties. Be sure to test with the Chrome browser while the developers tools are running and the focus is on the
console.*

Objectives

After completing this exercise you will be able to do the following:

- Listen for the error event.
- Send output to the console that describes the error event.

Step 1   Open the file "error-starter.html" located in the webWorkers-API folder.

Step 2   Locate the event listener that listens for the message event and add the listener for the error event below it as shown in bold below:

```
$(document).ready(function(){
        if(typeof(Worker) != "undefined"){
                worker = new Worker("scripts/bmi_finished_error.js");
                worker.addEventListener("message", messageHandler, true);
                worker.addEventListener("error", errorHandler, false);
        //console.log("Your browser supports Web Workers");
        }
        else{
                console.log("Your browser DOES NOT support Web Workers");
        }
```

Step 3   Write the onError() event handler function.

```
function errorHandler(evt) {
        console.log("Error in File: " + evt.filename);
        console.log("Error occurred on line #: " + evt.lineno);
        console.log("Error description: " + evt.message);
}
```

Step 4   Save and test the file in the Chrome web browser using the url: http://localhost, then locate this file from the directory shown in the web browser . Be sure to use Chrome Developer Tools or Opera Dragonfly and view the console as you attempt to interact with the application. You should see the error messages in the console.

Step 5   You may now close all open files.

Exercise outcome

This exercise should result in log statements to the console on the Developers Tools panel indicating a JavaScript error. There should be one log statement indicating the filename with the error, a second log statement indicating the line number the error occurred on and a third log statement indicating the error description. The browser will also return the error message on a single line.

Exercise summary

In this exercise, you learned how to respond to errors in the web worker by listening for the ErrorEvent.

Creating shared workers

Shared web workers allow any window from the same origin or domain to share the use of a worker thread. Remember that beginning a new thread for a worker consumes a lot of memory both at start up and while the worker is running. The ability to share a worker thread could improve performance.

While the main benefit of a shared worker is its ability to allow multiple documents to access a single shared worker instance, the code for creating a shared worker is a bit more complex. To create a shared worker you use the following code:

```
var mySharedWorker = new SharedWorker("commonlyUsedJS.js");
```

The API for shared workers varies slightly. For example when posting and responding to messages, you must reference a port object as shown here:

```
mySharedWorker.port.postMessage("myMessage");
```

and

```
mySharedWorker.port.addEventListener("message", "messageHandler", true);
```

Exercise 20.5 Creating a shared web worker

In this exercise, you will be able to create a single web worker that can be shared among multiple web pages. The web worker in this file is a simple weight calculator, which converts grams to various other units of measurement. Remember that this JavaScript is intentionally simple for exercise brevity and the ideal candidate for a web worker script is one that involves lengthy computations and time-consuming calculations.

Objectives

After completing this exercise, you will be able to do the following:

- Create a Shared web worker.
- Access the shared web worker thread from multiple pages.

Step 1   Open the file "shared-worker-demo.html" from the webWorkers-API Demos folder and run it in a web browser using the url: http://localhost, then locate this file from the directory shown in the web browser. Be sure to interact with the forms.

The file sharedWorker-starter.html consists of two iFrames. Each iFrame contains a reference to a web page that utilizes a single shared web worker. The web worker file includes the functions that convert grams to kilograms, ounces, pounds and tons.

In this exercise, you will create this shared web worker.

Step 2   Open the file "sharedWorker-starter.html" from the webWorker-API folder.

Step 3   Create a script block between the closing `</form>` element and the closing `</body>` elements.

Step 4   Declare a variable to store the shared worker:

```
var sharedWorker;
```

Step 5   Add a click handler to the "Calculate" button as shown in bold:

```
<input type="button" name="calculate" id="calculate" value="Calculate" on-
Click="getResult()">
```

Step 6   Write the getResult() function which will:

a.   Create the shared worker object that references the JavaScript convert.js file

b.   Add an event listener to the shared workers port*

c.   Connect to the port with the start() method

d.   Declare a "grams" variable and assign it the value of the grams text input field

e. Cast the "grams" variable as a number object

f. Invoke the postMessage() method to pass the shared web worker two pieces of information: the conversion unit as "LB" and the number of grams via the "grams" variable.

```
var sharedWorker;
function getResult() {
    sharedWorker = new SharedWorker('scripts/convert.js');
    sharedWorker.port.addEventListener("message", messageHandler, false);
    sharedWorker.port.start();
    var grams = document.getElementById('grams').value;
    grams = Number(grams);
    sharedWorker.port.postMessage({'units':'LB', 'measure':grams});
}
```

The port attribute must return the value it was assigned by the object's constructor. It represents the MessagePort for communicating with the shared worker.[5]

Step 7 Open the convert.js file from the scripts folder and examine the file with your instructor.

Step 8 Notice line 3 in convert.js. An event listener is added that listens for the connect event. A variable is then declared to store the port property of the event object. The port listens for the onMessage event and invokes the messageHandler event handler passing both the message event object (which contains the message in the data property) and the port. Notice line 40 which calls the postMessage() method of the port object and posts the result variable back to the page that spawned the web worker. Next, you will listen (from the HTML page) for this message from the web worker.

Step 9 Return to "sharedWorker_starter.html" and add the messageHandler result handler. This function will be called as a result of step 6-b above.

```
function messageHandler(evt){
    document.conversionForm.pounds.value = evt.data;
}
```

Step 10 Save the file and test it in the browser. A value of 1200 grams should be equal to 2.645549304220533 pounds.

Step 11 Open the file called "sharedWorker-a-starter.html" and create a worker that uses the same shared worker thread to convert grams to ounces. If you get stuck, look at the finished file.

Step 12 Try adding another unit of measurement to the frame-based demo page "sharedWorker-demo.html."

Step 13 You may now close all open files.

Exercise summary

In this exercise, you learned how to use a shared web worker that can be accessed by multiple pages. You learned how to configure the port property and listen for messages.

Chapter summary

In this chapter, you learned what a web worker is and how to use it. You also learned how to communicate between web workers and the pages that spawn them. You used a dedicated worker, but learned that there are shared workers as well.

---

5 http://www.whatwg.org/specs/web-apps/current-work/multipage/workers.html#shared-workers-and-the-sharedworker-interface

Additional APIs

Look for revisions to this courseware for additional APIs. In the meantime, be sure to research the following up and coming HTML APIs

- Service Workers (alternative to the deprecated AppCache)
- High Resolution Time API
- User Timing API
- Network Information API
- Page Visibility API
- WebGL
- WebRTC
- For more APIs, check out the links provided on page 7 for W3C and WHATWG announcements.

www.ingramcontent.com/pod-product-compliance
Lightning Source LLC
Chambersburg PA
CBHW050822220326
41598CB00006B/293